Measuring the Value of Information Technology

Han Van der Zee
Nolan Norton Institute &
Tilburg University, The Netherlands

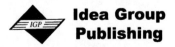 Idea Group Publishing

 Information Science Publishing

Hershey • London • Melbourne • Singapore • Beijing

Acquisition Editor:	Mehdi Khosrowpour
Managing Editor:	Jan Travers
Development Editor:	Michele Rossi
Copy Editor:	Maria Boyer
Typesetter:	LeAnn Whitcomb
Cover Design:	Deb Andre
Printed at:	Integrated Book Technology

Published in the United States of America by
    Idea Group Publishing
    1331 E. Chocolate Avenue
    Hershey PA 17033-1117
    Tel: 717-533-8845
    Fax: 717-533-8661
    E-mail: cust@idea-group.com
    Web site: http://www.idea-group.com

and in the United Kingdom by
    Idea Group Publishing
    3 Henrietta Street
    Covent Garden
    London WC2E 8LU
    Tel: 44 20 7240 0856
    Fax: 44 20 7379 3313
    Web site: http://www.eurospan.co.uk

Library of Congress Cataloging-in-Publication Data

Zee, Han T.M. van der.
  Measuring the value of information technology / Han Van der Zee.
    p. cm.
  Includes bibliographical references and index.
  ISBN 1-930708-08-4 (paper)
    1. Information technology--Evaluation. I. Title.
  HD30.2 .Z44 2001
  658'.05--dc21   2001024432

British Cataloguing in Publication Data
A Cataloguing in Publication record for this book is available from the British Library.

NEW from Idea Group Publishing

- **Data Mining: A Heuristic Approach**
  Hussein Aly Abbass, Ruhul Amin Sarker and Charles S. Newton/1-930708-25-4
- **Managing Information Technology in Small Business: Challenges and Solutions**
  Stephen Burgess/ ISBN:1-930708-35-1
- **Managing Web Usage in the Workplace: A Social, Ethical and Legal Perspective**
  Murugan Anandarajan and Claire Simmers/1-930708-18-1
- **Challenges of Information Technology Education in the 21st Century**
  Eli Cohen/1-930708-34-3
- **Social Responsibility in the Information Age: Issues and Controversies**
  Gurpreet Dhillon/1-930708-11-4
- **Database Integrity: Challenges and Solutions**
  Jorge H. Doorn and Laura Rivero/ 1-930708-38-6
- **Managing Virtual Web Organizations in the 21st Century: Issues and Challenges**
  Ulrich Franke/1-930708-24-6
- **Managing Business with Electronic Commerce: Issues and Trends**
  Aryya Gangopadhyay/ 1-930708-12-2
- **Electronic Government: Design, Applications and Management**
  Åke Grönlund/1-930708-19-X
- **Knowledge Media in Health Care: Opportunities and Challenges**
  Rolf Grutter/ 1-930708-13-0
- **Internet Management Issues: A Global Perspective**
  John D. Haynes/1-930708-21-1
- **Enterprise Resource Planning: Global Opportunities and Challenges**
  Liaquat Hossain, Jon David Patrick and MA Rashid/:1-930708-36-X
- **The Design and Management of Effective Distance Learning Programs**
  Richard Discenza, Caroline Howard, and Karen Schenk/1-930708-20-3
- **Multirate Systems: Design and Applications**
  Gordana Jovanovic-Dolecek/1-930708-30-0
- **Managing IT/Community Partnerships in the 21st Century**
  Jonathan Lazar/1-930708-33-5
- **Multimedia Networking: Technology, Management and Applications**
  Syed Mahbubur Rahman/ 1-930708-14-9
- **Cases on Worldwide E-Commerce: Theory in Action**
  Mahesh Raisinghani/ 1-930708-27-0
- **Designing Instruction for Technology-Enhanced Learning**
  Patricia L. Rogers/ 1-930708-28-9
- **Heuristics and Optimization for Knowledge Discovery**
  Ruhul Amin Sarker, Hussein Aly Abbass and Charles Newton/1-930708-26-2
- **Distributed Multimedia Databases: Techniques and Applications**
  Timothy K. Shih/1-930708-29-7
- **Neural Networks in Business: Techniques and Applications**
  Kate Smith and Jatinder Gupta/ 1-930708-31-9
- **Managing the Human Side of Information Technology: Challenges and Solutions**
  Edward Szewczak and Coral Snodgrass/1-930708-32-7
- **Cases on Global IT Applications and Management: Successes and Pitfalls**
  Felix B. Tan/1-930708-16-5
- **Enterprise Networking: Multilayer Switching and Applications**
  Vasilis Theoharakis and Dimitrios Serpanos/:1-930708-17-3
- **Measuring the Value of Information Technology**
  Han T.M. van der Zee/ 1-930708-08-4
- **Business to Business Electronic Commerce: Challenges**
  Merrill Warkentin/ : 1-930708-09-2

Excellent additions to your library!

**Receive the Idea Group Publishing catalog with descriptions of these books by
calling, toll free 1/800-345-4332
or visit the IGP Online Bookstore at: http://www.idea-group.com!**

Measuring the Value of Information Technology

Table of Contents

Preface

This book is to provide some answers to business managers, management consultants, and researchers who regularly question whether the contribution of IT to business performance can be measured at all. Of course, there are a number of dilemmas in appropriately measuring the value of IT. To mention two: it is increasingly difficult to isolate the role and function of IT from other aspects that make up a product, a service, a distribution channel, a business process, and so on; and there's an enormous time lag between IT investments and their results. Yet, the adagium, "if we cannot measure, we cannot measure" still holds true, also when the value of IT is concerned.

Based on my 15+ years of experience in this field, gained as a management consultant and scholar, I have known for quite some time that measurement of IT value is possible, at least to some extent. A few years back, I felt more emphasis was needed on the theoretical framing of my thoughts and concepts. Consequently, I worked on my PhD, resulting in an academic thesis on IT value measurement, which was published in 1996.

Then, I began to work on this book some three years ago with a simple question: how do you link the many lessons learned in practice with theoretical approaches for IT measurement already available? The concepts, frameworks and cases described in this book lean heavily on authors, researchers, and management consultants who understand and have captured the management perspective on organizational renewal, technological innovation, and IT managerial issues. Many insights in the themes of managing and measuring business value from IT and improvement in IT supply were drawn from the work of Dick Nolan, Dave Norton, Mike Hammer, Jim Champy, Peter Keen, Howard Rubin, Michael Scott-Morton, Bob Benson, Eric Brynjolfsson, John Henderson, Venkatraman, and other experts in this field, predominantly based in the Boston, Massachusetts area. I have always been greatly impressed by the innovative yet practical approaches to address complex business and IT-related issues devised by a number of thought leaders at "the other side of the Atlantic." I have been privileged to have worked with a number of them, and I would like to thank them to convey how much I value my interactions with and learning from them.

Special thanks are due to Michele Rossi, development editor at Idea Group Publishing, who carried out the tough parts of editing texts and turning the manuscript into a real book. She has been wonderfully responsive, capable, and persistent, in short: crucial in making this book a reality.

Driebergen, the Netherlands, 2001

Prof. Dr Ing Han T.M. van der Zee

Director Nolan Norton Institute
Nolan, Norton & Co.
P.O. Box 155
3454 ZK De Meern
The Netherlands

Professor of Business Transformation and IT
Tilburg University
Faculty of Economics and Business Administration
P.O. Box 90153
5000 LE Tilburg
The Netherlands

E-mail: vanderzee.han@kpmg.nl
Internet site: www.nolannorton.com

Chapter I

The Need to Measure the Value of Information Technology

Living as we do in the Information Age, an immense amount of information is readily available through high-powered workstations, laptop computers, Personal Digital Assistants (PDAs), and other smart devices, connected through high-bandwidth data communication networks, including the Internet, Wide Area Networks (WANs), Local Area Networks (LANs), and upcoming Personal Area Networks (PANs). Evolving technologies are directly changing the speed and shape of competition and how business is done, rewriting the rules of the game in industry after industry. The rate of change in today's business environment has pushed the need for technologies and acceptance of them to a continuously accelerating pace. The new technologies are enabling organizations to be flatter, networked, and more flexible, redefining our notions about everything from R&D to distribution, and in the processes making possible smarter, more customized products and services.

As a result of these forces, organizations spend enormous sums of money on computer hardware, software, communication networks, databases, and specialized personnel, collectively known as Information Technology (IT). Leading-edge companies all over the world in all industries have increased their overall IT expenditures by double-figure percentages annually. Many organizations currently observe that up to 50 percent of their total capital expenditure is for IT.

Yet there is a great deal of questioning and soul-searching about the payoff of these large investments in IT. The question of what companies are getting in return for the many dollars or euros they spend on IT remains unanswered. Does IT yield tangible productivity, or strategic benefits? And are they measurable?

Scholars, researchers, business managers, and consultants have divergent views about the business value of IT investments. A host of annual surveys by consulting companies, market research groups, and the like, as well as a more limited number of formal research studies, give contradicting answers to the question of whether investments in IT are worthwhile. Some investigations reveal severe discouragement about IT investments, while other studies demonstrate that they have a better return than any other sort of investment. It is clear that to date, research results provide little evidence of a correlation between IT investments and business performance. Nor does a uniform answer exist to the question of whether it is possible to measure the value of IT.

ATTEMPTS TO MEASURE THE VALUE OF IT

Many attempts have been made to measure the value of IT according to a variety of criteria. Brynjolfsson, a leading researcher in the field of IT economics, in 1993 summarized the principal studies of IT and productivity at that time. Brynjolfsson concluded that: "The relationship between information technology and productivity-the fundamental economic measure of a technology's contribution-is widely discussed but little understood." He termed the shortfall of evidence of increased business productivity through IT the "*productivity paradox.*"

Many of these studies address the value question at the macroeconomic level and are generally based on public data sets such as those from the U.S. Bureau of Economic Analysis (BEA), the Bureau of Labor Statistics (BLS) and Life Office Management Association (LOMA). Other studies are based on data sets such as those from the Profit Impact of Market Strategy (PIMS) research program, and Management Productivity and Information Technology (MPIT) research.

At the macroeconomic or national level, the focus is on the relationship between aggregate IT spending as input, and worker productivity in an entire sector, country, etc. as output. For example, a study performed by Roach indicates that during the 1970s and 1980s, the service sector's productivity did not increase relative to its outlays in IT. Other studies report that investments in IT have not resulted in improved productivity of the workforce in Corporate America. There is no reason to believe that this situation is different in other parts of the developed world.

Other researchers, such as Steiner, subscribe to short-term benefits of IT for an individual organization yet over that a sector's longer-term benefit of IT is not plausible at all:

> "There's no question ... that the technology over a long period of time clearly does produce the efficiency of a particular organization. However, efficiency does not mean profitability persé. Efficiency can mean the opposite. The automation of whole industries increases the volume of transactions executed and processed, at a lower cost per unit. Industries become more efficient, causing organizations' profits to decline."

Brynjolfsson, in writing of the productivity paradox, warns against over-interpreting the findings of the above-cited studies. A shortfall of *evidence* of IT productivity is not necessarily evidence of a productivity shortfall itself. He notes that the lack of evidence of IT productivity can be due to the relative lack of reliability of data sources, mismanagement ("not appropriately adjusting output targets, work organization and incentives to bring the benefits of IT to the bottom line") and a lack of explicit measures of the value of IT. Traditional measures of the relationship between inputs and outputs fail to account for non-traditional sources of value that IT can bring, such as increase in quality, greater variety and customization of products, customer service, speed and responsiveness, and, through the Internet, the access to complete new markets.

MANAGING THE COSTS / BENEFITS EQUATION OF IT

At the business level, managers seek to measure the application of IT in terms of costs and benefits. But they are hard pressed to do this because they need to be provided with measures and a measurement framework to help them relate IT investments to business performance.

Historically, IT spending in business was considered an administrative expense rather than a business investment. The costs and benefits of systems were relatively easy to identify and compute. The goal of today's IT investments is more often revenue increase than cost displacement. Many of today's IT applications enable and support far-reaching changes in the industry and business structure, and can have a huge impact on organizational forms, interfaces with suppliers and customers, distribution channels, products, services, and markets. Therefore, the context of the costs / benefits equation for IT has changed immensely, and equally has, as a result, the management of this cost / benefits equation of IT.

IT Costs

There are at least three related reasons for management concern about the cost side of the cost/benefit equation of IT:

- IT spending is substantial.
- It is unclear how large the growth in IT investment really is.
- A growing portion of the IT expenditures is invisible and therefore not (actively) managed by upper management.

Tracing and tracking the costs of IT is becoming more troublesome in most organizations, particularly because a growing portion of the expenditure in IT is "hidden" by user departments. This means that actual IT costs are not traceable and not included in central IT budgets, so both the actual expenditure level and its growth rate are unknown. The more decentralized the organization is, the more hidden the IT costs might be. Increasingly hardware, software and networking costs are scattered across business units' budgets and difficult to spot. It is even more difficult to trace the costs of outside IT services and of dispersed personnel who carry out IT-related activities, since these costs are seldom included in IT budgets. Some market research organizations (e.g. the Gartner Group) estimate that today hidden IT costs equal around 30-50 percent of known spending.

The growing tendency for business units to control their own IT and IT budgets is consistent with the trend of organizations to devolve autonomy and authority to line functions. The invisibility of IT spending, however, causes a problem when benefits of IT are doubted and overall IT budgets become the subject of investigation. Only with the help of well-developed inventory mechanisms, a standard "chart of accounts," strict definitions for each cost category, and much managerial effort to collect cost data on a regular basis, is it possible to trace and track overall IT costs. Besides, a company can only implement a policy of cost control when it understands what is driving IT costs.

IT Benefits

While the cost side of the cost/benefit equation of IT may be difficult to manage and measure, the benefit side is even tougher. Identifying and obtaining external and internal performance data to measure and valuate IT appears to be very difficult in practice. Some of the complicating factors in the measurement of IT benefits are mentioned by Keen, a well-known writer on the subject of IT management:

- *IT spending does not directly create benefits.* As with R&D, human resources management, and many other business activities, benefits are seldom directly linked to immediate and visible costs that give rise to them. IT benefits, like those of management education, do not necessarily translate directly and tidily into cost savings and increased revenues, especially when the investment is made to enhance service, effectiveness, and company image.
- *The same investment in the same IT technology can have very different outcomes.* Although every company in a given industry may have access to the same base of technology, it is the management process rather than the technology that determines the benefits.
- *Many of the value-added benefits of IT do not show up in the accounting system.* Just as the accounting system hides many aspects of the costs of IT, it overlooks many of the ways in which IT contributes to organizational performance. In addition, traditional financial measures distort the value of IT that is managed as budgeted overhead. No one can measure the business value of overhead.

Keen notes that in searching for the value of IT, business managers should not be like the drunkard who searches for his lost keys under a lamppost, far from where he dropped them, simply because it provides light for him to look.

Combining the views of Brynjolfsson and Keen, the common causes of the shortfalls in measuring the benefits of IT are:

- insufficient management (including planning) of IT and value of IT,
- inappropriate measures to determine the value of IT,
- lack of frameworks to measure the value of IT.

The general unease and the blurred discussion about the determination of benefits of IT confirm the need for better measurement, frameworks, and tools to assess and monitor its value. The demand for measurement of IT is especially intense in organizations under pressure or seeking major performance improvements, and in those where management perceives IT investments to show diminishing returns. In my experience, companies that are generally perceived as "successful" companies are also interested in conducting systematic measurement as a means of maintaining superior performance and as protection against the uncertainties of constantly changing business and technical environments.

MEASURING THE VALUE OF IT

It is widely accepted that measurement can provide a systematic way for managers to find out what they do not know, confirm what they do know and decide how to act. It was the scientist Lord Kelvin who said, "When you can measure what you are speaking about, and express it in numbers, you know something about it; but when you cannot measure it, when you cannot express it in numbers, your knowledge is of a meager and unsatisfactory kind; it may be the beginning of knowledge, but you have scarcely in your thoughts advanced to the stage of science." Later, this statement was abbreviated to "if you can measure it, you can manage it," and "if you cannot measure it, you cannot manage it." Both the long and the short forms demonstrate the importance of measurement in general as a tool for management. The same holds for IT.

Managers generally use a set of decision rules and tools that help them to make choices and to prepare their organization to achieve objectives. A "dashboard" of vital performance indicators provides management with a tool to gauge how the company is faring in terms of financial performance, continuous innovation, customer care, competitiveness, organizational control, etc. A dashboard, consisting of the measures required to monitor strengths and weaknesses, and to direct resources and organization, acts as a guide for management and forms the core of planning and control. It allows management to valuate the contribution of a variety of factors that impact the overall performance of the organization.

The application of IT is one of those factors. But, the measurement of IT's impact seems to be difficult. Evolving Information Technology does not stand on its own, but is interwoven with many aspects of doing business. Moreover, IT delivery processes are varied and the technology is increasingly complex. As a result, while business executives and IT managers would like to rely more heavily on systematic measurement, and be able to gain more leverage for improvement from that, they are often frustrated in their attempts to measure the value of IT and the efficiency and effectiveness of IT supply.

To develop an effective and systematic measurement approach for IT, reference can be made to more established measurement disciplines. For example, there is a rich and long tradition of management accounting and accounting systems, based predominantly on financial performance indicators. In fact, historians have demonstrated that accounting reports have been prepared for thousands of years. Bookkeeping records have been found engraved on stone tablets, dating back to ancient civilizations. The art and science of management accountancy are phenomena that have existed for some 150 years.

With regard to IT, important lessons can be learned from systems of management accounting, cost measurement, and cost management. According to Johnson and Kaplan, leading thinkers in this field, the basic functions of management accounting systems are to:

- allocate cost for a periodic financial statement;
- facilitate process control;
- evaluate product costs;
- support specific, *ad-hoc* studies;
- assess overall business performance.

The objective of the first and the last functions is to be able to assess periodically the health of the business with the support of financial indicators. According to Johnson and Kaplan, the second function, although important, is not standard throughout the organization. There cannot be just one process or cost control system; process control must be accomplished at the level of the organization where the process occurs. The third function, to evaluate product costs, aims to measure the long-term costs of each product, rather than the short-term costs. Finally, the fourth basic function may not be an overtly operational goal of a management accounting system, since it is hard to know in advance what data will be most relevant for a special study. "We only can hope that whatever system we do design will produce and retain data relevant for special studies," Johnson and Kaplan say.

Simons, a Harvard Business School professor, broadens the scope of management accounting to management control by introducing the term diagnostic control systems: "*Diagnostic control systems* are feedback systems; the backbone of traditional management control, designed to ensure predictable goal achievement. They can be used to set standards and measure outputs for individual managers or for parts of the business. Output variables depend on the level of analysis. A set of output variables identified for monitoring the performance of a shift supervisor will be different from the set identified for monitoring the performance of the overall business."

As in management accounting and management control, a systematic approach to measuring the value of IT should be capable of fulfilling basic functions of periodic assessment and of supplying feedback of the health of the application and supply of IT. Also, it must be able to facilitate the control of IT application and IT supply processes. Finally, it should allow for the evaluation of costs of IT products and services, and support specific, *ad-hoc* studies into either real or perceived problems with the application or supply of IT.

APPLYING AN IT VALUE MEASUREMENT APPROACH

Companies need to build a clear and thorough picture of the connection between business strategy, business processes, and business activities on the one hand, and the opportunities and constraints of current IT application and supply on the other. Like management accounting and diagnostic control systems, IT value measurement should aim systematically and consistently to bring together a variety of indicators of IT value at *different* levels of the organization. This helps manage the complexity of IT at each distinct level.

To launch effective, systematic and consistent measurement of IT, management must:

- clearly understand what to measure-- use of an overall *management framework* links planned activities with the valuation of their results;
- select *a set of key measures for IT value* to assess the many facets of the application and supply of IT;
- implement and incorporate *an effective measurement program* into the organization as a management tool to consistently and systematically measure the value of IT;
- develop *norms* for the application and supply of IT, through benchmarking for example.

The figure below illustrates these main thrusts of effective measurement of IT.

In the remaining chapters of this book, a *framework* for IT management and measurement will be developed. As any framework, it must be treated as a tool to help navigate difficult terrain, rather than as an end in itself. But because the applications of IT in organizations are so complex, a conceptual scheme for simplifying and ordering *measures* is desirable. Coined the "BTRIPLEE" framework, it provides a context in which organizations in search of the value of their IT can define related questions and find answers. The framework asks value questions at *multiple* organizational levels and places the answers in their business and planning contexts.

These questions, and associated value levels, explore the extent to which:

- IT contributes to business objectives and to business strategy, called the *Business value of IT*;
- IT effectively supports business processes, activities and employees, called the *Effectiveness of IT*;
- IT supply aligns with business requirements, called the *Effectiveness of IT supply*, and is supplied at minimum cost, called the *Efficiency of IT supply*.

Figure 1.1: Effective IT Measurement

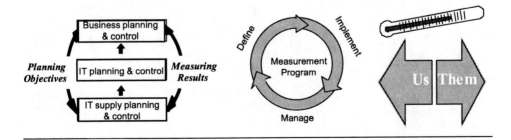

Link IT planning to IT valuation, ... measure IT, and ... benchmark IT

Hence, the B and three Es of the acronym BTRIPLEE. To get a quantitative handle on IT, one has to bear in mind that IT value measurement can be practiced in various ways, for a variety of purposes and for different audiences. It is therefore necessary to select measures that match the purpose of measurement and align with their context. In other words, selected measures will vary according to the objectives of the organization and the different levels of the organization.

Because measurement and measures influence people's motivations and attitudes, a *measurement program* must be systematically and cohesively introduced and maintained, to attain the long-lasting and embedded improvements sought. It is also essential to recognize the extreme difficulty and sometimes ultimate impossibility, given the practical circumstances, of measuring certain things in precise and quantified ways. These practical limitations impact the implementation of measurement programs into the organization.

Finally, companies may engage in comparative analysis, measuring their IT value against the value of business and technology peers. Such *benchmarking* approach can be very helpful to arrive at norms of IT value, as long as generally accepted and objective norms of IT value do not yet exist.

Through these key attributes, IT measurement can be used to achieve four goals. First, it can show to different stakeholders whether investments in IT are or have been valuable. Second, as the number of technical, organizational and strategic innovations and alternatives increases, measurement can improve quantitative assessment of different options. Third, measurement can be used by senior management and IT management as a basic tool to monitor activities, provide good stewardship of IT resources, and develop improvement strategies. Fourth, whether it is sophisticated or a more rudimentary start, IT value measurement can help bridge the communication gap between the worlds of business executives and suppliers of IT, by replacing opinions with facts. It directs discussions away from emotional opinions towards measurable improvements in the application and supply of IT.

REFERENCES

Brynjolfsson, E. (1993). The productivity paradox of information technology. *Communications of the ACM*, December, 36(12), 67-77.

Gartner Group. *Annual IT Budgets and Practices Survey*. Stamford, CT: Gartner Group.

Johnson, H.T. and Kaplan, R.S. (1987). *Relevance Lost: The Rise and Fall of Management Accounting*. Boston, MA: Harvard Business School Press.

Keen, P.G.W. (1991). *Shaping the Future: Business Design Through Information Technology*. Boston, MA: Harvard Business School Press.

Lord Kelvin of Largs. (William Thomson), An English scientist in mathematics, who lived from 1824 until 1907, developed various instruments for many kind of measurement purposes.

Loveman, G.W. (1986). *The Productivity of Information Technology Capital*. MIT, Management in the 1990s working paper, January 31.

Roach, S.S. (1991). Services under siege-The restructuring imperative. *Harvard Business Review*, September-October, 82-91.

Steiner, T.D. (1990). Wall Street's technology agenda for the 1990s. *Wall Street Computer Review,* April, 20-30.

Simons, R. (1995). *Levers of Control: How Managers Use Innovative Control Systems to Drive Strategic Renewal*. Boston, Mass.: Harvard Business School Press.

Van der Zee, J.T.M. (1997). *In Search of the Value of Information Technology*. Tilburg, The Netherlands: Tilburg University Press.

Chapter II

The Role of IT and Planning for IT Value

To determine the value of IT once it has been put into place and used, it is important to understand the context of the application of IT. Basically, the role of IT is to enable strategic change and improve business performance in several dimensions. IT enables the rapid delivery of top-quality, increasingly customized products and services, it supports organizations in meeting high standards in customer care, and it provides the means to compress design and development times in order to be the first to market. IT helps to launch new products more frequently, to explore and enter new markets faster, and to seek new distribution channels. All of these dimensions can give companies a powerful competitive edge, and IT is increasingly woven into them. IT does not stand on its own but contributes to realizing business objectives in today's competitive, often global environment.

To determine the value of IT once it has been put into place and used, it is important to first understand the context of the application of IT since it does not stand on its own but rather contributes to realizing business objectives. The first part of this chapter provides a review of the evolution of the role and application of IT, leading to its role in today's information-based organization. Secondly, it is obvious that the best value from IT is gained if the "right" investment decisions for IT are made. To make the right decisions about IT in the context of business objectives, organizations need to carry out some form of IT planning. Planning-for-success is therefore the second main subject of this chapter. The evolution of IT planning practices is briefly described, leading to the most important attributes of contemporary, effective IT planning approaches. Finally, the chapter links the distinct roles of IT with the planning and valuation approaches for IT investments in relation to their business purpose.

THE ROLE OF IT

With organizations increasingly depending on information and Information Technology, and business changes needing to be implemented almost overnight, the ubiquitous availability of IT is a key ingredient of overall business performance in many industries. Of course, IT has not always played such an essential role; its importance has evolved over time and in stages.

The evolution of IT is handsomely described by the framework, which Professor Venkatraman developed as part of the Management in the 1990s Research Program. This program was conceived as a close collaboration between academic researchers at the MIT Sloan School of Management and representatives of major companies. The results of their research include the various types of applications of IT in today's organization.

Venkatraman suggests five stages of growth, as illustrated in Figure 2.1.

- *Stage 1: Localized exploitation of IT* within business functions. This stage denotes the well-known examples of supporting IT such as order entry systems, customer support systems, computer-integrated design and manufacturing systems, payroll and bookkeeping systems, and so on. Functional departments specify their requirements and expect the systems department to respond by delivering systems accordingly, with maximum efficiency. Implementation of a system is typically followed by several years of maintenance (including enhancement) to keep it aligned with functional requirements, which inevitably change as the goals of the business change.

The benefits of exploiting IT relate to the efficiency of business processes and task efficiency and accuracy. Exploiting IT reduces delays and cuts or reduces clerical labor costs. The value of IT investments at this stage is relatively easy to

Figure 2.1: Venkatraman's Five Stages of Growth

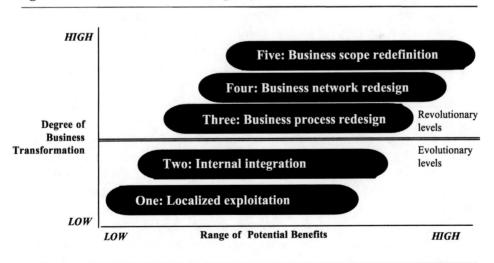

demonstrate in cost/benefit equations, since costs are comparatively simple to calculate and benefits are relatively obvious and tangible.

- *Stage 2: Internal integration of IT*, building the internal IT infrastructure, or platform, that permits the support of business processes and the integration of functions and tasks trough IT. At this stage, business activities are interconnected along a chosen direction (e.g., increased interdependence between marketing and R&D or between marketing and manufacturing). The organization typically deploys a common IT platform to interconnect its business activities, expecting such a platform to permit the exploitation of efficiency-related benefits of information sharing across the business processes. For example, a U.S. leisure travel company saw a productivity improvement of 30 percent after they combined previously separated tasks into the new function of travel counselor. Travel counselors were provided with easy access to the four applications that previously had to be accessed by different employees through separate log-on procedures. A control-panel-like user interface, acting as the counselor's private command center, provides access to all support required, including workstation applications like spreadsheets, text processors, and e-mail, as well as information on the reference sheets that previously were tacked up on the cubicle partition and stuffed into drawers.

At this stage, relatively minor organizational adjustments typically follow implementation, while the functional divisions of the business and their working methods remain largely unchanged. The value of IT already becomes much harder to demonstrate in comparison with Stage 1, since infrastructure investments only pay off over a longer period of time and only if sufficient IT applications that make use of this infrastructure are installed.

- *Stage 3: Business process redesign*, resulting from a fundamental rethinking of the most effective way to conduct business. Hammer and Champy, amongst others, have extensively elaborated on this phenomenon. At this stage, the driving assumption is that IT leverages the re-engineering of business processes. IT is not simply overlaid on the existing organizational structure; instead of treating the existing business organization and the configuration of its processes as a constraint in the design and development of IT, the configuration of the business activities itself is questioned. Business processes are developed that maximally exploit available IT capabilities, aiming at a high level of alignment between organization and technology. Figure 2.2 illustrates the aims of process redesign.

At this stage, rapidly developed and implemented IT enables the fast and flexible manufacturing of products and services with intelligent and flexible production planning and work flow management systems. IT allows for effective product development with help of expert systems, and supports customer service with comprehensive databases containing vast information about the customer. With flexible access to company-wide information and decision support tools, employees become multi-skilled, more effective and more productive, servicing larger numbers of satisfied customers.

Figure 2.2: Transformation of Business Processes

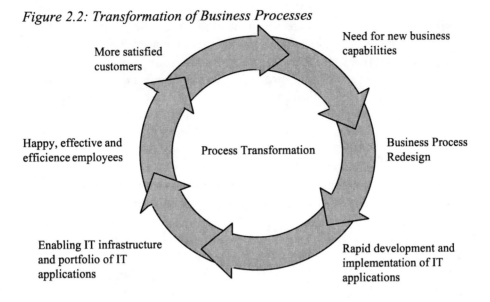

For example, Lex Electronics, a worldwide electronic parts distribution business, faced with a shrinking industry, more demanding customers, rigid decision-making practices, and a perception that advantage could be gained by applying technology beyond simple automation, decided to redesign key business processes. According to Lex Electronics' CEO, the number-one result of this effort was that they created a process for continuous self-improvement. There were other key results as well: huge monetary savings; motivated, involved, and empowered employees; dramatic restructuring of workflows; and a high level of teamwork. The vision of a high performance company was made real by a dramatically reduced cost structure, by effective efficient business systems, and by the power of IT.

To transform any process well, organizations need to make sure they have the right resources in place and in time: people, facilities, information, and technology. IT at Stage 3 is broader in scope, and business requires it to be delivered more rapidly. It is more complex to plan and implement than Stage 2 IT, since it is aimed at allowing significant and extensive organizational change. The benefits, however, should far exceed those arising from the incremental improvements through IT in Stages 1 and 2, although they are more difficult to quantify. It is often impossible to distinguish the contribution of IT to the business success from the many other influencing factors.

- *Stage 4: Business network redesign*, the use of IT by the organization to reconfigure the scope and tasks of the business network involved in the creation and delivery of products and services. This stage includes anyone who can contribute to the firm's effectiveness. IT substantially changes the nature and degree of inter-relatedness within an industry and amongst organizations that work together. IT changes the collaborations and business transactions of an organization with suppliers and customers. IT can be used to acquire raw materials and intermediate goods, and sell products. Levi Strauss & Co, for example, has simplified its ordering, stocking, receiving, and invoicing by deploying LeviLink, a merchandising and inventory management system. More than 3,500 of Levi Strauss's customers use some aspect of the system, which pre-tickets merchandise for customers, generates electronic packing slips that arrive before shipments, and tracks sales to create reorders. Many organizations use EDI and multimedia techniques such as the Internet, telephone, and TV to interact with their customer base. Centraal Beheer, a Dutch direct writer insurance company, sells its policies through interactive, electronic selling. Of course they use the Internet as a sales channel, but they also employ the combination of the telephone (as voice transmitter) and the TV set (as a picture and video-stream transmitter) to show and discuss the calculations and specifics of a potential insurance policy to its prospects.

Finally, IT can change the way in which customers pay for the products they receive from their suppliers, other than with cash, plastic or check. Several electronic payment techniques are feasible, including micro-payments and "cyber bucks" or "cyber euros."

At this stage, IT is a major contributor to the necessary any-to-any communication, while workflow management tools make coordinated parallel activities possible, eliminating geographical, time-based, and organizational boundaries. In this stage, calculation of the value of IT is even more complex. IT is an integrated part of the strategic business options that organizations consider. Projects are not straightforward to cost, and the benefits are often partly intangible and difficult to predict with some precision. IT investments are justified as such, meaning that uncertainty or risk factors must be included in the cost/benefit calculations that are made to evaluate Stage 4 IT.

• *Stage 5: Business scope redefinition* pertaining to the possibilities of enlarging or shifting the business mission and scope. This stage relates to the decision to break out and exploit the new technology in the marketplace and in products and services. Particularly the immense popularity of the Internet makes this option a viable one for almost every company in any part of the world. IT can enrich products in the form of additional information, and IT can substitute traditional products with IT-enabled products (e.g., electronic travel guides rather than traditional paper guides). IT can even be a new product itself, traded by new players such as infomediaries.

At this stage, IT is no longer part of the strategic options; IT rather *is* the focus of business strategy. The value of IT is determined by the top and bottom lines of the annual financial statements of the organization.

Business success increasingly depends on the organization's ability and understanding of how to fuse the potential power of IT into products, services, business activities, processes, and business networks. Many of today's organizations should therefore consider constantly how IT can be applied to enable and improve the functioning of the organization as a whole, both internally as well as within its environment. Only if IT is woven into every aspect of the organization and

Figure 2.3: Weaving Information Technology into the Organization

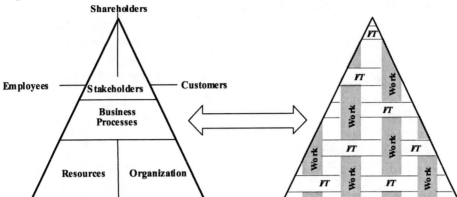

into the planning and decision-making processes at all organizational levels, can it contribute optimally to business performance.

Many of today's organizations apply IT at all levels of Venkatraman's model. IT has a significant impact on market and product strategies as well as on strategies developed to satisfy the needs of the main stakeholders (shareholders, customers, and employees). IT has a great impact on how enterprises align their business processes with these strategies and on how organizations organize and commit their resources to business processes. Organizational structures, policies, culture, performance measures, reward systems, jobs scopes, and training are equally impacted by today's IT. It is safe to say that in many of today's organizations, IT is almost literally woven into every aspect of the business, as illustrated in Figure 2.3.

Given the overarching importance of IT, many of today's organizations increasingly rely on an appropriate, flexible IT infrastructure that can easily adapt to organizational changes, geographical shifts, shifting forces of centralization and decentralization, and new technological capabilities. The flexible IT infrastructure is so important because it allows business activities and processes to be interconnected.

Ms. Coleman, a vice president in Apple's Information Systems and Technology area during the 1990s, talks about "putting in place a triple E (Essential, Enduring, and Enabling) infrastructure to support doing business and facilitate business restructuring and turnaround." Her definition of the characteristics of an IT infrastructure, in two phrases, is intriguing and noticeable: "New Economics" and "Turbo-Charged Service." New economics in this context means for Apple: focusing IT cost on a high-value IT infrastructure, including flexible, worldwide transaction systems and data warehouses. Turbo-charges service at Apple's Information Systems and Technology organization means: increased functionality, at a lower cost (they reduced their cost structure by 23 percent) in dramatically less time (reduction of 50 percent).

The IT infrastructure combines a vast array of technologies and integrates different types of data and information such as sound (e.g., voice), pictures (e.g., video and graphics) and data (e.g., numbers and text) into workstations, laptop computers, PDAs, and other smart devices. According to Keen and Cummins, the IT infrastructure permits the exploitation of efficiency-related benefits of compression of time and distance, as well as effectiveness-related benefits of information sharing across the organization and across partners in the organization's business network of suppliers and customers. To be able to reap these benefits, the IT infrastructure must be in balance with the organization's (and hence, the business network's) structure and culture, processes, and business and technology strategies. The organization, with its IT infrastructure in place, must be in balance with its external environment, including the emerging technology.

Progress in technological capabilities is particularly made in three areas, each of which is central to the ability of IT to change the way work in organizations is performed:

- *Extensive communications*: continued expansion of public and private networks; the interconnect availability that will come from the continued adoption of standards; and the ability to combine voice, images, data, and computation.
- *Accessibility of distributed databases and knowledge bases*: continued expansion and linkage of traditional "mainframe" databases, local area network "file servers," and emerging "database machines".
- *Enhanced workstations and user devices*: continued development of "smart" (software-enabled) human interfaces that permit ready, "natural" use and powerfully leverage the work to be done by anyone, anywhere, anytime, with any device.

The IT infrastructure might be considered as one of what Pralahad and Hamel call the "core competencies" of the information-based organization. Core competencies coordinate diverse production skills and integrate multiple streams of technologies; the expertise upon which they are built can be considered to be the basis of an organization's competitive advantage.

The IT infrastructure as a core competence is a combination of skills, processes, procedures, organizational structures, physical systems, and components, forming the continuing basis for a firm's competitiveness. It enables business networks for the "connectivity" and "accessibility" of anything, anyone, anywhere, anytime. McKay and Brockway define the IT infrastructure as the roll-up of technology into three distinct layers of service, held together by procedures and knowledge, that directly support business processes (Figure 2.4.). They distinguish:

- *Shared IT Components*: IT components are the basic building blocks of hardware and software that are acquired to perform specific activities, such as the storage, transport, and processing of data. Processors, related input/output devices, printers, mobile communication devices, and local area networks would all qualify as IT components.
- *Shared IT Services*: IT services are produced by combining IT components to create a broader base of IT function. Universal database access, an information

or video conferencing center, and a file restoration service are examples of IT services.

- *Shared Business Capability*: business capabilities are created by combining IT services to produce a broader base of business function and value that directly supports an existing business activity. IT services, such as network services, workflow services, electronic mail services, database access services and EDI, intranet and extranet services, could be combined to provide an interactive order processing capability that interlinks suppliers and customers with the purchasing process.

These "bricks," comprising the three layers of IT infrastructure, are held together by the mortar consisting of the specific knowledge and skills required to combine the IT infrastructure components into robust IT services and business capabilities. The body of knowledge consists of the policies, procedures, standards, packaging, and documentation that is woven into the assembly of technology, as well as the combined knowledge, experience and expertise of the planning, design, construction, and support personnel involved in the development and operation of the IT infrastructure.

The components of this infrastructure model are in constant evolution. Procedures and knowledge in the form of mortar, once in place and understood, tend to be codified into software and eventually hardware components. Hence, the evolution of formerly labor-intensive data centers into the almost "lights-out" operated computer rooms of today.

In designing an IT infrastructure, the degree of tailoring to specific business requirements increases as one moves up the model to the business capability level. The functions found at the component level are essentially commodities that are acquired to fit into the overall structure. A basic set of IT services is also generally available across companies in the form of electronic mail systems, local and wide

Figure 2.4: The IT Infrastructure

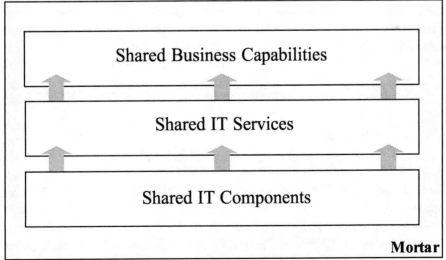

Figure 2.5: The Planning and Control Cycle

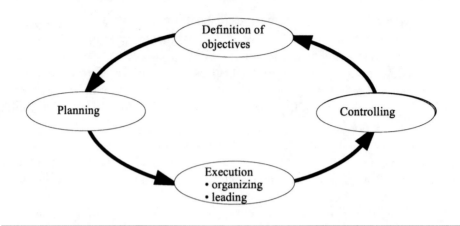

area networks, and end-user computing systems. The enrichment of IT services and the tailoring of them by the company's mortar to meet business requirements is where unique and distinctive business capabilities and market advantage are achieved.

Although strategically important as a competitive weapon, an IT infrastructure does not provide any benefit in and of itself, and the acquisition and maintenance costs are often considerable. It is only over time that the full effects of how people use IT and indirectly use the underlying IT infrastructure in the organization can be realized, and even then these effects can be unpredictable and unexpected.

PLANNING FOR IT

As the application of IT and the importance of an IT infrastructure have evolved over time, so has the art and science of planning for IT. Planning--in general--is an integral part of the overall, continuous planning and control cycles, also called management, of the business and the activities that a business comprises. The traditional planning and control cycle is illustrated in Figure 2.5.

Management is typically defined as *a systematic process of planning, organizing, leading, and controlling the efforts of organization members and of using all other organizational resources (finances, equipment, and information) to achieve stated organizational goals.*

Further to this definition, four key words are defined as follows:
- *Planning*: thinking through goals and actions in advance, based on some method, plan or logic, rather than on a hunch.
- *Organizing*: coordinating the deployment of human, financial and material resources of the organization. The effectiveness of an organization depends on its ability to arrange its resources to attain its goals.
- *Leading*: directing and influencing people to get things done.
- *Controlling*: assuring that the organization is moving towards its goals.

This continuous cycle of planning and control requires standards, measures and norms. Before managers can organize, lead, and control, they must make the plans that give purpose and direction to the organization, deciding what needs to be done, when and how it needs to be done, and who is to do it.

Planning is a process that does not end when a plan is agreed upon; plans must be implemented. At any time during the implementation and control process, plans may require modification. Management must continually monitor relevant environmental and internal factors so that the organization can adapt to new situations as quickly as possible. To do this, the ongoing planning process should include the collection of external data on products and market potential, competitive positioning, and the economic, technological, ecological, socio-demographic, political, legal, and environmental factors. The process also includes the ongoing collection of data on the organization's internal functioning.

Another important aspect of planning is decision making, the process of developing and selecting options and related courses of action. With the help of the collection of external and internal data, and comparisons with previously established standards or benchmarks of performance, corrective actions can be taken and new directions set.

Traditional Planning for IT and Problems Experienced in the Past

In relation with IT, planning has traditionally been performed at three distinct levels:
- business planning,
- IT planning,
- IT supply planning.

Objectives of business planning

Business planning is aimed at configuring skills and capabilities, including IT, in such a way that the most profitable and competitive advantage is attained in the future. The first objective of business planning is to creatively and innovatively answer the question "What business are we really in?" A railroad company, for example, could perceive itself in the business of operating trains and tracks, or transportation of passengers and goods. Either perspective can be acceptable: it depends on the strategic view and ambition of the organization's leaders, while different answers undoubtedly provide a different focus and lead to very different implications for the application of IT.

The next objective of business planning is to develop the strategies to satisfy the needs of stakeholders *vis-à-vis* the organization's competitive positioning. To manage the future, a preferred corporate structure is determined, and might include possible mergers, acquisitions, alliances, or divestments. For each business segment (may be a strategic business unit), further planning aspects include the product and services portfolio; identification and flow of primary and secondary business processes (either carried out by the firm or outsourced to specialists outside the firm); organizational structure and culture; and allocation of core competencies, core capabilities (including an IT infrastructure), and the required financial, human and capital resources.

Problems of traditional business planning in the past

There are some serious limitations to traditional business planning approaches, as Gray concluded from the strategic business planning practices of 300 managers in the U.S. in the second half of the 1980s. Although this seems to be a long time ago, more recent investigations seem to confirm his findings. Gray views planning as a two-step process: development of the strategy being the first step, strategy execution and implementation the second. He found that the managers who were surveyed do not perceive the first step as a problem. The second step however, often breaks down because of faulty preparation and implementation. The design and management flaws identified by Gray appear in Exhibit 2.1.

The application and supply of IT is dependent on a well-accepted and committed business plan, as is assumed by the traditional IT planning approaches. Unfortunately, it appears that the availability and reliability of such a plan are questionable at best. In any case, the main point is that the processes of strategy development and business planning are not as sequential, not as logical and straightforward, and not as reliable as one would hope when planning for effective IT. Rather, they are goal-driven approaches for changing organizational objectives, structures, and allocations of resources within a company.

Objectives of IT planning

Like business planning, IT planning is concerned with the overall direction of the application of IT within an organization. The term "IT planning" is used to indicate the planning activities undertaken by an organization to systematically

Exhibit 2.1: Shortcomings of Business Planning

- Line managers are poorly prepared for their leadership in strategic planning, once they take over the responsibility from staff specialists.
- Business (unit) boundaries are wrongly defined and/or inherited from the past; the strategic planning process is not supposed to cross pre-defined, but often inappropriate, Borders.
- Goals are too vaguely formulated or too general, and no one maps out the pathways leading to these general thrusts.
- Managers just below top management lack the information and motivation necessary for good strategy execution.
- Business unit plans are badly reviewed and reconciled. Gray describes the review process as "backdoor dealing, across-the-board cutting, goal posts moving" while reconciliation should happen, including "queuing, downsizing, redirection, and recycling."
- Strategic planning does not link adequately with other control systems, such as budgets, information systems, and reward systems.

determine its IT requirements in broad terms so that it can prepare to meet its short-term (1-2 years), medium-term (2-4 years), and long-term (5-7 years) IT needs. It defines objectives for IT systems (such as the benefits to the organization) and provides directions for the IT infrastructure. The most important goals of IT planning are to allow for:
- alignment of IT with the business objectives and business requirements;
- decision making on the scope, scale, and pace of IT projects;
- investment decisions and IT budgeting;
- allocation of resources to IT activities;
- communication between IT management and top management of an organization;
- overall quality of IT.

Since the 1980s, there are many methods of IT planning, often called "Information Systems Planning." Traditional IT planning methods typically share the underlying assumption that IT planning is aimed at translating an organization's business strategy and business objectives into a structure and plan for IT. They are top-down methods and have at least the following sequential steps in common:
- *Documenting* the:
  - business vision, mission, and objectives;
  - business strategy;
  - business structure, business processes and/or business functions.
- *Deriving:*
  - an information strategy;
  - the IT architecture: information systems, data structures, hardware and communication systems.

The common deliverables of IT planning processes are an IT strategy and IT architecture. An IT strategy can be defined as "the determination of the objectives, strategy, policies, functions, and organizational aspects for the development and acquisition of automated information systems and technical facilities for data processing and data communication within an organization." The IT architecture describes the structure of IT, as previously introduced. The architecture consists of high-level blueprints for key categories of IT: information systems, data, hardware, and communications.

Problems of traditional IT planning in the past

On top of the problems with business planning approaches, there are some serious problems with traditional IT planning processes as well. The Exhibits 2.2 and 2.3 demonstrate the methodological and practical problems that many of us have faced with past information systems planning methods. The main conclusion to be drawn from these lists is that traditional IT planning approaches have poorly aligned with business planning approaches from methodological and practical perspectives. What can be learned from the two exhibits is that IT planning should not be regarded as primarily being a rational, analytical, and technical activity, as it was perceived to be during the 1980s and 1990s by many business managers, consultants, and scholars.

Exhibit 2.2: Methodological Shortcomings of IT Planning

- To be successful, IT planning methods require concise articulation of organizational objectives and strategies. We have seen that this is a major bottleneck in everyday IT planning exercises.
- Management has to choose the best strategy from various alternative structures for IT and decide on the overall IT architecture. One might wonder if management has the know-how to make the right decision, especially since the deliverables of the planning process are generally hardly readable or understandable.
- Methods for IT planning generally require significant time to collect, analyze, synthesize, and verify information. Many managers and workers must be interviewed to understand the organization's processes, and exhaustive, detailed facts need to be assembled. The translation of large volumes of data into a viable plan is therefore extremely difficult, time consuming and too technical in nature.
- Results of an IT planning process are difficult to implement, because they are not easily translatable into the technical specifications that computer suppliers and system developers require.
- Some methods for IT planning (such as BSP) have been designed for centalized environments only. Nothing in these methods helps an organization if its computer resource has become organizationally or physically decentralized.
- Structuring oft the future IT architecture is mainly based on analysis of existing business processes and information systems if the approach is based on the functional decomposition of business activities (as most IT planning methods are). Strategic opportunities and qualitative aspects are easily neglected, or in other words: the results of IT planning are not truly strategic.

Exhibit 2.3: Practical Problems of IT Planning

- Top managers might not be able to successfully control the IT supplier (either the internal IT department or organization or an external supplier of IT services), and they are not inclined to express themselves in the IT language and terms of entities, attributes and data relationships.
- Top management is insufficiently involved with IT and sometimes not aware of the potential business opportunities that IT can offer
- Often information analysts are the key players in IT planning processes, responsible for elaborating strategic objectives and developing alternative designs for the overall IT architecture. One might wonder whether they have the capabilities and whether they are the best equipped to build successful links between business objectives, the IT strategy and the IT architecture.
- The IT supplier might not be given access to the corporate strategy: a corporate strategy might not exist, or might be incomplete, or outdated, or too confidential to divulge
- The IT supplier or IT planners might have too poor a track record to be asked to perform an IT planning process.

Objectives of IT supply planning

IT supply planning is concerned with planning IT supply activities–IT operations and development and implementation of new or enhanced IT products and IT services (e.g., information systems)–within an organization. It defines the objectives, directions, guidelines, performance targets, and organizational structures for the supply of IT-related services, for the establishment and deployment of the IT infrastructure, and for the creation, implementation, and maintenance of information systems.

New IT products and services must be planned in response to business needs, and should be guided by an IT architecture. For each project, its functional scope and depth as well as its resource needs and throughput time are laid down in individual plans. Together with users' requirements for changes and enhancements to existing systems, and requirements to maintain existing systems, these plans are then consolidated into an aggregated IT development and maintenance plan. The associated cost structures, time frames, and milestones are reviewed and authorized by business management.

Problems of traditional IT supply planning in the past

Many organizations have encountered problems with the planning aspects of IT supply. Historically, planning approaches for the supply of IT revolved around the use of large central utilities, large system development projects, and central IT organizations. The emphasis of IT supply planning was on the efficiency of operations and use of scarce resources, and most organizations had a centralized, full-service IT department as a staff function. From an IT planning and user perspective, the organizational structure of that centralized IT function was unimportant, and it was taken for granted that these departments delivered high-quality services without charging users a fee.

Nowadays, however, many organizations have decentralized parts of IT supply to business functions and outsourced other parts to external, commercial IT service providers. High-quality levels are no longer taken for granted but have to be negotiated and agreed upon. The same applies to the price paid for the delivery of services. Both elements explain the growing popularity of Service Level Agreements (SLAs) and formal contracts between the users and the suppliers of IT services. The popularity of SLAs can be seen as an indicator of managerial dissatisfaction with how planned supply of operational IT services has been realized by the traditional IT supplier–the internal IT organization. So is the trend to outsourcing arrangements for IT services. Many organizations have outsourced their entire IT departments or have turned over pieces of their IT operations to improve service, reduce cost, or free up management attention. Global companies in the U.S. and Europe, like Eastman Kodak, Merill Lynch, Philips, GM, BP, Heineken, and many, many others have outsourced large portions of their IT functions–including data center operations, network management, systems development and maintenance–to IT service providers such as EDS, CSC, IBM, Andersen, Origin, and Perot Systems, just to name a few of the big players in this market.

Managerial dissatisfaction with planning and execution of IT development projects can be illustrated by studies into this matter, revealing the track record of in-house system development organizations: about 40 percent of IT projects exceed their estimated cost or time scale. Typically, time scale slippage and effort (and budget) overruns range from 30 percent to 40 percent but can be much larger. It should be noted that these slippage and overrun data are based on estimates made upon the completion of the functional design stage, when all requirements have been defined and specified, and probably halfway through the project. Other data, recorded for estimates at the start of projects, show that close to 70 percent of IT projects exceed their estimated cost or time scale, and slippage and overruns are significantly greater than 30 percent or 40 percent. Clearly, there is substantial room for improvement in the planning of IT supply.

Contemporary Business, IT, and IT Supply Planning

Since the outcomes of IT planning and IT supply planning, in line with business goals, should offer the basis for the valuation of the application and supply of IT, a closer look at today's practices of business, IT, and IT supply planning is needed. It is clear that in order to attain and further develop the information-based organization, the traditional, rigorous, and exhaustive top-down planning processes have not been adequate. While business, IT, and IT supply planning have caused many problems as performed in a large number of organizations, solutions have been identified and are increasingly implemented. As the business and its environment have changed, IT management (hence, planning) practices have also changed. And as the capabilities of IT have changed, business planning approaches have changed accordingly to incorporate the potential power of IT.

To pragmatically plan for the portfolio of IT applications and a flexible IT infrastructure, the levels of business planning, IT planning, and IT supply planning have increasingly become more interdependent, in such a way that they can no longer be treated as purely sequential activities. Today, the distinct levels of business, IT, and IT supply planning are still identifiable, but the planning approaches for each have become more flexible and open to incorporating ideas from other levels.

Today's business planning

At the business level, quoting Mintzberg, "companies must differentiate between planning and strategic thinking, which captures what the manager learns from all sources, and then synthesize that learning into a vision of the direction that the business should pursue .... The outcome of strategic thinking is an integrated perspective of the enterprise, a not-too-precisely articulated vision of direction .... Such strategies often cannot be developed on schedule and immaculately conceived. They must be free to appear at any time and at any place in the organization typically through messy processes of informal learning that must necessarily be carried out by people at various levels who are deeply involved in the specific issues at hand .... Search all those strategic planning diagrams, all those interconnected boxes that supposedly give you strategies, and nowhere will you find a single one that explains the creative act of synthesizing experiences into a novel strategy .... In short, we should drop the label 'strategic planning' altogether."

When (strategic) business planning arrived on the scene in the mid-1960s, corporate strategic planners embraced it as the one best way to devise business strategies, as well as step-by-step instructions for business managers for carrying out those strategies. In fact, and in hindsight, strategic planning, as it has been practiced, has really been strategic programming, the elaboration of strategies, or visions, that already exist. Of course, there's a need to clarify and express strategies in terms sufficiently clear to render them formally operational, so that their consequences can be worked out in detail. But this requires a good deal of interpretation and careful attention to what might be lost in articulation: nuance, subtlety, and qualification. Mintzberg calls the steps of this detailing process codification, elaboration and conversion. The basic message here is that strategic thinking should occur anytime, anyplace, while neither "a rigid, sequential process" nor "the strategic planners" should hinder creative strategic development. In other words, a methodology should not always be followed per se, step-by-step, as a goal in itself. Nor should the people

Figure 2.6: IT Planning Aspects

IT Planning Aspects	Key Points
1. IT Risk-Taking issues	All efforts to introduce new technologies into an organization involve the risk of dysfunctional and unanticipated consequences. Effective planning must first determine an appropriate risk posture for the organization and then assess the extent to which this risk posture is embodied in the existing and planned application portfolios.
2. Technology issues	Business planning must incorporate tracking key developments in relevant product and process technologies. This is particularly important when the dominant technology must be assessed. Such a concern has proven especially important with IT.
3. Business Market issues	Business market analysis is based on an understanding of the markets within which an organization operates, not only the firm's relative stance *vis-à-vis* its competitors, but also those external agencies crucial to the organization's survival. This is useful in recognizing opportunities for developing inter-organizational information systems.
4. Business Strategy issues	Business strategies can be developed through a systematic examination of clearly defined choices and alternatives available to the organization. Business strategy analysis must surface choices and alternatives through identification of an organization's weakness and strengths.
5. Intra-Organizational Political issues	Understand the relative influence held by an organization's key coalitions; the distribution of power within an organization invariably influences strategic choice.
6. Organizational Learning issues	When business plans involve the introduction of new technologies to an organization's subunits, the capabilities of subunits to accept, use and institutionalize the technology must be assessed. Such a concern has proven especially important with IT.
7. Organizational Culture issues	An organization's culture is closely linked to the success it can expect to achieve. Planning must consider the organization's current culture and anticipate how this culture may impact or be used to affect information technology efforts.
8. Intra-Organizational Market issues	Analyze the various consumer segments within the organization to identify schemes for marketing IT services to each segment.
9. IT Infrastructure issues	Effective planning, by definition, must include an analysis of the constraints of resource capacities and limitations under which the information system's function operates. Such an analysis should cover hardware, software, telecommunication channels, data resources, personnel resources, end user capabilities, organizational maturity and the application portfolio.

who are assigned to planning tasks be the only ones who are authorized to come up with strategic initiatives. In fact, a more fluid, iterative, cyclic, and broader strategy development approach should be aimed at, compared to the traditional planning processes.

Today's IT planning

Obviously, there is close relationship between IT planning and business planning, classified by nine critical aspects for effective planning of IT as is stipulated by Figure 2.6. As the overview indicates, an organization's IT management (and thus, planning) practices are contingent on both the role that IT serves within the organizational context and the management by which IT resources are made available to users.

At the IT planning level, the traditional top-down planning process has been gradually replaced by a more iterative, goal-oriented, evolutionary, and continuous process of organizational learning and some degree of experimentation for a great deal of IT planning aspects. Such an IT planning process is much more dynamic and interactive, allowing for the incorporation of good ideas that bubble up from the operational level and making sure that planning results are understood early on by making the deliverables visible and tangible.

The traditional top-down planning process could be labeled as "alignment planning," the bottom-up process as "impact planning." A contemporary IT planning process combines both directions, starting from the business organization and needs, generating an IT architecture (top-down); while opportunities from existing IT and IT supply can be generated and deployed to change business plans and/or to align with business needs (bottom-up). Such a pragmatic IT planning approach consists of the following principal steps:

- The business identifies a broad, but clearly articulated strategic vision–a combination of challenging but attainable medium-term goals, and a more general expression of the organization's strategic intent, its values, and beliefs. The vision typically comes from the chief executive, and the top-management team shares it.
- In parallel with the development of the business vision, the main thrusts of the application and development of IT are expressed in a series of IT principles. They generally are defined in such a way that the combined set of principles fits on a few pages of paper. IT principles are the overarching rules, values and beliefs that relate to the IT architecture and infrastructure, the organization of IT including the distribution of responsibilities over the business side and IT supply side, and the management approaches for the initiation, coordination, and monitoring of IT projects.
- The business identifies and defines its key and supporting processes. Processes are neither objectives nor goals; processes are structured sets of activities, ordered across time and place, with a beginning, an end, and clearly defined inputs and outputs. They should be stated in action words, such as *provide after-sales service*. Examples of main processes are: create products,

supply sales, support customers, and create markets. Examples of supporting processes include: manage human resources, manage finance, manage IT, and manage physical infrastructure. It begins by preparing a shortlist of main processes, and then identifies the principal ones that are critical to its success. Most organizations find that they have between 8 and 15 main processes. Porter's "value chain" has been widely used as a guide for identifying the main processes.

- Having identified the principal processes critical to the business's success, another step is to analyze the workflow and work activities and the locations where work is performed, and improve (re-engineer) them. The processes are analyzed and improved in terms of their structure, their interdependencies, the business functions involved, the information needed, their decision points, and the main parameters such as cost, time, and quality. And last but not least: the impact and power of IT-based solutions are considered to cope with otherwise almost irresolvable problems and bottlenecks. Typically, preparing and evaluating activity flowcharts (simpler, but basically similar to those first used by organization and methods specialists and industrial engineers more than 30 years ago) do this. The charts, now rapidly created with modern automated tool sets, can be used to indicate such things as time delays, costs and errors, corrections and rework, so that the improvements to be gained from reducing time delays at functional boundaries, for instance, can be assessed. The modified activity charts, displaying the reengineered processes, provide an important input to the development of computer-based prototypes, from which requirements for IT applications can be specified.

- Based on the reengineered processes, new jobs--or rather roles of employees, customers, and other participants within the renewed business processes--are identified. Examples of roles are "customer," "customer service representative," and "account manager". To perform a role, an individual works in an environment, called the role environment. The *role environment* in the information-based organization is typically a (fixed or mobile) workstation-based interface with IT services that support the work of the role. It is custom designed for a specific business role and is a window on all underlying applications and workflow/communication services. The crux of a role environment is that it enables user interface screens to be prototyped, designed, and built for the totality of a business role. User interfaces are thus associated with business roles, not applications. In this way, visualization of interwoven work and IT is a specific form of the prototyping technique, already included in the IT planning process rather than in application development activities.

- The total set of reengineered business processes, workflows, locations, roles, and information needs is further expanded into the target *IT architecture*: the modeling on a conceptual level of the IT applications, data models, hardware and communications classes, organizational structures, and IT service delivery requirements. The IT architecture is constructed on a fairly high conceptual level, not describing the details that are necessary to develop future IT applications. The boundaries of the ultimate IT applications, databases, and IT infrastructure needs are only broadly defined. The IT architecture might therefore be called a "road map" for further IT application design. Ideally, the whole model should fit on not more than a few sheets of paper, presented in a visual format of arrows (processes) and blueprints (for each generic location the activities, roles, information needs, IT applications, and technology requirements are listed).

The process of developing such IT architecture is typically iterative. Although it starts with the business vision, the developed models are made possible, even suggested, by emerging technologies. During the process, the model is continuously tested and enhanced by reviewing whether the advantages of appropriate technological opportunities are included.

Although many applications of IT can be planned as described, some exceptions have to be made. The process as depicted here is valid for the planning of those applications of IT that are more or less broadly used by defined groups of users (e.g., by business process) and collectively form the portfolio of IT applications. It is this class of IT applications that should be planned as pragmatically, iteratively, and cyclic as described. Contemporary planning for IT, however, in fact requires a mix of different planning approaches to effectively manage different types of IT. On top of the described approach, we can distinguish at least three different management and therefore planning approaches:

- *Venture management*: planning of new, high-risk but strategic business ventures, e.g., new Internet-based business initiatives, with high potential impact and a high IT content. For such ventures, we don't have the time to follow the approach as described. Typically, applications are prototyped and realized using packaged and parameter-controlled software, which is quickly brought to an acceptable level for initial usage. Once the venture has proven successful, it is incorporated in one of the other planning and management approaches. If not successful, the venture can be easily discarded without damaging other classes of IT, and without too much waste of investment.
- *Retail management*: distributed planning of low-cost technology where justification lies in the hands of end users. Planning activities and related budgeting decisions for this technology are focused on improving the effectiveness of users, and are based on efficient, standardized, and often centrally organized support. The ultimate example of such technologies is the PC or laptop computer for end-user computing, configured with standard text processing, Internet access, office suite software, etc. The IT planning approach mainly deals with the development of standards and compatibility, and aspects related to the volume of this technology such as expense planning and acquisition controls.
- *Utility management*: planning of a central, shared resource with emphasis on efficiency and management of capital-intensive and vital resources. For example, the technical complexity of a contemporary, flexible IT infrastruc-

ture that meets the demands of connectivity and accessibility of anything, anyone, anywhere, anytime, calls for a more rigorous, structured and detailed planning approach. The planning activities focus on formal standards and minimization of risk of failure while substantial capital investments are involved. IT specialists who understand the capabilities, risks, and constraints of today's technology should perform the more detailed planning of an IT infrastructure.

Today's IT supply planning

At the IT supply planning level, a mix of different planning approaches to effectively manage different types of IT supply can be observed. The majority of improvements in the planning of IT supply, compared with the past, have aimed at meeting agreed-upon deadlines (thus reducing the uncertainty of results delivery), cost reduction, and improved quality levels of IT supply. For example:

- For many operational services carried out on a daily basis by, e.g., a data center, SLAs are put into place. SLAs include a set of performance measures such as applications availability, timeliness and accuracy, responsiveness of user support, and cost of operation. The purpose of an SLA is to provide a basis for objective assessment of operations performance, and to establish clear procedures for problem resolution. Performance targets are accompanied by standards or criteria for success and specific measures to employ. Procedures govern how and when to measure and report the results, how to respond when targets are missed, how to revise the SLA should that become necessary, and who is responsible for these activities.

- In many cases, standard software packages might be preferable to the development of IT applications. A software package will often be available that meets most of the essential users' requirements. Although the costs of implementing packages are relatively high (flexible packages require a high degree of tailoring and customizing), the total cost of acquisition and maintenance of a package are generally substantially less than the cost of development of an equivalent IT application. Besides, the required time to select and implement packages is much better to plan and control than traditional, in-house IT development projects.

- For remaining application development projects, the conventional, sequential "waterfall" application development process is being replaced by a more iterative, goal-oriented, and continuous process of evolutionary development. The planning practices for this type of projects include setting of predefined timeframes (*time-boxes*) for the delivery of each updated version of the application being built on a regular basis. If tradeoffs have to be made between meeting the time commitment or delivering the planned content, the deadline wins over completeness.

- For many application maintenance activities, organizations tend to formalize and organize their work around "releases" of changed applications. Releases contain the modifications and enhancements to applications, grouped together as a result of the assembly of change requests over a given period of time. Releases are implemented according to predefined time intervals that have been agreed upon by both business representatives and the IT supply organization.

These and other examples of today's planning practices for IT supply will be further explored in Chapter 6, in which the specific performance measures for IT supply will be discussed.

Altogether, today's planning for IT is less rigid and elaborate than traditional IT planning approaches. While IT might follow an organization's strategic direction, at the same time the business strategy can also be led by IT opportunities. Those who understand the strategic direction of the company, those who are deeply involved with the business issues at hand, and those who are able to think in terms of business results increasingly carry out the process. IT supply, and IT infrastructure resources in particular, are managed (and planned) more rigidly, while the supplier of IT is increasingly held accountable for observing agreed-upon performance levels in terms of time, quality, and cost.

PLANNING FOR VALUE FROM IT

As the role, application, and planning of IT have evolved over time, so have the art and science of planning for value from IT. Most organizations have little history of planning and monitoring the achievement of benefits from IT. But it is increasingly understood that value from IT can be generated mainly by only a limited number of decisions made at the pre-investment planning stage of IT projects. This is due to the fact that the cost of operating, maintaining, and servicing an installed base of IT applications originates from decisions in the past to engage in IT development projects. Once applications are in use, the level of relatively fixed costs can only be influenced by reviewing the effectiveness and efficiency of the activities and resources that are put into place to deliver these IT products and services.

IT investment decisions are not materially different from other investment decisions. It is through the decision-making process and applied decision criteria for IT investments that the future achievement of value from IT is planned. It is therefore important that cost/benefit calculations for IT projects do take into account the full life-cycle cost, including costs of operations, maintenance, and user support.

IT investment decisions indeed share many characteristics with other investment decisions. They all must reflect the needs of the organization. The benefits of investments in IT must therefore be evaluated in relation to the business purpose of the investment. The criteria that are appropriate for justifying different types of IT investments differ according to the purpose of the investment and the type of IT. The value of IT should be managed and measured by distinguishing different classes of

IT in relation to their business purpose.

From a business perspective, five main business purposes of IT investments can be identified. These distinct business purposes lead to five classes of IT investments. Each class of IT investment requires different evaluation criteria, since the classes of IT investment differ according to the purpose of the investment, and in particular, to the kind of benefits that are to be achieved by the specific application of IT. The act of organizing IT investments in these terms offers management a framework to decide on IT investments and apply the appropriate decision criteria *vis-à-vis* business objectives.

- The first class is *mandatory IT*, required to satisfy regulatory requirements (such as changes to the payroll system), to meet internal organizational requirements (such as consolidation of financial reporting for a multinational company), or to provide IT applications that are a competitive necessity (for example, the need to join an industry-specific EDI service or e-marketplace initiative). Although the value of this class of IT investments, or rather expenditures, may not be clear, the business reason is. Expenditures are considered sunk costs, also called *threshold expenditures* on IT, and represent the amount of money that an organization must spend on IT if it is simply to survive. Because the organization has no choice but to spend on mandatory IT, the main investment consideration is how efficiently these IT activities can be supplied, maintained, and operated.

- The second class is IT to improve the efficiency and *effectiveness* of the organization, aimed at reducing or avoiding operational and labor costs, increasing business productivity and revenue, and monitoring business activities. IT may contribute in various ways, and its contribution can be evaluated with measures of cost, quality, and speed of internal business processes. Cost/benefit assessment is, in principle, the most common approach of valuating this class of IT investment.

- The third class is IT to *change the business, the business network*, and *the business scope*. This class of IT, often called "Strategic IT," is meant to improve competitiveness, aimed at gaining a sustainable advantage over competitors, improving the organization's share of, or position in, existing and new markets, all aimed at winning and retaining profitable customers. This IT is designed to achieve a major competitive leap for the organization, and includes the application of IT as a product or as a service, often involving Internet functionality. Valuating such IT, however, is more than simply assessing the extent to which revenues or profitability may be increased. Business value can be determined by cost/benefit calculations, modified to account for the organizational and technological risk of failure, while IT investments of this class must also be evaluated in the light of longer-term business success, strategic match, and competitive advantage. The investment decision for strategic IT is similar to other (non-IT) investments, where management judgment is ultimately the most critical factor.

- The fourth class is *IT infrastructure*, which enables the benefits of other IT applications to be realized. These are investments in the basis on which IT applications are built. They do not offer direct benefits, but enable the benefits of other IT investments to be realized. The value of this type of investment is contingent on the value that accrues from future applications making use of the infrastructure. It is actually not possible to valuate investments in IT infrastructure themselves, just as it is impossible to valuate infrastructure investments in other areas of the business (office buildings, warehouses, corporate libraries, and so on) or at the national level (roads, rail tracks, harbors, etc.).

Ultimately, top management must form a judgment as to whether the potential benefits of the proposed infrastructure investments will pay off. However, such an evaluation process for IT infrastructure investments can be made easier by establishing performance standards for the IT infrastructure and by including a share of infrastructure costs when evaluating investments in IT application.

- The fifth class is *IT research*, executed to ensure that the business is not left behind by technological progress. Many organizations devote a portion of their IT budget to researching technologies and experimental systems to help ensure that their information needs will continue to be met adequately in the future. Allocating a predefined amount of money for research projects and setting clear objectives and budgets for the projects is the common way of funding such activities. However, the business benefits of research projects, if any, usually take several years to become evident, and many research projects just don't deliver results. Hence, how much to spend on researching future applications and products is a question of judging the future needs of the business, and the value of individual research projects in preparing the organization to meet those needs.

CONCLUSION

IT has evolved, over time, from a purely supportive resource into a truly strategic asset. Many of today's organizations apply IT for both purposes and for those at different "stages of growth" in between, which complicates the management and valuation of IT and hence, the planning for value from IT enormously.

Achieving appropriate planning results for IT is and will remain difficult. The traditional exhaustive and long-lasting top-down planning exercises at the business planning, IT planning, and IT supply planning levels are not adequate and in fact never have been. Contemporary planning approaches, relying on five basic principles, have gradually been introduced in many of today's organizations:

- IT not only supports and changes business operations, it also introduces IT-enabled products and distribution channels and it allows individuals and organizations to work together effectively and efficiently, while simultaneously weaving in the enabling IT applications and IT infrastructure.
- The whole process of IT planning is more appropriately thought of as "work transformation" and "business scope redefinition." Application of IT needs to

be a broad, cross-functional, and cross-business process that entails under-standing business goals and strategies, refashioning business processes, and weaving IT into the fabric of the organization.

- IT planning can be moved for a great deal of its application to fast-tracked, iterative, prototyping-oriented approaches that involve business executives in every step of the process. The ultimate user of IT–the people who ultimately have the biggest impact on satisfying the end-customer, including the people who design, manufacture, and market new products and services–all have to be involved. The business people need to comfortably sit in the driver's seat of planning IT and planning value from IT.

- Although in principle the business leads and IT follows, reality shows synergistic interaction and partnerships between IT and business people, business and IT initiatives. Top-down/alignment and bottom up/impact plan-ning are merged into a pragmatic, appropriate approach for IT planning.

- A contemporary IT planning approach acknowledges that variations exist in the degree of rigor to be applied to planning different classes of IT. Of critical importance is a detailed planning approach to define an appropriate, flexible IT infrastructure that embraces standards for networks, distributed databases, and user interfaces.

REFERENCES

Boynton, A.C. and Zmud, R.W. (1987). Information technology planning in the 1990s: Directions for practice and research. *MIS Quarterly*, March, 59-71.

Cox, B. (1990). Project estimating. *PEP Paper 16*. London: Butler Cox.

Gray, D.H. (1986). Uses and misuses of strategic planning. *Harvard Business Review*, January-February, 89-97.

Hammer, M. and Champy, J. (1993). *Reengineering the Corporation, A Manifesto for Business Revolution*. New York: HarperCollins.

Keen, P.G.W. and Cummins, J. M. (1994). *Networks in Action*. Belmont, California: Wadsworth Publishing Company.

McKay, D.T. and Brockway, D. W. (1989). Building the IT infrastructure for the 1990s. *Stage by Stage*, Number 3, Lexington, MA: Nolan, Norton & Co.

Marwaha, S. (1993). The role environment perspective: Gearing technology to the needs of the business. *Connect*, Number 3, Cambridge, MA: Arthur D. Little.

Mintzberg, H. (1994). The fall and rise of strategic planning. *Harvard Business Review*, January-February, 107-114.

Morton, M. S. (Ed.) (1991) *The Corporation of the 1990s: Information Technology and Organizational Transformation*. New York: Oxford University Press.

Parker, M.M., R.J. Benson and H.E. Trainor (1988), *Information Economics: Linking Business Performance to Information Technology*. Englewoods Cliffs, NJ: Prentice-Hall.

Porter, M.E. (1985). *Competitive Advantage: Creating and Sustaining Superior*

Performance. New York: The Free Press.

Porter, M.E.(1980). *Competitive Strategy: Techniques for Analyzing Industries and Competitors*. New York: The Free Press.

Pralahad, C.K. and Hamel, G. (1990). The core competence of the corporation. *Harvard Business Review*, May-June.

Pruijm, R.A.M. (1990) *Corporate Strategy and Information Systems*, Doctoral Dissertation Erasmus University, Rotterdam.

Van der Zee, J.T.M. and de Jong, B. (1999). Alignment is not enough. *Journal of Management Information Systems*, Fall, 16(2), 137-156.

Van der Zee, J.T.M. and Strikwedra, H. (2001). *Capturing Value in the New Economy*. Amsterdam, The Netherlands: Financial Times/Prentice-Hall.

Chapter III

The Link Between IT Planning and IT Valuation: The BTRIPLEE Framework

Managers, when faced with choices, generally use a set of decision rules and tools that help them to make choices to best achieve their objectives. This should not be different for decisions about IT, especially since IT has become part and parcel of the business strategy of virtually any business. An important aspect of planning for IT, as we have seen, is decision making, the process of developing and selecting options and related courses of actions. The application of IT has a cost and a benefit side, and business managers are in search of the IT with greater benefits than costs. Both parts of the cost/benefit equation must therefore be planned and then evaluated in a business context.

While the cost side may be difficult to plan and manage, the benefit side is even tougher to manage and measure: identifying and obtaining external and internal performance data to measure and valuate IT appears to be very difficult in practice. As was stated earlier, the common denominators of the shortfall of evidence of the value of IT are:

- insufficient management (including planning) of IT and the value of IT,
- deficiencies in frameworks to measure the value of IT,
- deficiencies in appropriate measures to determine the value of IT.

The first point, the subject of planning for value of IT, was addressed in the previous chapter. This chapter aims to provide a currently lacking, comprehensive measurement framework, answering the basic questions: *What* to measure, and *How* to measure, to compare results from IT investments with performance improvements in the business, and in the application and supply of IT. The following three chapters are dedicated to the determination of appropriate measures.

MEASURING THE VALUE OF IT

Organizations need to build a thorough picture of the connection between business strategy, business processes, and business activities on the one hand, and the opportunities, (im)possibilities, and current application and supply of IT on the other. Like commonly applied management accounting systems and other diagnostic control systems, an IT value measurement system should be aimed at a consistent attempt to systematically bring together different indicators of IT value at different levels of the organization. IT valuation at different levels helps manage the complexity of IT at each distinct level. Besides, IT value measurement must be aimed at multiple stakeholders. Whether it is sophisticated or a more rudimentary start, IT value measurement should be capable of bridging the communication gap between the worlds of the business and IT. It replaces opinion with fact, focusing discussions away from the emotional side, and it directs towards measurable improvements in the application and supply of IT.

In short, a systematic and consistent measurement of IT value must be based on two key attributes:

- *An overall management framework*: Because the realities of IT application in organizations are so complex, a conceptual scheme for simplifying and ordering them is desirable. Although "the use of any framework provokes the temptation to treat the framework's abstractions as if they were the whirling reality, or alternatively, the temptation to dismiss the model as mere jargon," as Cohen puts it, a framework must be treated as a tool to help navigate difficult terrain, rather than as an end in itself. To manage, monitor, and provide feedback on the value of IT, measurement of IT value must be based on a management framework (coined the BTRIPLEE framework) which links the levels of business planning, IT planning, and IT supply planning with comparable valuation levels. By assigning value to IT at each level, and in its full context, the overall value question can be answered.
- *A set of key measures for value*: These allow the management of IT, varying according to the objectives of the organization and the level of the framework for which the measures are constructed. The appropriate measures to assess the value of IT at three levels will be discussed in the next three chapters, on the basis of the BTRIPLEE framework.

The BTRIPLEE framework and associated measures are designed to determine the value of the application and supply of IT.

THE BTRIPLEE FRAMEWORK FOR PLANNING AND VALUATION OF IT

As IT is almost literally woven into every aspect of the business, IT has become an indispensable part of the business *fabric*, described in the previous chapter. The fabric analogy is elaborated in the following sections.

Figure 3.1: The Value of IT as Part of the Business Fabric

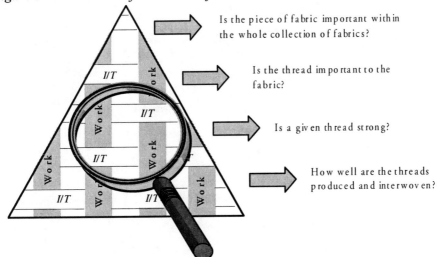

IT Value Questions

It can be argued that individual IT applications and IT services, being it Internet applications, bookkeeping systems, or text processing services, are all threads in the pieces of fabric representing business activities and processes. Several questions about these threads are meaningful and appropriate. Figure 3.1 shows these questions, together with the fabric of business processes and IT.

The questions are:

- Is the piece of fabric itself important within the whole collection of fabrics that make up the business? In other words, how do products and services, and business processes contribute to overall business objectives and performance?
- Is the thread important to the fabric? In other words, how does IT contribute to the products and services, or the performance of the business processes and business activities? What is the functional alignment of IT applications and services with customers and suppliers, business processes, and how do IT applications and services successfully support the employees in an organization?
- Is a given thread strong? In other words, what is the technical quality of the IT involved?
- How well are the threads produced and interwoven? In other words, how well are IT applications and services developed, implemented, and supported by its producer ("process quality")?

We might conclude the analogy by stating that the only way to assign value to the IT threads is to ask all four (value) questions together, and to place each IT thread or group of IT threads in the context of business processes.

This is an interesting approach; however, it should be noted that the value of mandatory IT, IT infrastructure, and IT research (three important IT investment classes as discussed in the previous chapter) cannot be measured by a possible direct

Figure 3.2 (a): Planning and Control at Different Levels

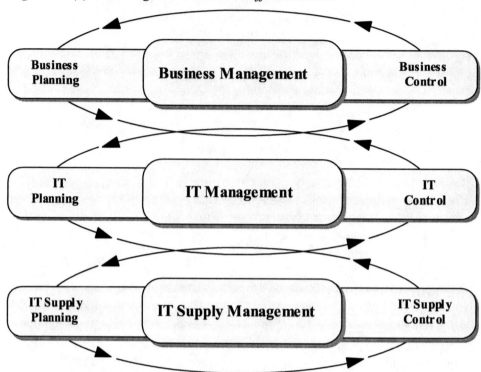

contribution to the performance of IT-based products and services, nor by a possible direct contribution to the performance of business processes. Mandatory IT, IT infrastructure, and IT research rather contribute to the organization's strategic goals, and ultimately, to the top and bottom lines of the annual financial statements.

This means that questions that cannot be answered directly include: "What is the value of a given individual thread (an IT application or IT service)?" or "What is the value of the collection of threads known as IT?" To explore the overall business value of IT, value questions must be asked at different but interdependent levels, and answers must be placed in their full business context, as discussed below.

Linking Value to Planning Levels

The different value questions can be linked to the different *planning* levels defined in the previous chapter: business planning, IT planning, and IT supply planning, as shown in Figure 3.2 (a). At each level, different value questions are asked. Although the levels of planning are interdependent and iterative, allowing for top-down and bottom-up initiatives, as previously discussed, value can be measured at each *distinct* level by applying *distinct* sets of measures. This will result in relevant answers to the questions specific to each level.

Business plans are derived from business objectives and business goals through some kind of business planning process. Business plans determine how the

Figure 3.2 (b): Planning, Deliverables, and Control at Different Levels

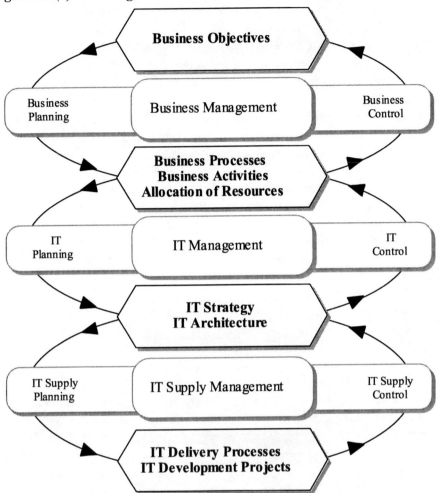

things that have to be done will be done through the configuration of products, services, distribution channels, business processes, and business activities, along with the allocation of resources. The linkage of business objectives with its products, services, distribution channels, processes, activities, and resources, called business management, is illustrated in Figure 3.2 (b).

As explained in Chapter 2, an IT strategy and an IT architecture are not hierarchically derived from business plans; IT planning processes rather *align* an IT strategy and an IT architecture dynamically with business objectives and plans, and business processes, activities, and resources. This alignment, called IT management, is also illustrated in Figure 3.2 (b).

Equally, the IT strategy and IT architecture are used to guide IT supply planning processes, which result in the construction of IT delivery processes and the definition of IT development projects. In Figure 3.2 (b), the link between the IT strategy and IT architecture on one hand, and IT delivery processes and IT development projects on the other, is called IT supply management.

Replacing "Control" with "Value Measurement"

The term "control" at the three levels in Figure 3.2 (b) is too broad and not specific enough to express what has to be measured at the levels of business management, IT management, and IT supply management. Therefore the term *value*, already used many times in previous sections, is re-introduced and further explored. As at each distinct level different value questions must be answered and distinct sets of measures applied, as said before, value must be defined differently at each distinct level.

Webster's New World Dictionary defines *value* as "the worth of a thing in money or goods," and "that quality of a thing which makes it more or less desirable, useful, etc.," and "a thing or quality having intrinsic worth."

According to the first definition, the value of IT relates to the worth of IT expressed in money. Parker, Benson, and Trainor's description of value of IT broadens the monetary interpretation of *value*, introducing the notion of *organizational improvement* through IT:

> "*The concept of benefit remains important as a measure of discrete economic effect such as cost reduction or direct revenue production, and these benefits are certainly worth something to a business. We propose value as a broader concept based on the effect IT [investment] has on the organizational performance of the enterprise. Cost reduction and revenue production-traditional benefits-are two of several components of value. Cost reduction or direct revenue production are important effects on organizational performance, but so is competitive advantage and increased market share. Value is assessed by adding organizational performance factors to discrete benefits.*"

According to Webster's second definition, the value of IT also relates to the quality of IT that makes it desirable. A review of the term *quality* is appropriate, since it is often wrongly used in relation to both the application and supply of IT. Quality, according to Van Reeken, includes both *effectiveness* and *efficiency* aspects. This implies that the application and supply of IT can only be desirable and valuable if they are effective and efficient. Again, these terms must be defined somewhat more precisely.

Webster's New World Dictionary describes *effectiveness* as "producing a desired effect," which basically means, "doing the right things." An appropriate synonym for efficiency might be "doing the right things right." *The Concise Oxford Dictionary* defines efficiency as "the ratio of useful work performed to the total energy expended." Webster's defines *efficiency* as "producing the desired result with a minimum of effort, expense, or waste." The words "useful work performed" and "desired result" are important: they capture the need for effectiveness to be present for something to be efficient. For example, it is not sensible, by definition, to discuss efficiency of business processes, activities, and resources, if they are not effective. Equally, IT delivery processes and IT development projects can never be efficient if they are not effective. Webster's definition of efficiency underpins the notion of "*minimum* of effort or expense" rather than just "the total energy expected" so that this definition is preferred.

Returning to the framework of Figure 3.2 (b), if business processes, activities, and resources are well aligned with business objectives, so that these objectives are realized, business management is effective. If it is effective, and business processes and activities are executed with a minimum of effort and resources, business management is also efficient. In relation to IT: business management is effective if the potential benefits of IT capabilities are optimally reflected in business objectives, and if business processes, activities, and resources are optimally enabled by IT. Potential benefits of IT include apparent financial effects of cost reduction and revenue production through IT, and strategic effects of competitive advantage, increased market share, and the like. In other words: the business management level incorporates the effectiveness of IT in reconfiguring, redesigning, and aligning the business scope, the business network, business processes, business activities, and resources.

If IT is exploited and used with a minimum of effort and resources, business management may not only be called effective, but also efficient, in relation to IT. Effort and resources at the business management level include the cost of all IT, including mandatory IT, IT infrastructure, and IT research.

The measurement at the business level of aggregate effectiveness and cost of IT (in other words: the business value of all IT) refers to the extent to which IT enables and contributes to meeting business objectives, thus improving organizational performance, at minimal cost. The label "Business Control" in Figure 3.2 (b) should therefore be replaced by the label *Business value of IT*.

At a lower level, IT value measurement relates to the determination of the results of effective IT planning and hence the determination of the value of IT in its alignment with, and support of, the business processes, activities, and resources, and its costs. IT management is effective if business processes, activities, and resources are optimally supported by the IT strategy and IT architecture, and as a result: the IT applied. If alignment of IT is realized with a minimum of effort, IT management is efficient as well.

At this level, however, the cost of IT, and thus the efficiency aspect, is excluded because of three practical reasons. Firstly, IT is only part of a wide-ranging set of cost components that impact the efficiency of business processes, activities, and resources. It is virtually impossible to allocate the proportion of any efficiency improvement, which can be determined to stem from any cost component. It is only possible to evaluate efficiency improvement in business processes, activities, and resources of the whole package of components, not just of IT. Secondly, since a large part of IT expenditure is on IT infrastructure, supporting multiple business processes, activities, and resources, and aimed at building a strategic "core competence," it is a practical problem to comprehensively allocate such IT costs to specific business processes, activities, or resources directly. Thirdly, like the costs of IT infrastructure, it is practically impossible to allocate the costs of mandatory IT, IT research, and IT in products and services to specific business processes, activities, and resources. For these practical, yet important reasons, IT costs are not included at this level.

IT costs are taken into account, as said, at the business management level. However, it may still be important to determine whether the IT strategy and IT architecture are efficiently translated into IT at this level. The best solution to tackle this problem is to measure the efficiency of making IT products and services available, at the third level of the BTRIPLEE framework: IT supply management. What remains at the second level of IT management is the measurement of the extent to which IT satisfactorily supports business processes, business activities, and business employees, called the measurement of the *Effectiveness of IT*.

To assess the results of IT supply planning, the *Effectiveness and Efficiency of IT supply* is determined. This category of value measurement relates to the measurement of the effective and efficient supply of IT products and services. At this level, IT supply management is considered to be effective if IT delivery processes and IT development projects conform to the requirements defined by the IT strategy and IT architecture. If IT is supplied by an external IT supply organization, its efficiency might be of less relevance, unless inefficiencies are reflected in the price to be paid for IT products and services. However, in the case of IT supply, "useful work" is represented by IT products and services that match the requirements of the IT strategy and the IT architecture, while "effort and expenses" corresponds to the costs of resources committed for that purpose. Committed resources may be found both in the supplying internal or external IT organization, as well as in the user's organization. Users are often involved in the supply of IT as well, for example to determine specifications and to test IT supply deliverables. Their efforts should be taken into account when measuring "effort and expenses," as IT supply is regarded as a set of supply processes, consuming several types of resources and crossing organizational borders. In fact, it is not the organizational structure that defines which resources should be counted, but rather the IT delivery processes as such.

In conclusion, the following definitions apply:
- The *Business value of IT* can be defined as the worth of IT for an organization as a whole, expressed in terms of organizational performance improvement at minimum cost.
- The *Effectiveness of IT* is defined as the extent to which IT satisfactorily supports business processes, business activities, and business employees, regardless of associated costs.
- An appropriate definition of *Effectiveness of IT* supply is the extent to which the supply of IT products and services aligns with the business's requirements as defined by an IT strategy and an IT architecture, regardless of associated costs.
- The definition of *Efficiency of IT supply* is the extent to which effective IT is supplied at minimum cost.

As said, it is only sensible to discuss efficiency if effectiveness is present.

Effectiveness (doing the right things) and efficiency (doing the right things right) are complementary terms as long as they are attributed to the same level of Figure 3.2 (b). Ideally, things are both effective and efficient, at any level.

However, the degree of effectiveness at a lower level impacts efficiency at a higher level (it goes without saying that efficiency at a lower levels adds to efficiency at a higher level as well). For example, the IT strategy is executed more efficiently and the IT architecture is "filled" in an efficient way, if IT supply is effective. If the IT strategy and IT architecture are effective, business processes and activities can be executed more efficiently since IT is optimally aligned and users of IT face fewer problems in employing it. Similarly, if business processes are executed effectively, stakeholders' goals can be met efficiently. This concept of effectiveness at lower levels impacting efficiency of higher levels is reflected in Figure 3.3. The concept underpins the need to assess the value of IT at the distinct levels indicated.

The BTRIPLEE Framework

The discussion of (business) value, effectiveness, and efficiency of the application and supply of IT results in the translation of these concepts into the three-layer framework of business management, IT management, and IT supply management as presented in Figure 3.2 (b).

The measurement of aggregate cost and ultimate effectiveness, together called value, of all IT (including IT to support business processes and reconfigure the business network, IT in products and services, mandatory IT, IT infrastructure, and IT research) relate to the business management level of our framework. The extent

Figure 3.3: Effectiveness and Efficiency at Different Levels

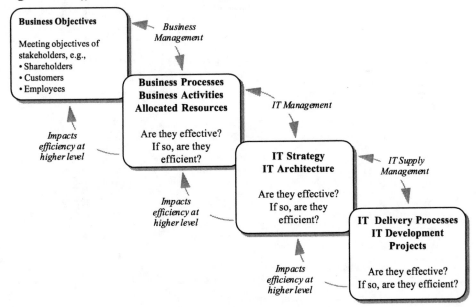

to which all IT enables and contributes to meeting business objectives effectively and efficiently has been coined the *Business value of IT*. The label "Business Control" is therefore replaced by the label "Business value of IT," as shown in Figure 3.4.

The IT management level including the measurement of the results of effective IT planning and hence the determination of the effectiveness of IT in supporting business processes, activities, and employees, regardless of associated costs, has therefore been called the *Effectiveness of IT*. This is also reflected in Figure 3.4.

The third layer, IT supply management, includes the measurement of the results of IT supply planning. At this level, the effectiveness and efficiency of the supply of IT products and services are measured, therefore called *Effectiveness and Efficiency of IT supply*.

Figure 3.4: The BTRIPLEE Framework for IT Planning and Validation

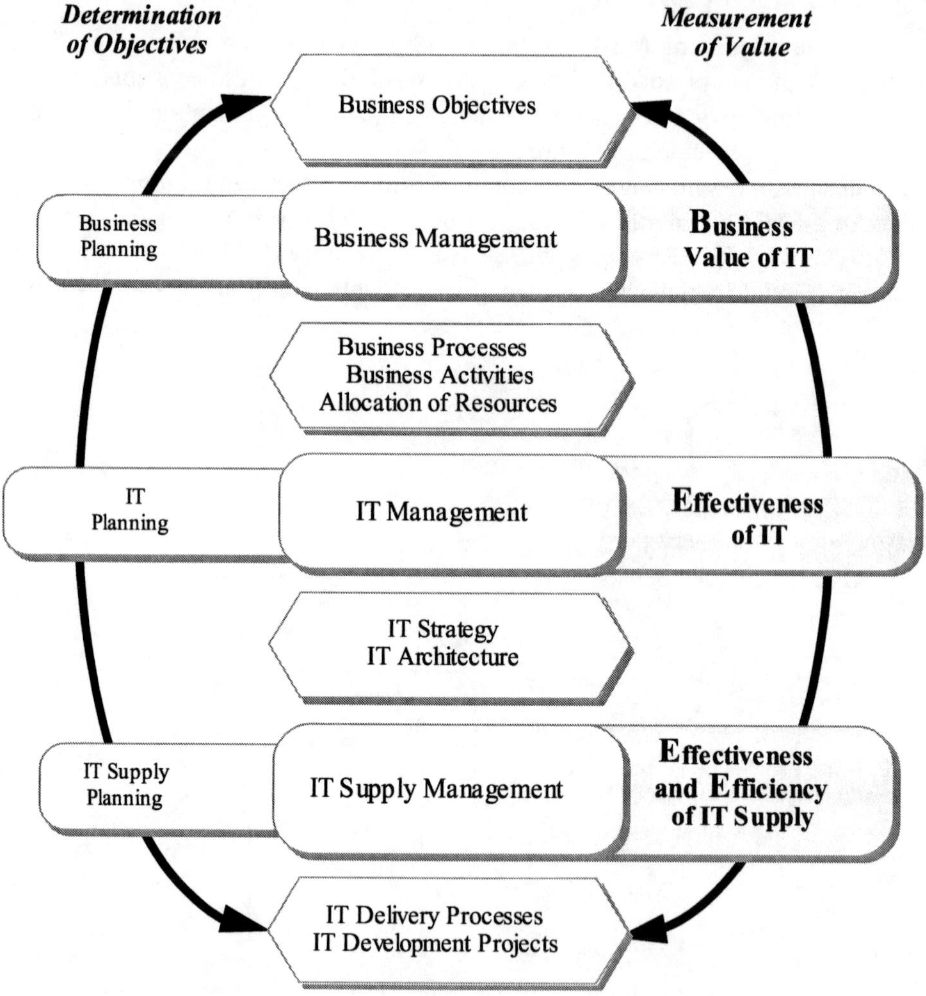

The framework that links IT planning with the valuation of IT at the defined levels is called the **B**T**RIPLE**E framework, after the first letter of the name of each level of value measurement. Since the levels of planning and value are interrelated, both downwards and upwards, any IT planning and valuation framework must support both top-down alignment as well as bottom-up impact planning initiatives. The bi-directional arrows in Figure 3.4 reflect these aspects.

In conclusion, to assign value to IT is to ask questions at the different levels together and to place answers in context. Although the different planning levels are interdependent and iterative, the value of IT must be measured at each distinct level, by applying distinct sets of appropriate measures. Only at the IT management level, the efficiency aspect of the value of IT is excluded, for practical reasons.

Reading the B**TRIPLE**E framework from bottom to top, value of IT is realized, if:

- Required IT products and services are satisfactorily developed, maintained, and operated (IT supply effectiveness), consuming a minimal amount of resources (IT supply efficiency).
- IT has successfully contributed to the performance of business processes, activities, and employees (IT effectiveness).
- IT is used to its full potential in terms of its possible contribution to organizational performance, at minimal cost (Business value).

MEASURING THE BUSINESS VALUE OF IT

Throwing money at IT and expecting instant business value does not make much sense. Quite some research has been devoted to measuring the business value of IT costs at the business level, but none provides conclusive proof that money spent on IT automatically leads to improved organizational performance. Strassmann has convincingly shown that no correlation exists between company performance and total IT cost. He investigated many possible correlations between levels of IT cost and business success, expressed in financial ratios such as returns on assets or shareholders' investments, without results. Harris and Katz proved that high-performance firms spend a significantly higher proportion of revenues on IT than low-performance firms do; however, it is unlikely that IT expenditure alone ensures a firm's superior performance.

The main conclusion from this research is that no single performance measure at the organization, business, or SBU level (depending on the scope of interest) is available to determine the value of IT, and therefore multiple measures to reflect different relationships at different levels are needed. The underlying principle for an assessment of the business value of IT must be that it can only be derived from the improvement in performance of the organization, as a result of the application of IT. Measuring the business value of IT should therefore be linked to the measurement of an organization's performance improvement in different aspects.

The business value of IT is likely to be thought of in terms of improving the organization's financial performance, because "the language of upper management is money," as Juran indicated more than 25 years ago (see Figure 3.5).

Figure 3.5: Languages in an Organization

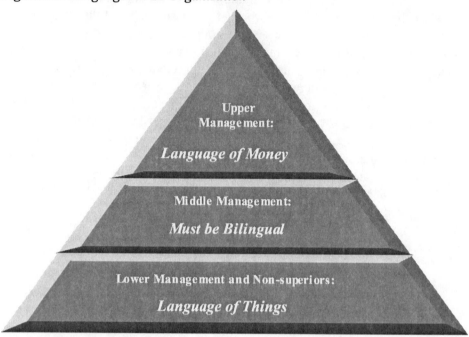

However, an organization can improve its short and longer-term performance in many different ways. Three are important in relation to the application of IT:

- improving *financial* performance (reducing or avoiding operational and labor costs, increasing business productivity and revenue) through the traditional application of IT to improve the effectiveness and efficiency of the organization;
- improving *business* performance (enlarging market share, improving customer satisfaction, shortening order fulfillment times, etc.) through the innovative application of IT (e.g., through Internet, intranet, and extranet applications);
- enhancing *strategic* performance by reconfiguring the network of businesses involved in the creation and delivery of products and services, and by incorporating IT in products and services, or even completely replace them by IT, thus reconfiguring the business scope.

The measurement of the business value of IT is thus concerned with the relationship between the costs of IT and its contribution to the improvement of an organization's performance, measurable in three related dimensions:

- *financial performance*, measured by financial indicators such as profitability, productivity, earnings, etc.;
- *business performance*, measured by non-financial indicators such as competitiveness, new product sales, product development lead times, manufacturing lead times, distribution lead times, customer satisfaction, etc.;

- *strategic performance*, measured by indicators that match specific management objectives (management's critical success factors).

Therefore, a closer look at the three relevant value dimensions is taken, leading to an aggregated approach to correlating IT costs with business value.

IT Costs and Financial Performance

The first valuation dimension is the relation between IT costs and financial performance. One important financial performance indicator is profitability. Profitability can be increased when operating costs are decreased, e.g., by means of improving productivity and efficiency through IT. The business value of IT at the organizational level in that case is clear. Another financial performance indicator is revenue. It is often assumed that the total level of IT spending, measured as a percentage of the revenue of the organization, may be used as an indicator of the "right" spending level. This ratio is benchmarked (compared) with that of other organizations to judge whether it is right. If the organization's IT spending is about in line with those of others in the same industry, management might stop worrying because the numbers show they are at industry average. Figure 3.6 shows an example of IT spending-to-revenue data of the Gartner Group, one of the companies that assembles and analyzes such data on a regular basis.

Although the percentage of revenue spent on IT is not a valid and reliable value-for-money indicator, as stated earlier, an analysis of IT costs for comparative purposes within the same industry at a gross level and in combination with other indicators can be worthwhile to perform. Such an analysis may reveal abnormal patterns in IT spending and may lead to further, more focused investigations into the value question. To investigate, it is necessary to look at relations between financial performance and IT costs from different points of view. The appropriate indicators of IT value measurement are developed in the next chapter.

Figure 3.6: IT Spending as a Percentage of Revenue

Industry Group	IT Spending as % of Revenue				
	1991	1993	1995	1997	1999
Communications (Telcos)	4.7	5.8	4.1	6.7	13.9
Electric/Water/Gas/Sanitary Services	1.6	1.6	1.8	2.8	3.4
Finance, Insurance, Banking	3.6	2.6	2.5	6.5	8.6
Hospitals and Health Care	2.3	2.5	2.3	3.9	5.3
Manufacturing	1.9	2.0	1.8	1.8	3.0
All Industries	3.0	2.5	2.6	4.1	5.5

Adapted from Gartner Group

IT Costs and Business Performance

The second valuation dimension is the relation between IT costs and business performance. Business performance can be measured by using non-financial performance indicators, complementary to and in combination with financial performance measures.

Non-financial performance indicators have always been used in organizations, many of them for internal control. To relate IT costs to improvement in business performance, a focus on the results of the organization's activities in the market is necessary, so that external-oriented measures of business performance are needed. Number of customers served would be an example of an external-oriented measure to indicate business size. Business output can be measured by tons of final products produced in a manufacturing environment, number of insurance policies issued and number of claims processed for an insurance company, amount of KWh produced for an electrical utility, etc.

Kaplan classified non-financial measures into organizational improvement, organizational learning, product design improvement, and production planning and evaluation. Adding the external perspective, this classification resulted in Kaplan and Norton's "Balanced Scorecard" concept which combines non-financial and financial performance indicators in a structured way. To further illustrate the linkage of IT costs with non-financial business performance indicators, the Balanced Scorecard concept will be applied in the next chapter. This concept has become quite popular over the past few years, mainly because of its practicality.

If IT costs are linked to non-financial business performance indicators, e.g., IT costs per customer served, such ratios help in determining the business value of IT from an historical perspective (trends) or an external comparative perspective (benchmarking).

IT Costs and Strategic Performance

The third dimension of measuring the business value of IT is to relate IT costs with the strategic performance of the organization. Strategic performance can be measured by the extent to which an organization realizes its critical success factors--the most critical activities of the organization that contribute most to its success.

The idea of focusing on a limited number of important activities, or business priorities, has been a popular and useful management tool for several decades, and has become even more important lately as a result of the Core Competence management approach. Drucker coined the term "Management by Objectives" in the 1950s to describe the process whereby managers establish a few key objectives and follow them with detailed action plans. Zani suggested that "Key Success Variables" might identify the most important elements of the firms' success and help specify priorities for information systems development. Rockart further developed the concept of "Critical Success Factors (CSFs)" as "the limited number of areas in which results, if they are satisfactory, will ensure successful competitive performance for the organization. They are the few key areas where things must go right for the business to flourish. If the results in these areas are not adequate, the organization's efforts for the period will be less than desired."

It is possible to determine whether the best value of IT is obtained by relating IT spending to these critical success factors. In other words, the level of "strategic alignment of IT," can be revealed by determining whether IT costs are aligned with the business strategy and distributed over the CSFs. This approach is based on the notion that IT costs should be focused on areas that give the greatest return: areas of greatest relative importance to the organization's business. The next chapter elaborates on the practical application of this approach to valuating IT.

MEASURING EFFECTIVENESS OF IT

The next level of the BTRIPLEE framework deals with the value of IT measured by its contribution to improvement in the performance of business processes, activities, and employees. Striving for optimal effectiveness of IT is increasingly

Figure 3.7: Effectiveness Factors for IT

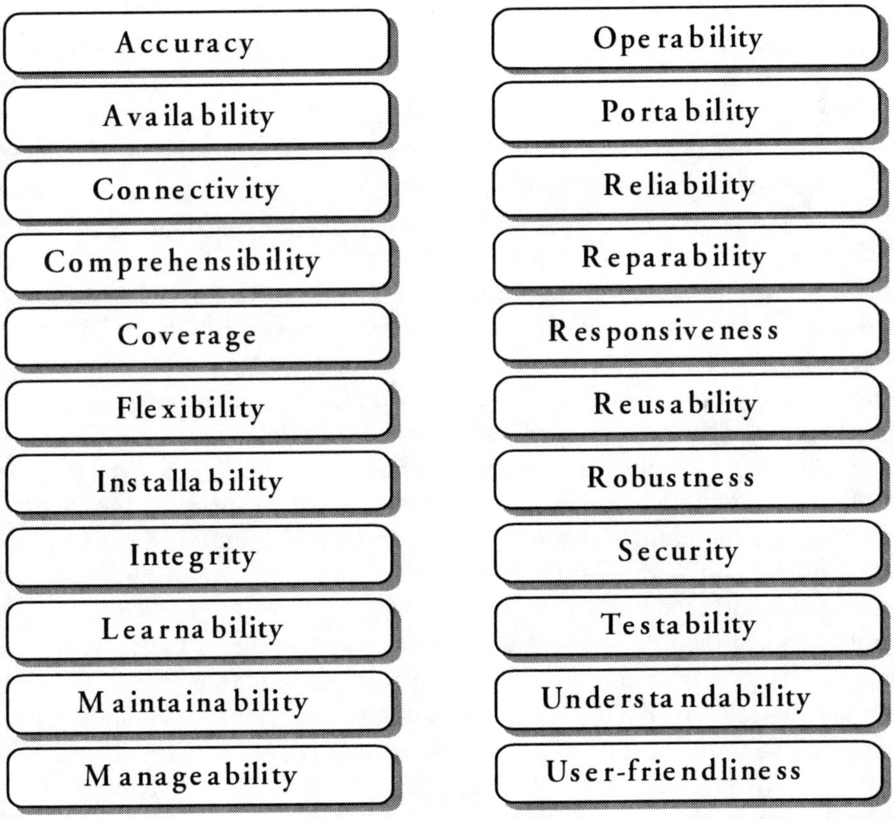

Accuracy	Operability
Availability	Portability
Connectivity	Reliability
Comprehensibility	Reparability
Coverage	Responsiveness
Flexibility	Reusability
Installability	Robustness
Integrity	Security
Learnability	Testability
Maintainability	Understandability
Manageability	User-friendliness

Alphabetical order

important as dependence on IT grows and as IT is increasingly woven into every aspect of the business.

The Software Engineering Research Center (SERC) as part of their Quint project (Figure 3.7) compiled an extensive set of effectiveness factors for IT applications.

Based on the research of several leaders in the field, SERC described the specific definitions of effectiveness factors, related effectiveness measures, basic data items to collect and calculate, the degree of reliability of the measures, and the relative complexity of assembling the necessary data.

The list of effectiveness factors for IT in Figure 3.7 is really a mixed bag of user-oriented effectiveness indicators and indicators that rather stem from the more technical requirements of IT. Three dimensions must be taken into account when determining the effectiveness of IT. These dimensions are derived from the objectives and requirements of business products, services, processes and business activities, users of IT, but also from the objectives of IT supplying functions in relation to different types of IT.

Measurement of the effectiveness of IT is thus related to the:

- support and enabling of business products, services, processes and activities, and its availability to business employees;
- effectiveness as perceived by the people who use it;
- technical aspects that stem from architectural and infrastructure requirements expressed by IT supplying functions.

The first measure to determine the effectiveness of IT is the degree to which IT capabilities exist to support the effective and efficient execution of business processes and activities. In fact, it is the degree of automation of business processes and business activities that is assessed (called coverage), indicating the extent to which human labor has been eliminated from all of them. Also, the availability from the users' perspective of IT applications and, in particular, customized user interfaces and workstations is determined. Whether IT applications and databases reside locally on users' workstations, across the Local Area Network on a mainframe or server, remotely across a Wide Area Network, or across cellular connections at a third-party location, is of less importance.

Secondly, users (either customers, suppliers, or employees) must be satisfied with the context and content of IT to be effective, which are measured in ease-of-use, accessibility, flexibility, reliability, and security. Measuring the users' satisfaction with available IT capabilities is a way to measure their requirements and needs for effective IT; at the same time the need for education, training, and coaching for users to employ available IT to the maximum is revealed. User satisfaction with IT capabilities is important, since the most common obstacles to IT effectiveness encountered by companies pioneering the advanced stages of IT are people- and culture-related, rather than the complexity of IT itself, as a host of research results points out. MIT's "Management of the 1990s" research supports this finding, declaring organizational implementation to be the key challenge companies face with respect to advanced IT.

Consequently, the measurement of the effectiveness of IT in relation to the requirements of users of IT has to do with establishing and maintaining a high level of user satisfaction and, thus, employee effectiveness. In the end, it is the user (again, either a customer, a supplier, or an employee) who determines whether IT is supporting his or her requirements, role, and business activities effectively.

Thirdly, requirements that stem from the IT supply functions (maintainability and operability of IT applications, adherence to architectural standards, etc.) are important to include in effectiveness measurements. Although they don't have a direct impact in the business sense, they are important for the effective and efficient supply of IT services and its ongoing maintenance. Indirectly, they are important to meeting effectiveness requirements for IT applications in the long run. Because the availability and delivery of (IT-based) products and services, the execution of (changing) business processes, the supply of IT to users, and individual IT applications all depend on the ubiquitous availability of a solid, stable, and thoroughly planned IT infrastructure, IT infrastructure-related requirements deserve special treatment when developing IT effectiveness measures.

In Chapter 5, the appropriate effectiveness measures will be further discussed on the basis of these three IT effectiveness aspects.

MEASURING THE EFFECTIVENESS AND THE EFFICIENCY OF IT SUPPLY

Measuring and evaluating the performance of IT supply (either through an internal IT department or organization, or an external IT services supplier) has always been a sensitive issue. In the case of an internal IT supply function, either the actual or the perceived levels of effectiveness and efficiency of IT supply remain a major concern for many organizations. Ouellette puts it mildly when he states: "In most corporations the IT department is not considered to be foremost in the daily business thrust." Expressing it more bluntly: many of today's IT organizations have a very poor image. Measuring the performance of IT supply is therefore very important, yet difficult, to accomplish.

The performance of the IT supply function is as difficult to evaluate as many other functions in the organization. Van Weele focused in 1994 on research into the measurement of the performance of the purchasing function in the late 1950s. The research concluded at that time that the purchasing function was one of the more difficult departments to evaluate. Van Weele asserts: "From our own experiences we would say that, certainly in comparison with other business areas, things have progressed only in a limited way since then." The valuation of R&D functions also has its problems, according to Vantrappen and Metz: "When executives examine how smart their innovation processes are, the soul-searching involves questions of effectiveness, efficiency, and risk. Traditional performance measures do not provide the answers to these questions." Measuring the performance of marketing departments, human resources departments, accounting departments, etc., poses the same sort of problems, not only in the 1990s but also today.

According to these and other researchers, problems include:

- *Lack of definition.* Although frequently used in practice as well as in theory, terms like performance, effectiveness, and efficiency have not been precisely defined; these concepts are often used interchangeably.
- *Lack of formal objectives and performance standards.* Objectives of functions are often not clearly defined; likewise, most functions operate without the guidance of well-defined performance standards. If there are any measures used at all, they tend to be lagging indicators, while future-oriented management needs leading indicators. This seriously limits the possibility of measuring activities accurately and comprehensively.
- *Inexact measurements.* Functions are not isolated; performance is a result of many activities which, due to their intangible character, are difficult to evaluate. In general, direct input-output relationships are difficult to identify.
- *Difference in scope.* Tasks and responsibilities differ greatly from one company to another, and many processes are creative processes that do not lend themselves to tidy routine checks. This precludes the development of broadly based, uniform evaluation systems.

These four problems seriously limit objective and accurate assessment of the performance of IT supply, and need to be addressed.

Defining IT Supply Performance

To tackle the first problem of definitions, the term "IT supply performance" must be defined. According to the BTRIPLEE framework, IT supply performance is considered the result of two elements: IT supply effectiveness and efficiency. Both aspects have been defined before and relate to the extent to which previously established goals or standards are being met. It has also been discussed, however, that planning of IT supply activities is not so straightforward but, rather, inherently dynamic. Triggers from many sides evoke actions of IT supply, necessitating continuous adaptation and change. In line with what Henderson and Venkatraman coined "alignment of IT," IT supply must also be aligned, aimed at establishing a state of harmony between the activities that make IT available, and goals and activities of an organization, its business processes, activities, and employees.

Effectiveness Versus Efficiency of IT Supply

The second problem, lack of formal objectives and performance standards, must be addressed by looking at the conflicts that might arise when matching effectiveness requirements against efficiency requirements. Our definitions of effectiveness and efficiency capture the need for effectiveness to be present for something to be efficient. In practice, however, efficiency is often treated as a synonym for cost. When overly effective IT supply is requested, IT may become very expensive. As a result, it will not always be perceived to be very efficient.

Figure 3.8: Effectiveness Versus Efficiency of IT Supply

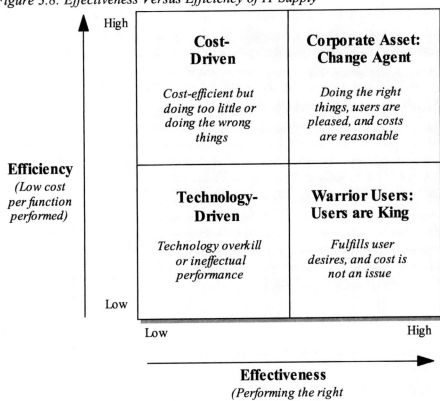

Trade-offs may have to be made, especially in the case of an internal IT supply function. Two fundamentally different approaches for IT support might be distinguished: efficiency-oriented and effectiveness-oriented. Efficiency-oriented approaches are concerned with technical issues and optimization of production capability, while effectiveness-oriented approaches are concerned with issues of information content, superb IT support, use of systems, and impact on user and organizational performance. In fact, it is the combination and balance of effectiveness of IT supply and the minimization of costs that determine its success. The Gartner Group published an interesting matrix to illustrate this notion (Figure 3.8).

The degree to which effectiveness or cost levels are sacrificed for the sake of the other is very much contingent on the goals of an organization, its business characteristics, its maturity in dealing with IT issues, and the affordability of its options. The problem of lack of formal objectives of IT supply can be solved by choosing a desired position in the above matrix or, more specifically, in derived matrices for distinct IT supply activities (to be presented in Chapter 6). An appropriate set of well-balanced performance measures, matching the objectives of IT supply, can then be derived (also presented in Chapter 6). Further, norms or targets can be defined for each performance measure to define specific and concrete objectives, as described in Chapter 7–the implementation of an IT (supply) measurement program–and with the help of benchmarking of IT supply (Chapter 8).

Measuring IT Supply Performance

The third problem of inexact measurements of the many activities, which are difficult to evaluate due to their intangible character, must be addressed by making these activities more tangible and measurable. This can be done by analyzing IT supply processes; their influencing and enabling factors, such as resources and means, workflows, and work activities in terms of their structure; interdependencies; decision points; and main parameters such as cost, time, and effectiveness. Such an analysis includes evaluation of the main factors that affect the levels of effectiveness and efficiency of IT supply (Figure 3.9).

The central core of this model consists of the IT supply processes, executed to effectively and efficiently supply IT products and services. The arrow at the top illustrates the distribution channel to the customers: the business alignment and customer interface between the IT delivery processes and the users of IT. This interface might consist of, e.g., electronic interfaces (help screens, electronic bulletin boards etc.), human interfaces (help desks, account management, etc.), and procedural interfaces (Service Level Agreements, production schedules, etc.).

For processes to work well, the right resources have to be in place to execute them. The first type of resource is people, including their relevant experience, knowledge, and skills. Their capabilities and performance must be assessed, as well

Figure 3.9: Factors of Effectiveness and Efficiency of IT Supply

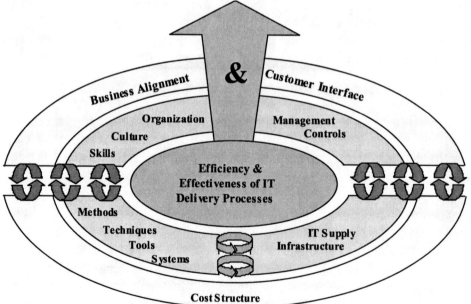

as organizational characteristics such as structure and culture, which provide the contextual motivation for them to perform IT supply processes well. Effective and efficient people further use the methods, techniques, tools, and systems (office automation systems, workflow systems, etc.) that match the requirements of the work to be done.

The second type of resource consists of the technology, facilities, information, expert support, etc., which in the model is labeled as IT supply infrastructure. Its impact on the overall effectiveness and efficiency of IT supply processes can be enormous, and must therefore be included in any credible performance assessment.

Management controls such as principles, procedures, guidelines, performance measures, and reward systems are put into place to run IT supply as a professional business. This means that IT supply activities are planned, executed in a controlled fashion, and tracked and verified afterwards.

One of the specific means to measure IT supply activities is tracking the costs associated with IT supply. In fact, money is the third important type of resource to be considered, so the cost structure of IT supply must be assessed as well. The cost structure of IT supply should be consolidated into financial statements like the balance sheet and profit-and-loss-statement, just as is done in any other aspect of the business.

Scope and Tasks of IT Supply

Finally, the fourth problem of difference in scope of tasks and responsibilities as a consequence of the differences between companies can be overcome by first evaluating the possible organizational structures of IT supply and then taking a *process view* rather than a functional perspective, as follows.

One of the important aspects of the effectiveness and efficiency of IT supply is the question of how it should be organized, since many discussions have been held about centralization and decentralization of IT supply over the past decades. Because the role of IT has changed in most organizations from a support tool for processing internal transactions to a strategic resource that is almost literally woven into every aspect of the business, the traditional centralized IT supply function is often no longer adequate. Organizational theorists have shown that the structure of IT supply is influenced by the organization's external environment and strategy. Blanton, Watson, and Moody researched which organizational structure would offer the most effective IT support, and which differences in IT organizational structures appear to facilitate that support. Their conclusions are as follows:

- How companies organize IT activities may have a significant impact on the overall effectiveness of IT support.
- Environments with a high degree of complexity, change, and uncertainty may improve the effectiveness of IT support by implementing IT organizational structures with higher states of *differentiation* (i.e., dividing the organization into separate groups with authority, that deal with different components of the environment) and *integration* (i.e., coordinating the interrelated activities of

groups so that they complement and support each other and obtain unity of effort).

- Environments with a high degree of complexity, change and uncertainty place pressures on organizations to process information more quickly, requiring a proactive IT decision-making process rather than a reactive one. A proactive process can only be achieved by having appropriate integrating mechanisms in place before decision situations arise,
- Effective integrating mechanisms are those that promote feedback on IT performance, gain cross-functional participation in IT planning, and facilitate communication amongst and between IT groups and user groups through liaison functions.

Blanton, Watson, and Moody argue for decentralizing IT functions physically toward business environments as much as possible, while maintaining functional integration. In contrast, Von Simson puts heavy weight on the integrating factor, in his view leading to physical integration of at least the more capital-intensive IT functions such as data processing centers. He identifies three factors driving a trend to "recentralization" resulting from a need for improved efficiency and management control:

- High cost of multiple data-processing facilities: companies can no longer ignore the cost-effectiveness of consolidation.
- Changing demographics of the information systems profession: demand is growing as supply is declining.
- Emphasis on company-wide information systems that integrate business functions and support new business opportunities: calls for a central staff with a broad overview of the company's information needs.

The implication of these different points of view is clear: there is not a straightforward best way to organize the activities for IT supply and support. However, a Nolan, Norton & Co. survey on the organization of IT revealed the most common structure in place in the majority of 50 large European companies. The features of this structure take advantage of the best of both effectiveness and efficiency worlds:

- IT management responsibility is positioned where business planning takes place (often in autonomous business units), with the exception of the management of the technical infrastructure.
- IT management is coordinated by a small, high-level IT management function at the corporate level.
- IT infrastructure management is a group-wide responsibility that takes place at the corporate level.
- Data center operations, network installation and management, and the development and maintenance of corporate IT applications are shared group-wide. Often they are centralized, as a resource pool, either in a profit center or a service (cost) center, and, in an increasing number of occurrences, partly or completely outsourced. Economies of scale and necessary management control are optimally profited from, especially for assets-intensive operations.

- End-user computing support and dedicated systems development and maintenance are either decentralized or centralized, depending on size (economies-of-scale, span-of-control, and critical mass).

This "federal IT management structure" is in place in the vast majority of large companies in the United States as well, featuring distributed responsibility for IT with some central functional leadership or guidance, and a combined IT services supply unit.

A Process View of IT Supply

Since no single organization chart for IT supply and support activities is applicable in every situation, it is most appropriate to discuss effectiveness and efficiency of different IT supply and support processes, regardless of how they are organized. Business processes are often modeled on Porter's Value Chain. Focusing on the key primary IT supply processes, and with just a little tweaking of his concept, Porter's Value Chain can be translated into IT supply processes as follows:

Inbound Logistics	-	Development of IT Applications
Operations	-	Operations of IT
Outbound Logistics	-	Communications Management
Marketing & Sales	-	Account Management
Service	-	Client Support

The Balanced Scorecard concept of Kaplan and Norton introduced earlier can be applied to measure the performance of each of these IT supply processes. For each IT supply process, a Balanced Scorecard will be developed in Chapter 6, plus one for the aggregate IT supply organization to be able to include Porter's support processes, such as IT human resources management, financial management and administration, procurement, etc. Because Operations of IT and Communications Management are similar and closely attached activities from a measurement standpoint (both are continuous, repetitive activities aimed at effective and efficient infrastructure asset and service management), only one scorecard will be developed for them under the label of IT infrastructure Management.

This leads to five scorecards, covering the performance measures for each process:

- IT Supply Management, often named Management of the IT organization.
- IT Development Management, often named System Development and System Maintenance.
- IT Infrastructure Management, often named Data Center Management and Data Communications Management.
- Account Management.
- Client Support, often named End-User Computing Support and Help Desk Support.

CONCLUSION

The shortfall of evidence of increased business value through IT has propagated a good deal of research into and discussion on the valuation of IT and delivered results. The business manager, however, still needs to know how to measure the value of IT. The BTRIPLEE framework has been developed to meet this need.

The BTRIPLEE framework does not, however, provide a direct "yes" or "no" answer to the question, "Do we get value for money from our IT expenditures?" since it is impossible to reply in a simplistic way to such a complex question. The framework provides a context for organizations in search of the value of their IT, in which to define related questions and find answers. It asks value questions at multiple levels and places the answers in their business and planning contexts.

These questions, and associated value levels, explore the extent to which IT:

- contributes to business objectives and to the business strategy, called the *Business value of IT*. Business value can be measured by linking IT costs with organizational improvement, measured by the organization's:
  - financial performance;
  - business performance, applying the Balanced Scorecard concept;
  - strategic performance, applying the concept of Critical Success Factors.
- effectively supports business processes, activities, and employees, called the *Effectiveness of IT*. It can be measured by assessing the degree to which it meets requirements that stem from:
  - business processes and activities;
  - employees, in requirements related to the availability of IT and to its use;
  - IT supply, in requirements related to IT applications and to the IT infrastructure
- supply aligns with business requirements, called the *Effectiveness of IT supply*, and is carried out efficiently, called the *Efficiency of IT supply*. Both effectiveness and efficiency of IT supply can be determined for the main IT supply processes:
  - IT Supply Management;
  - Account Management;
  - IT Development Management;
  - IT Infrastructure Management;
  - Client Support.

REFERENCES

Blanton, J.E., Watson, H. J. and Moody, J. (1992). Towards a better understanding of IT organizations: A comparative case study. *MIS Quarterly*, December, 531-555.

Cohen, A.R. (1990). Managing people: The R factor. In Collins, E.G.C. and Devanna, M.A. (Eds.). *The Portable MBA*. New York: John Wiley & Sons.

The Concise Oxford Dictionary. (1976). New York: Oxford University Press.

Gartner Group. (1994). *Inside Gartner Group This Week*, 10(4). Stamfort, CT: Gartner Group.

Guralnik, D.B. (Ed.). (1982). *Webster's New World Dictionary*. New York: Warner Books.

Harris, S.E. and Katz, J.L. (1989). Predicting organizational performance using information technology managerial control ratios. *Proceedings of the 22th Annual International Conference on Systems Sciences*, 4, (January), 197-204.

Henderson, J.C. and Venkatraman, N. (1993). Strategic alignment: Leveraging information technology for transforming organizations. *IBM Systems Journal*, 32(1), 4-15.

Juran, J.M. (1974). *Quality Control Handbook*. New York: McGraw-Hill.

Kaplan, R.S. (Ed.). (1990). *Measures for Manufacturing Excellence*. Boston, MA: Harvard Business School Press.

Kaplan, R.S and Norton, D.P. (1992). The balanced scorecard-Measures that drive performance. *Harvard Business Review*, January-February, 71-79.

Nolan, Norton & Co. (1997). *Transformation of IT Organisations*. Utrecht: White Paper, Nolan Norton Institute.

Ouellette, L.P. (1992). *How to Market the I/S Department Internally*. New York: AMACOM.

Parker, M.M., Benson, R.J. and Trainor, H.E. (1988) *Information Economics: Linking Business Performance to Information Technology*. Englewoods Cliffs, NJ: Prentice-Hall.

Porter, M.E. (1985). *Competitive Advantage: Creating and Sustaining Superior Performance*. New York: The Free Press.

Rockart, J.F. (1979). Chief executives define their own data needs. *Harvard Business Review*, March-April, 81-93.

SERC. (1992). *Het Specificeren van Software-Kwaliteit: Een Praktische Handleiding*. Deventer, NL: Kluwer Bedrijfswetenschappen.

Strassmann, P.A. (1990). *The Business Value of Computers*. New Canaan, CT: The Information Economics Press.

Van der Pijl, G.J. (1993). *Kwaliteit van Informatie in Theorie en Praktijk*. Doctoral Thesis, Tilburg University, Tilburg.

Van der Zee, J.T.M. (1997). *In Search of the Value of Information Technology*. Tilburg, The Netherlands: Tilburg University Press.

Van Reeken, A.J. (1987), "Begrippen rondom kwaliteit," *Bedrijfskunde, Tijdschrift voor Modern Management*, vol 59, nbr 2, 173-182.

Van Weele, A.J. (1994). *Purchasing Management: Analysis, Planning, and Practice*. London, UK: Chapman Hill.

Vantrappen, J.J. and Metz, P.D. (1994). Measuring the performance of the innovation process. *Arthur D. Little's PRISM* (fourth quarter), 21-33.

Von Simson, E.M. (1990), "The Centrally Decentralized IS Organization", *Harvard Business Review*, July-August.

Zani, W.M. (1970). Blueprint for MIS. *Harvard Business Review*, November-December, 95-100.

Chapter IV

Measures of the Business Value of IT

In any business a "dashboard" of vital performance indicators is needed to gauge how the company is faring. Such a dashboard, consisting of the appropriate measures to indicate strengths and weaknesses, provides a guide for management and forms the core of planning and control. A dashboard of performance indicators allows management to valuate the contribution of several factors that impact the overall performance of the organization. One of these factors is the application of IT.

To valuate IT, a dashboard of relevant performance indicators for IT must be developed. The BTRIPLEE framework offers the structure of the dashboard and identifies the distinct but interdependent levels of **B**usiness value of IT, **E**ffectiveness of IT, and **E**ffectiveness and **E**fficiency of IT supply. This chapter aims at developing the appropriate performance indicators (the gauges) at the first level within this structure: measures of the business value of IT. The following two chapters are devoted to the other two levels.

Measures are not all of the same kind: different types of measures exist to support different purposes and sorts of measurements (a discussion on different attributes of measures can be found in Appendix A). In any situation, it is necessary to select the appropriate measures from the many measures that will be proposed and discussed in this and the following chapters. Choices between possible measures have to be made to valuate IT and to interpret actual measurement results in the context of the specific situation and the company's ultimate business objectives and goals. For instance, one organization might choose a cost leader strategy, while another organization might opt for, let's say, a niche player strategy. Such choices have implications for IT, and thus, for the measures to valuate IT. In other words: the dashboard of IT value gauges has to be custom designed to reflect the specific internal and external issues at hand

(Chapter 8 describes how to construct and put in place a custom-designed performance measurement system).

As stated earlier, the business value of IT is measurable on three related dimensions. Measuring the business value of IT is concerned with the relationship between the costs of IT and its contribution to the improvement of:

- *financial performance*, measured by financial indicators such as profitability, productivity, earnings, etc.;
- *business performance*, measured by non-financial indicators such as competitiveness, new product sales, product development lead times, manufacturing lead times, distribution lead times, customer satisfaction, etc.;
- *strategic performance*, measured by indicators that match specific management objectives (management's critical success factors).

A key component in the discussion of business value is the level, purpose, and categories of IT costs, followed by an investigation into the impact of IT on the performance of an organization. First, we will take a closer look at the cost dynamics of IT and the different purposes of IT spending. Then, we will review the three relevant valuation dimensions to arrive at an aggregated approach to correlating IT cost with business value.

Figure 4.1: Cost Dynamics of IT

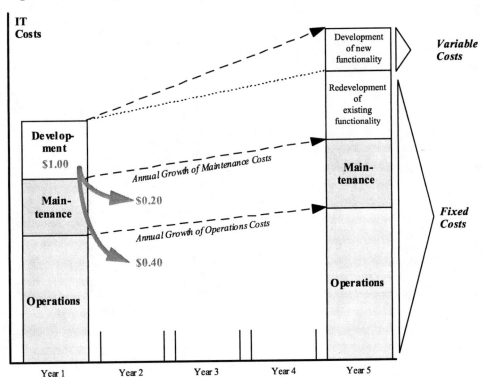

DYNAMICS OF IT COSTS

To manage and measure the value of IT, attention should be given to the cost side of the cost-value equation. IT costs are not all discretionary and subject to management's decisions; they follow defined patterns as described by, amongst others, Van der Zee and Koot and Keen. These patterns suggest that every dollar spent on IT development automatically generates follow-on costs for IT maintenance and IT operations. According to Keen, each dollar of new development generates 20 cents of maintenance and 40 cents of operations in each subsequent year, indicating that the larger the existing portfolio of IT applications, the larger the proportional IT spending on maintenance and operations. So, when a company budgets $1 million to develop a new IT application, it is, in fact, committing to spend more than $4 million over the next five years of usage. These costs are considered fixed for a certain period of time, called the lifecycle of the developed IT

Figure 4.2: Options to Deal with Cost Dynamics of IT

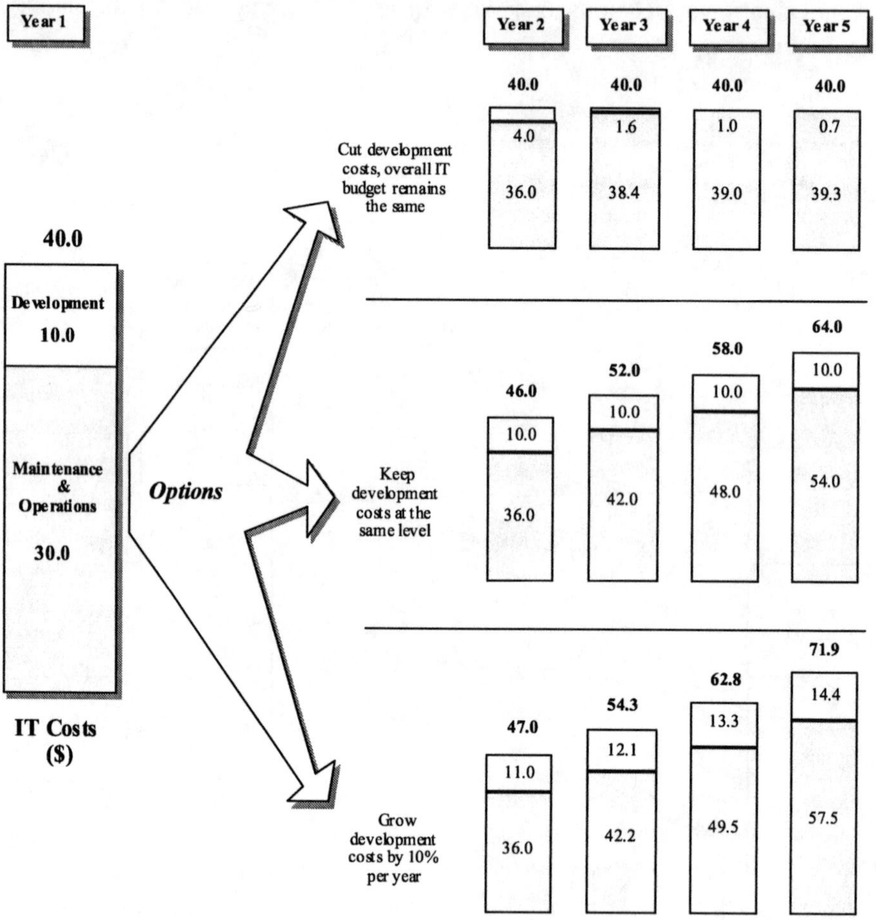

Source: P.G.W. Keen, Shaping the Future

application. On the broader level of the installed base of IT applications, the conclusion must be that the larger part of most IT budgets is quite fixed, as Figure 4.1 indicates.

Organizations have options for dealing with the cost dynamics of IT. This is important to understand, both at the time of planning for IT (ex-ante) to determine what to do, and at the time of valuating IT afterwards (ex-post) to place IT costs in the context of past (explicit or implicit) decisions. Three scenarios follow, as indicated in Figure 4.2, adopted from Keen:

- *Cut development costs*. If the overall IT budget is to remain the same over a period of five years, development costs must be cut by a cumulative 93 percent over that period. Only 7 percent of the original development budget will remain.
- *Keep development costs at the same level*. The compounded IT budget grows 15 percent per year over 5 years as a result,
- *Grow development costs*. Growth of development costs of 10 percent per year results in a compounded growth of the IT budget of 18 percent per year.

Statistics from the Gartner Group show that after initial IT cost cutting, up to the mid 1980s, companies have decided to follow a growth strategy. The numbers point to a steep growth in IT spending, as a percentage of overall revenue (see Figure 4.3). But, at least three factors should be considered when evaluating the statistics:

- Increasingly, the so-called "hidden" costs of IT (actual IT costs that are not included in central IT budgets and therefore were not easily traceable) have been included in the above numbers, so that the average growth rate has artificially increased. Recent Gartners' annual IT Budgets and Practices surveys estimate that hidden IT costs equal 30-50 percent of known spending, indicating a much faster overall growth rate traditional IT budget growth suggests,
- The fact that each dollar of new development generates 20 cents of maintenance and 40 cents of operations in each subsequent year might have been true in the 1980s and early 1990s, when mainframe computing and third generation mainframe IT applications dominated, but much has changed over the past few years. Technology has become cheaper, while many IT supply organizations have increased their efficiency levels, especially in the computer operations area, by combining data centers and by outsourcing parts of their data center activities, thus taking advantage of economies of scale. They automated operations and eliminated non-standard computer systems to increase efficiency. On the application development and maintenance side, efficiency levels have been increased by embarking on policies for standard software packages rather than roll-your-own development, while remaining development activities have become more efficient through, e.g., Rapid Application Development approaches that include the use of CASE tools, reusable components, code generators, and other efficiency boosters.
- E-business is dramatically changing the way businesses operate, and the necessary investment to make this happen is not small. Gartner predicts e-

Figure 4.3: Annual Rate of IT Budget Growth

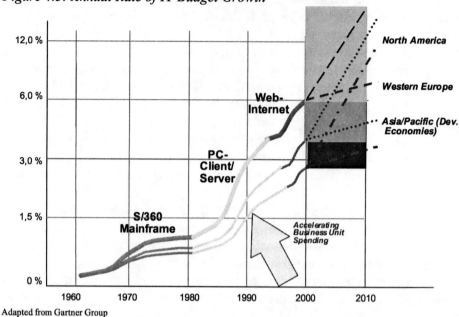

Adapted from Gartner Group

business will cause IT spending as a percentage of revenue to exceed 10 percent by 2005, with 67 percent of large enterprises redeploying funds previously devoted to ERP and Y2K activities to e-business initiatives, and with e-business initiatives consuming between 30 percent to 50 percent of enterprise IT spending. Spurred on by e-business, more of the corporate capital budget will likewise be devoted to IT. In fact, the U.S. Department of Commerce reports that IT's total share of the enterprise capital budget is 50 percent. Estimates in Europe look similar. While this figure includes IT spending embedded in broader plant and equipment, a "pure IT" capital spending rate of approximately 30 percent emerged in the late 1990s.

As the above discussion indicates, aggregate annual IT costs might be segmented by activity to understand the cost dynamics of IT and to perform trend analysis and comparison with other companies. Such a comparison might indicate a relatively large proportion spent on one of the cost categories, perhaps at the cost of others.

Generally, IT costs are categorized into the activities of:
- development of new IT capabilities,
- maintenance of existing IT capabilities,
- operating IT capabilities (production),
- end-user computing support,
- planning and administration of IT and IT activities, and "other" costs not directly related to activities, such as costs of occupancy, furniture and fixtures, etc., on behalf of IT supply.

Figure 4.4 illustrates such a breakdown of the aggregate IT spending level.

Figure 4.4: IT Spending by Activity (%)

Activity	1991	1993	1995	1997	1999
Development/ Major enhancements	9	15	16	19	18
Maintenance/ Minor enhancements	16	20	19	23	25
Production/ Operations	47	44	43	29	26
End user computing/ Help desk	10	11	11	18	21
Planning, administration, other	18	10	11	11	10
	100	100	100	100	100

Derived from Gartner Group

Each activity can be further analyzed. For example, costs of "development" can be divided into the costs of development of new IT functionality and the cost of re-development of existing IT. Another example would be the segmentation of "maintenance and enhancement" into the generally accepted categories of adaptive maintenance, corrective maintenance, and perfective maintenance.

It might be possible to carry out each activity more efficiently and/or effectively. This is a matter of supply efficiency and effectiveness, which will be discussed later in this chapter.

A second, complementary approach to segmenting the total IT cost is to split IT costs by mix of resources: technology costs (hardware and software), personnel costs, costs of outside services, and "other" costs, again, to perform trend analysis and comparison with other companies. Figure 4.5 illustrates such segmentation by resource.

Neither the analysis nor benchmarking of the total percentage of revenue spent on IT nor the measures of IT cost by activity or by resource have been proven by research to be valid and reliable "value for money" indicators on their own. However, an analysis of IT costs for comparative purposes within the same industry, and ideally within the same geographical region or currency, may reveal "abnormalities" and may lead to further, more focused investigations into the value question. From a practical point of view, it is recommended to include the measures of overall IT costs as a percentage of revenue, annual rate of IT budget growth, IT spending by resource, and IT spending by activity in the set of measures of business

Figure 4.5: IT Spending by Resource (%)

Resource	1991	1993	1995	1997	1999
Hardware	29	26	26	22	18
Software	8	8	8	13	13
Personnel	40	36	37	35	37
Outside Services	12	19	18	16	11
Datacom and other	11	11	11	14	20
	100	100	100	100	100

Derived from Gartner Group

value from IT, since they are relatively easy to calculate and to compare with public data. They should never be used in isolation to draw final conclusions about the value of IT, however. Rather, they complement the measures that relate IT costs to improvements of financial, business, and strategic performance of the organization.

MEASURES OF FINANCIAL PERFORMANCE THROUGH IT

During the 1990s, Strassmann was by far the most quoted researcher to have shown convincingly that there is no correlation between company performance and overall total IT cost. Strassmann investigated many possible correlations between levels of IT cost and business success, expressed in financial ratios such as revenues or shareholders' investments, without results. He therefore developed another measure of performance, based on the value added to an organization provided by management: ROM (return-on-management). To calculate management value added, he uses the financial results of the business, minus those items that are outside the control of management. The total value added of a firm is computed as the difference between net revenues and payments made to suppliers of raw materials, energy, contract labor, leases, and so on (revenue by itself is not regarded as a reliable measure, since it includes the cost of resources employed by others). The contribution of capital is then separated from the contribution of labor. This leaves labor value added. Taking out the direct operating costs leaves management value added. When divided by the costs of management, this gives an indicator of the total performance of management–return on management (ROM). The extent to which ROM is improved as a result of costs of IT provides a measure of IT's business contribution.

Although theoretically valid, Strassmann's approach has never been adopted widely, as far as known. Probably the ROM concept is too artificial and alien to most organizations. Also, it is questionable whether ROM really contributes to new insights vis-à-vis other indicators. In Strassmann's own words: "If your financial experts are concerned that the ROM index measure conflicts with the customary financial ratios, the trends for Return-on-Assets (ROA) and Return-on-Equity (ROE) compare with ROM." With that statement, he affirms that ROA and ROE could be used as equally valid ratios to measure the business contribution of IT.

A study in the 1990s of 47 companies by CogniTech and the DMR Group, Inc. uncovered that companies with high profit margins, earnings per share, and ROE tend to have highly effective IT. Another study, however, by Sethi, Hwang and Pegels, among more than 500 companies into correlations of IT investment criteria, business performance criteria, and the overall IT effectiveness index developed by Computerworld, excludes ROE as a viable financial measure that can tell something about the business contribution of IT. This study revealed that earnings per share is not a valid measure either, since it is highly correlated with ROE. This leaves ROA and profit margin as the only valid measures to include into our set of potential financial performance indicators. Although the measure ROA might be troublesome because depreciation policies can make this ratio depend on the accountants' choice of valuation methods, as Strassmann indicates, it may nevertheless be used for internal trend comparisons, assuming that depreciation policies remain consistent. Henderson, an Information Management professor at Boston University, also recommends ROA, to justify company-wide investments in IT infrastructure.

The study by Sethi, Hwang, and Pegels confirmed that the financial performance measured by ROE of the so-called "IS effective" companies (designated by Computerworld) is not significantly better than that of other firms. The financial performance measures ROI and ROS, however, appear to be appropriate to correlate with IT investment levels. The appropriateness of the ROS measure is consistent with the measure "profits margin" that CogniTech and the DMR Group indicated as valid.

Another result of the research of Sethi, Hwang, and Pegels reveals that it is not just the amount of money spent on IT resources that is important, but rather how those resources are aligned with business objectives. This is supported by the findings of Mahmood and Mann who were interested in finding useful measures of what they call "IT investments" and "strategic and economic performance." They selected "Computerworld's Premier 100" most effective information system users to supply them with the following ratios:

IT investments:
- IT budget as a percentage of revenue,
- value of an organization's IT equipment as a percentage of revenue,
- percentage of IT budget spent on IT staff,
- percentage of IT budget spent on training of IT staff,
- number of personal computers and terminals as a percentage of total employees;

Strategic and economic performance:
- return on investments (ROI),
- return on sales (ROS),
- revenue growth,
- sales by total assets,
- sales by employee.

The IT investment ratios were correlated with the strategic and economic performance ratios to investigate the possible presence and nature of relationships among the measures. The research indicated a weak relationship between individual IT investment measures and individual strategic and economical performance measures. When grouped, however, the correlation increased significantly, yielding some strongly related positive and negative findings:

- *Sales by total assets, sales by employee, ROS,* and *ROI* are positively affected by the IT investment measure IT budget spent on training. The more spent on the training of employees, assuming that the funds are effectively used, the better employees are expected to be at what they do, thereby pushing the organization to better performance, which, in turn, should result in increased net worth of the organization and ROI to shareholders.

- *Sales by employee* and *ROS* are positively affected by the number of PCs and terminals per employee, when combined with training (the number of PCs in itself is not related to increased sales by employee or ROS). This makes sense, as employees must be trained on this equipment before the organization can hope to achieve the benefits of investment, rather than merely providing PCs to employees.

- *Sales by total assets* is positively affected, but sales by employee and ROS are negatively affected by an organization's IT equipment value as a percentage of its revenue. Organizations with larger investments relative to revenues achieve a higher amount of sales relative to total assets. This supports the idea that total investment in IT is beneficial to organizational performance, or at least to the sales function. Second, any relationship between IT investment and sales by employee would depend to a large extent on the specific nature of IT; that is, whether it is decentralized, such as in the form of PCs, intranets, and extranets. Because IT value as a percentage of revenue represents much more in the way of IT than only PCs, it is a less precise measure than PCs per employee in evaluating relationships between IT investments, ROS, and sales by employee. Thus, the negative relationships found between these variables are considered of minor importance.

- *The percentage of IT budget spent on staff* was not significantly related to any strategic and economic performance measure; neither was growth in revenue significantly related to any IT investment measure.
- *ROI and sales by total assets* are significantly negatively affected by IT budget as a percentage of total revenue. Mahmood and Mann are not sure as to why this finding is the case. They suspect that some of the companies in the sample may be spending excessive amounts on IT as a percentage of total revenue without a proper business strategy. This may result in negative returns on IT investments for these firms. It is advised that an organization should find its optimum level of IT investment, perhaps by using relevant industry data as a basis for evaluating its own position with regard to costs. Like the indicator IT costs as a percentage of total revenue, the measure IT costs as a percentage of operating costs might be regarded as an additional, complementary measure. In my opinion, it should not to be used in isolation, however.

Mahmood and Mann draw the following conclusions from their research findings:

- Steady investments in IT should be considered for enhancing strategic and economic performance.
- To improve economic performance, IT investments must be accompanied by appropriate training.
- To evaluate the impact of IT investments on economic performance, performance measures such as sales by employee, sales by total assets, ROI, and ROS should be considered.

Figure 4.6: Relationships Between IT Investment Radios and Financial Performance Ratios

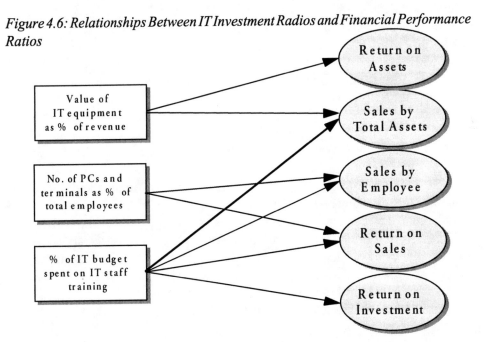

- Measures such as percentage of IT budget spent on IT staff training, number of PCs and terminals as a percentage of total employees, and IT equipment value as a percentage of revenue should be used as measures of IT investment.

The findings of Mahmood and Mann; Sethi, Hwang, and Pegels; the CogniTech/DMR research; and Henderson lead to the set of recommended measures and their relationships as illustrated in Figure 4.6.

Although only a limited number of relationships between IT investment and financial performance ratios can be drawn, the overall conclusion from this discussion is that investments in IT equipment (and thus IT infrastructure), together with the appropriate training, might positively influence the financial performance of organizations. This conclusion remains to be put in the context of the other dimensions of business value as well as the layers of the BTRIPLEE framework.

MEASURES OF BUSINESS PERFORMANCE THROUGH IT

Business performance is achieved through business activities, grouped together in business processes, and through the organization and allocation of resources to these business processes. Apart from using financial indicators, business performance can also be measured by using non-financial performance indicators, as we will now discuss.

To develop the link between IT costs and non-financial business performance indicators, the Balanced Scorecard concept will be applied. This concept has become quite popular over the past few years, mainly because of its practicality. Kaplan and Norton devised the Balanced Scorecard concept as a set of measures to give top management a fast but comprehensive view of its business.

The Balanced Scorecard includes financial measures that show the results of actions already taken. Financial measures are considered to be lagging indicators, focused on the past. The Balanced Scorecard complements financial measures with operational measures on customer satisfaction, internal processes, and the organization's innovation and improvement activities–operational measures that are the drivers of future financial performance. These are considered to be leading indicators, focused on the future.

Kaplan and Norton argue that senior managers understand that their organization's measurement system strongly affects the behavior of managers and employees: "What you measure is what you get." They advise executives and managers to concentrate on a balanced presentation of both financial and operational measures such that information overload is prevented by limiting the number of measures used. This balanced structure of business performance measures answers four basic questions from as many perspectives:

- How do customers see us? (customer perspective)
- What must we excel at? (internal perspective)

Figure 4.7: The Balanced Scorecard

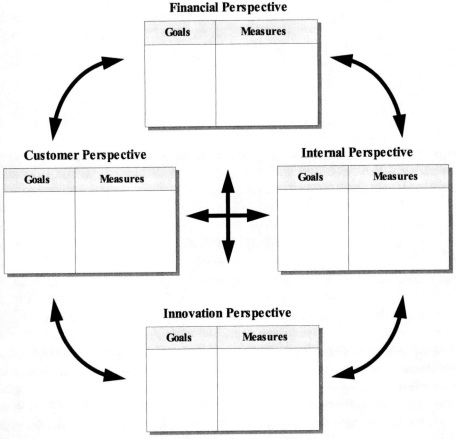

- Can we continue to improve and add value? (innovation and learning perspective)
- How do we look to shareholders? (financial perspective)

The customer perspective is based on the notion that many companies today have a mission that focuses on the customer. The Balanced Scorecard demands that managers translate their general mission statement on customer service into specific measures that reflect the factors that really matter to customers. These business measures typically fall into the categories: (lead) time, cost, quality, performance, and service. Lead time measures the time required for the company to meet its customers' needs. Quality might measure defect levels of delivered products and services, as well as on-time delivery. The combination of performance and service measures how the company's products and services contribute to create value for its customers, e.g., the price they pay for products and services, or the accuracy of delivery forecasts.

The *internal perspective* and the relevant measures for the Balanced Scorecard stem from the business processes that have the greatest impact on customer satisfaction–factors that affect cycle time, quality, employee skills, and productivity, for example. However, in my opinion, this is too narrow a view: not only the business processes that have the greatest impact on customer satisfaction should be taken into consideration. Companies should decide what processes they must excel at to satisfy all of the stakeholders: not only customers, but also employees and shareholders, and specify the relevant measures for each.

The *innovation and learning perspective* relates to the fact that targets for success keep changing. Many external factors require that companies make continual improvements to their existing products, services, and processes and should have the ability to introduce new products with expanded capabilities. A company's ability to innovate, improve, and learn ties directly to the company's value. That is, only through the ability to launch new products, create more value for customers, and improve operating efficiencies continually can a company penetrate new markets and increase revenues and margins – in short, grow and thereby increase shareholder value.

The *financial perspective* and financial performance measures indicate whether the company's strategy, its implementation, and its execution are contributing to bottom-line improvement. As discussed in the previous section, typical financial goals have to do with profitability, growth, and shareholder value; in other words: survival, success, and prosperity. Survival might be measured by cash flow, success by quarterly sales growth, and operating income by department/division, as well as by prosperity by increased market share by segment and return on equity.

The advantages of using the Balanced Scorecard to relate IT costs to business performance indicators are:

*   The Scorecard brings together many of the seemingly disparate elements of a company's possible competitive initiatives, such as becoming customer-oriented, shortening response time, improving quality, emphasizing teamwork, reducing new launch times, managing organizational learning, etc.
*   The Scorecard guards against sub-optimization; by forcing senior managers to consider all the operational measures together, the Balanced Scorecard lets them see whether improvement in one area might have been achieved at the expense of another. The conclusion whether that is good or bad is left to the discretion of the management, and depends on the organization's goals and objectives.
*   IT costs are directly linked to the business performance indicators with which management is already familiar. IT value measurement is thus less alien to the organization and easier to understand for all organization members.

Most non-financial performance indicators are specific to sectors. For example, car manufacturers measure the man-hours needed to assemble a car. An airline measures the number of passengers carried per year; an electricity company could count the total generating capacity per year; an insurance company could count the number of issued policies; while a bank might count financial transactions. In the retail industry, revenue per square meter is a widely used measure; transportation companies often measure truck utilization, etc. The tracking of IT costs to support the assembly of a car over time, in relation to the man-hours to assemble a

Figure 4.8: Relating IT Costs to the Balanced Scoreboard of an Airline

Performance Indicator	Year 1	Year 2	Year 3	Year 4	Trend (%)
IT costs ($m)	15	17	18	20	33
Revenues ($m)	300	350	400	450	50
Operating costs ($m)	280	315	350	390	39
Number of passengers (000)	600	640	690	735	23
Number of freq. flyers (000)	60	100	150	200	233
IT costs as % revenue	5.00	4.85	4.60	4.45	-11
IT costs as % operating costs	5.35	5.40	5.30	5.15	-3.5
IT costs per passenger	25.00	26.50	27.00	27.20	9
IT costs per frequent flyer	250.00	170.00	120.00	100.00	-60
Revenue per passenger	500	547	580	612	22
Operating costs per passenger	466	493	507	531	14

Relating IT costs to the:

Financial Perspective

Internal Perspective

Customer Perspective

Innovation Perspective

car, gives an indication of the business value of IT. In these scenarios, IT costs per passenger flown, IT costs per electricity-consuming household, IT costs per policy or per financial transaction could be used to relate IT costs to business performance. In the example of an airline, IT costs are related to the four business performance perspectives (see Figure 4.8):

- Growing revenue represents the financial perspective.
- Operating costs represent the internal perspective; they increase but at a lower rate than revenues, showing internal excellence.
- Growing number of passengers represents the customer perspective, assuming that the growth results from customer satisfaction.
- Expanding number of members of a new product, the so-called Frequent Flyer Program, represents the innovation and learning perspective.

From the example it is clear that although the total IT costs increase considerably over time, IT costs as a percentage of revenue decrease, as do IT costs as a percentage of operational costs and IT costs per frequent flyer. However, IT costs per passenger increase slightly, but not as much as the total operational costs per passenger. IT spending does not seem to be out of control or growing too fast. It might even be considered to further increase IT spending in order to decrease the growth of total operational costs. Investigation into the growth patterns of different operational cost components would be necessary to judge whether efficiency improvements through IT have been and could be made. For example, when the cost of fuel increases at a high rate, IT cannot help to diminish that cost directly. But if growing operational costs are due to increasing administrative costs, increased IT spending can probably enable that cost component to grow at a lower rate or even decrease.

The advantage of relating IT costs to the different categories of business performance measures is that it allows the contribution of IT to be assessed in a holistic manner, comparable with the Balanced Scorecard itself. Even though the trend in one of the ratios may be indicating that IT costs are increasing "too fast," others may be indicating that the level of cost is indeed helping to improve business performance. It may not be a cause for concern if IT cost as a proportion of revenue shows an undesirable trend, if the IT cost relates well to improved customer-related or innovation-related business performance measures. Certain measures of an organization (e.g., the financial measure revenue) can fluctuate considerably, especially in some industry sectors, so relating IT cost to other non-financial business performance indicators might indicate that IT is indeed adding value.

Using the four types of business performance measures listed above, each organization needs to establish its own set of ratios that relate IT costs to key business performance measures. It is recommended to relate IT costs to multiple measures for each category of business performance to reflect the different activities and objectives of the business in a balanced way. The key to using a balanced set of business performance measures lies in interpreting them in accordance with business priorities and realities at any one time.

MEASURES OF STRATEGIC PERFORMANCE THROUGH IT

The third dimension of business value of IT deals with the question to what extent IT costs are distributed over the limited, but most important, areas (the critical success factors, or CSFs) in which results are expected to generate strategic success. As Henderson and Venkatraman explain, economic and strategic performance of an organization is directly related to the ability of management to create a strategic fit between the organization's position in the competitive product-market arena and its capability to exploit IT functionality on a continuous basis. If the two match well, and continue to match well over time, IT is "strategically aligned" with the organization's objectives. The key to determining the business value of IT is to first determine the most critical areas of the business that contribute most to its success.

To do so, firstly, organizational objectives are determined. These are highly company specific, and differ because of the structure of the particular industry, the company's competitive strategy, its industry position and geographic location(s), and many other external and internal factors.

Secondly, critical success factors are determined and ranked. Rockart does not provide help on how to select these other than by interviewing people, but Kaplan and Norton, among others, suggest limiting the search for CSFs to one or more of four perspectives: priority products or services, priority processes, priority business functions, and priority job families. I believe the geographic dimension should be added to these perspectives, to reflect the global dimension of doing business today. The impact that each of these perspectives might have on the organizational objectives is examined and weighted, e.g., by their (potential) impact on revenue and profits.

Thirdly, the level of annual IT costs is determined for each of the critical success factors. An even more sophisticated and more complex approach would be to split overall IT costs into three classes in line with the business purposes of IT investments, as discussed in Chapter 2.3:

- *IT costs to maintain the organization's status quo*, the so-called "going concern" costs: the costs of IT maintenance and IT operations added together, as well as the costs of new mandatory IT development.
- *IT infrastructure and IT research costs*, to acknowledge the fact that these IT costs are generally corporate-wide investments in a "core competence" of the organization, enabling other IT investments to create direct value.
- *Development costs of new IT applications*, to improve the efficiency and effectiveness of the organization, or to change the business, the business network, or the business scope.

The matrix to distribute IT cost over CSFs is illustrated in Figure 4.9, albeit simplified: vertically, two possible CSFs are indicated, as well as two non-critical business activities. Horizontally, the classes of IT are defined. The distribution of IT costs across the resulting cells of the matrix provides insight into how money is spent. The confrontation of costs of classes of IT with the relative strategic importance of each of the CSFs allows determination whether money spent on IT is adding optimal business value. For example, if relatively large amounts of money

Figure 4.9: IT Costs by Critical Success Factor

IT Costs	Classes of IT				
	Going Concern IT		IT Infrastructure & Research	New IT Development	
	Maintenance & Operations	Mandatory Development		Business Improvement	Business Redesign
Rejuvenate Product Portfolio					
Develop Eastern European Market					
Payroll					
General Ledger					

Critical to Business Success

Not Critical to Business Success

are spent on "going concern" IT for non-critical purposes, and if relatively small amounts of IT costs are found in the row of CSFs, one might question whether the best value of IT is obtained from a strategic perspective.

A variation on this theme would be not to fill the cells with IT costs but rather to look at value of IT assets. This idea is not really new–already many years ago both Nolan and Keen described the importance of an "IT asset balance sheet" to reflect the huge investments in information, software, and technology that do not appear on companies' regular balance sheets. Nevertheless, only few companies I am aware of practice what Nolan and Keen preached. The IT asset balance sheet is not a legal financial statement, but instead a management report. For example, software is generally not capitalized, nor is data, although these assets represent enormous capital and associated business value. The values of the balance sheet categories are not easy to calculate. The easiest approach is to value the different components on the basis of replacement value, rather than book value or historical costs. I'll provide some guidance, by showing the IT balance sheet that was pulled together as part of a consultancy engagement for a large, European utility company (see Figure 4.10). The concept has not yet widely been used, to my knowledge.

The IT asset balance sheet capitalizes all IT equipment, software, and data resources currently in use. The first category is IT infrastructure. The most obvious and easiest-to-calculate component is hardware, comprised of central and distributed computers, network equipment, telecommunications equipment, and peripherals. These components are generally found on the financial balance sheet of an

Figure 4.10: The IT Balance Sheet

Replacement Value of IT Assets

Business Activities	Balance Sheet Categories			
	IT Applications	IT Infrastructure	Data	Total
Product Manufacturing	507	350	610	1,467
Product Shipping	20	*	*	20
Product Distribution	1,145	–	6,000	7,145
Administrative Support	760	–	2,275	3,035
Corporate	–	1,247	–	1,247
Total	2,432	1,597	8,885	12,914

* = Not available

organization. The second component of IT infrastructure is infrastructure software, including operating systems, database management systems, personal computer software, etc.

The second category of the asset balance sheet is IT applications. This component represents all the IT applications in use. Three types of IT applications can be distinguished: commercial software packages that are not modified, software packages that have been modified for one reason or another, and custom software that has been developed specifically for the organization at hand. The value of unmodified packages would be the costs of their acquisition; for modified packages, the costs of modification must be added to the acquisition costs. To calculate the value of custom-developed software, one could estimate the total number of function points of the installed base, and multiply that number by the system development costs per function point. The resulting figure represents the replacement costs of these types of applications.

The third category of the asset balance sheet is data. The associated value is the estimated capital cost of the salaries, processing, and storage incurred in creating the data resources within an organization.

The distribution of IT investments across the cells of the matrix introduced previously is not easy. Many costs will be classified as infrastructure costs, since a great deal of hardware, software, and data resources is used across the organization. This is not surprising, since an IT infrastructure enables the practical and efficient creation of more specific and individual IT applications. In the information-based organization, in which IT is woven into every aspect of the organization, there is no cheap and easy way to build the large-scale data, computer, workstations, and network platforms that constitute the corporate IT infrastructure as a core competence.

CONCLUSION

The key to determining the business value of IT is to apply an aggregated approach to correlate IT costs with the performance of the organization. Improved performance is expressed as improved financial performance, improved business performance, and realized strategic goals.

It is recommended to firstly determine the dynamics of IT costs of a particular organization by measuring overall IT costs as a percentage of revenue, annual growth rate of IT costs, IT costs by resource (personnel and technology), and IT costs by activity (development, maintenance, and operation). These indicators are relatively easy to calculate and to compare with historical trends and public data. They provide an insight in IT cost patterns and may reveal abnormalities in trends. An organization that is consistently and significantly deviating from industry averages and general trends should at least endeavor to understand why.

To determine the value of IT measured by improved economic performance of a particular organization, IT costs must be related with financial performance measures. Particularly the percentage of IT budget spent on IT staff training, the number of PCs and terminals as a percentage of total employees, and IT equipment value as a percentage of revenue should be used as measures of IT costs that can be related to the financial measures sales by employee, sales by total assets, ROI, ROA, and ROS.

To valuate the contribution of IT to improve business performance, it is recommended to relate IT costs with multiple business measures for different categories of business performance to reflect the different activities and objectives of the business in a balanced way. Business performance measures are specific to sectors and contingent on business priorities and realities at any one time. The improvement of business performance, determined by these measures, is an indicator of the business value of the associated supporting or enabling IT.

A refinement of the approach of valuating IT in terms of business performance is to measure the contribution of IT in realizing strategic goals. IT costs are for that purpose related with each of these goals, expressed by defined Critical Success Factors. This approach can be enhanced by distinguishing between "going concern" IT costs, IT infrastructure and IT research costs, and the development costs of new IT capabilities, for each CSF. Another approach is not to look at IT costs but rather at the value of IT assets. An "IT asset balance sheet" reflects the monetary value of investments in information, software, and technology per CSF (or per business process, organizational unit, or any other area of interest).

The relationships between IT costs and organizational performance measures add insight into the question of IT value, but only when additional value questions are asked at each level of the BᴛʀɪᴘʟᴇE framework, and answers are synthesized intelligently, is it possible to find the complete answer. The next level of the framework to be discussed in the next chapter is the level at which the effectiveness of IT is measured.

REFERENCES

Butler Cox (1990). Getting value from information technology. *Butler Cox Foundation Research Report 75*. London: Butler Cox.

Gartner Group. *Annual IT Budgets and Practices Survey*. Stamford, CT: Gartner Group.

Interview with J. Henderson. (1994), *Management & Informatie* (December).

Henderson, J.C. and Venkatraman, N. (1993). Strategic alignment: Leveraging information technology for transforming organizations. *IBM Systems Journal*, 32(1), 4-15.

Kaplan, R.S and Norton, D.P. (1992). The balanced scorecard-Measures that drive performance. *Harvard Business Review*, January-February, 71-79.

Kaplan, R.S. and Norton, D.P. (2000). Having trouble with your strategy? Then map it. *Harvard Business Review*, September-October, 1671-176.

Keen, P.G.W. (1991). *Shaping the Future: Business Design through Information Technology*. Boston, M: Harvard Business School Press.

Mahmood, M.A. and Mann, G.J. (1993). Measuring the organizational impact of information technology investment: An exploratory study. *Journal of Management Information Systems*, Summer, 10(1), 97-122.

Nolan, R.L. (1982). *Managing the Data Resource Function*. St. Paul, MN: West Publishing Company.

Russell, R. (1992). What difference does IT make. *Informationweek*, October 26.

Sethi, V., Hwang, K.T. and Pegels, C. (1993). Information technology and organizational performance, A critical evaluation of Computerworld's index of information systems effectiveness. *Information & Management*, 25, 193-205.

Strassmann, P.A. (1990). *The Business Value of Computers*. New Canaan, CT: The Information Economics Press.

Sullivan-Trainor, M.L. (1989). Leaders go beyond basics, Link is to business strategy. *Computerworld*, September 11.

Van der Zee, J.T.M. (1994). Rapid application development. *Informatie*, 1, 40-48.

Van der Zee, J.T.M. and Koot, W.J.D. (1989). I/T assessment, een kwalititatieve en kwantitatieve evaluatie van de informatieverzorging vanuit en strategisch perspectief. *Informatie*, 12, 837-851.

Chapter V

Measures of the Effectiveness of IT

Effectiveness of IT, although well researched (mainly under the label of "Quality of IT"), remains a confusing subject for many business managers in everyday life. This confusion is at least partly due to the lack of standard terms or definitions, a lack of generally accepted quality norms, and a proliferation of approaches to discussing the subject. A lot of "quality" might have been put into the IT applications built in many organizations, including features for extra durability, serviceability, reliability, and functionality, for which nobody actually asked, but which was included by the suppliers of IT to "anticipate possible future needs." But what actually is quality? And what is effectiveness?

Garvin has classified the various definitions of quality as follows:
- *Transcendent*: quality cannot be defined, "you know what it is."
- *Product based*: differences in quality amount to differences in the quantity of some desired ingredient or attribute.
- *User based*: quality is fitness for use.
- *Manufacturer based*: quality means conformance to requirements.
- *Value based*: quality means best for certain customer conditions.

Apart from the first definition, which is not helpful to deriving measures of IT effectiveness, this classification system can be used as a framework to discuss the different perspectives of IT effectiveness.

The effectiveness of IT should be related first to the role of IT in supporting and enabling the effective and efficient execution of business processes and business activities, and to the availability and characteristics of IT as perceived by the people who use it. These are the user-based and value-based dimensions of IT effectiveness. The more technical aspects, which stem from the architectural and infrastructure requirements of IT supplying functions, comprise the product-based and manufacturing-based dimensions of IT effectiveness.

In this section, the driving factors of IT effectiveness for each of these categories will be briefly discussed. The appropriate measures for IT effectiveness will be classified, based on business requirements of three perspectives:

- business products and services, processes, and business activities;
- users of IT;
- IT supply.

IT EFFECTIVENESS FROM A BUSINESS PRODUCTS AND SERVICES, PROCESSES, AND BUSINESS ACTIVITIES PERSPECTIVE

Research into the effectiveness of IT has focused predominantly on the quality attributes of IT, once it is installed and made available to users. With respect to the effectiveness of IT from a business products and services, processes, and business activities perspective, however, the first question to answer is whether IT is available in products and services, and to support business processes at all, and to what extent.

Techniques to measure IT availability (still) in use today were developed in the 1970s and 1980s mainly to measure the degree of data processing coverage of functionally organized business activities.

They measure, for each business function:

- The actual degree of automation, by first reviewing the output of the function, then estimating the amount of human work that would have been required to produce that output, and finally, estimating the part of human labor that has been eliminated by IT.
- The potential degree of automation, by estimating the maximum possible elimination of human labor by IT.
- Actual automation as a percentage of potential automation.

The result of this exercise is a picture of the aggregated level of automation, which is basically a balance sheet of opportunities for automation of business functions versus the actual degree of automation throughout the company, broken down into the levels of automation of each of the business functions. Note that automation in this context only refers to the elimination of human labor from a business function.

These basic concepts are still valid, albeit that under the realm of "digitized products and services," and "business process redesign," traditional products and services, as well as functionally organized business functions, have been (partly) replaced by digital products and services, and automated business processes. Also, traditional data processing has been accompanied by an array of other IT capabilities over time. Both aspects impact measurement issues of the level of automation, so that they must be discussed briefly here.

Business processes have become the primary organizational axis of today's networked organization. In definitional terms, a process is a structured set of activities, ordered across time and place, with a beginning, an end, and clearly defined inputs and outputs, as Davenport states. Davenport, among others, distinguishes between management processes (such as performance monitoring, finance management, human resource management, etc.) and operational processes (such as product creation, manufacturing, order fulfillment, etc.). There are inherent differences between characteristics of these types of business processes, their IT requirements, and hence, the types of measures of the effectiveness of IT.

After good old Anthony, three types of *management processes* can be defined:

- *Strategic management*: processes of deciding the objectives of the organization, changes in these objectives, the resources used to attain these objectives, and the policies that govern the acquisition, use, and disposition of resources. Strategic management processes tend to focus on highly unstructured problems involving many variables.

- *Management control*: processes by which managers assure that resources are actually obtained and used effectively and efficiently in the accomplishment of the organization's objectives. Management control processes tend to encompass many of the company's operations with the objective of initiating action conforming to the policies and precedents established in the strategic management processes.

- *Operational control*: processes of assuring that specific tasks are carried out effectively and efficiently. Operational control processes focus on the supervisory level of management where specific activities are executed: the operational processes themselves.

Other researchers distinguish between two types of *operational processes*: production-oriented and innovation-oriented processes. As I see it, three types of operational processes exist, namely:

- *Production-oriented processes*, such as the manufacturing of tangible goods, are clearly structured around predefined outputs, in accordance with well-defined rules and procedures and require relatively limited judgment and decision making. These processes are typically designed for a high level of repetition and efficiency, and low defect rates.

- *Innovation- or development-oriented processes*, such as product creation, are less structured; goals are less defined or even vague; activities are carried out in accordance with a set of guiding principles rather than strict rules and detailed procedures. Such processes leave much room for personal creativity. These processes are aimed at producing high-quality end results; effectiveness is more important than internal efficiency.

- *Problem-solving-oriented processes*, such as customer service, are reasonably structured, although outputs ("a solved problem" or "a happy customer again") are hardly defined; activities are carried out in accordance with a set of broadly defined guiding principles while the employees involved are empowered to resolve issues fast. These processes aim at the quick and adequate resolution of problems, so speed and effectiveness are the main design criteria.

For a specific organization, the stratification of business processes permits analysis of the extent of IT support of these processes along a number of dimensions. As mentioned earlier, apart from data processing, many types of IT exist today. For example, Weill and Olson distinguish strategic, informational, transactional, and threshold IT. Davenport elaborates even further and lists nine types of IT, each with the potential to improve the effective and efficient makeup of the products and services rendered by an organization, and the effective and efficient execution of business processes and business activities. They are:

- *Automational*: eliminating human labor from a process.
- *Informational*: delivering information to customers as a service or a product, and capturing process information for purposes of management.
- *Sequential*: changing process sequence, or enabling parallelism.
- *Tracking*: closely monitoring process status and objects.
- *Analytical*: improving analysis of information and decision making.
- *Geographical*: coordinating processes across distances.
- *Integrative*: coordinating between tasks and processes.
- *Intellectual*: capturing and distributing intellectual assets.
- *Disintermediating*: eliminating intermediaries from processes passing information.

These main types of IT can be mapped against the different types of business processes, resulting in a matrix showing the predominant IT opportunities for each type of process. Figure 5.1 illustrates this matrix.

Figure 5.1: IT Characteristics per Type of Business Process

Type of IT	Management Processes			Operational Processes		
	Strategic Management	Management Control	Operational Control	Production	Innovation/ Development	Problem Solving
Automational IT		✔		✔	✔	
Informational IT		✔	✔			
Sequential IT				✔	✔	
Tracking IT			✔	✔		✔
Analytical IT	✔	✔		✔	✔	✔
Geographical IT				✔	✔	✔
Integrative IT			✔	✔	✔	✔
Intellectual IT	✔	✔		✔	✔	
Disintermediating IT			✔	✔		

Figure 5.2: Normative IT Application Portfolio (Manufacturing Example)

| **Firm Infrastructure** |
| Office automation tools, workflow management tools, groupware tools, electronic mail, financial management systems, etc. |

| **Human Resources Management** |
| Human resource information systems, demand-supply and career development modeling tools, etc. |

| **Technology Development** |
| CAD/CAE, simulation tools, concurrent engineering systems, project management tools, etc. |

| **Procurement** |
| Inventory/production planning systems, vendor evaluation systems, EDI, JIT control systems, etc. |

Inbound Logistics	**Operations**	**Outbound Logistics**	**Marketing & Sales**	**Service**
• Production planning systems • Inventory systems • Incoming goods inspection and quality control • Management information	• Production planning & monitoring • Inventory systems • Fixed assets management • Materials mangement • Shop floor control • Management information	• Customer information systems • Distribution planning and monitoring • Truck planning • Route planning	• Customer information systems • Sales history • Inventory & production systems • Analysis and presentation tools • Order entry and billing systems • Accounts receivable system • Expense reports • Sales administration • Management information	• Customer informatin systems • Product information systems • Service history • Diagnosis support tools • Field repair systems • Dialog scripts • Management information

To further specify opportunities for improved effectiveness and efficiency of business processes and business activities, and to measure IT coverage in each business process, a detailed analysis must be made. Figure 5.2 depicts an example of IT opportunities in the form of a "normative" portfolio of IT capabilities for each of the key business processes, as Porter's Value Chain defines them. The picture is meant to be conceptual rather than exhaustive, and depicts a generic view of common business processes and IT opportunities of a manufacturing organization. The model could be used as a basis for the drawing of the specific processes for a company interested in measurement of the effectiveness of IT.

As in Figure 5.2, an organization should map its business processes and analyze the extent of current IT support versus today's IT opportunities. It goes without saying that some business processes cross organizational boundaries, so that links to other companies in the business network are included in such a mapping exercise. Determination of the degree of IT coverage in each process by type of IT support would indicate where IT currently is concentrated as well as the degree of IT coverage in total. Such an analysis offers a basis for discussion about the value of IT *vis-à-vis* company objectives, in conjunction with the distribution of "monetary" IT efforts as discussed before.

The above-described type of quantitative measurement of coverage does not yet show whether or not existing IT supports users effectively. For this reason, it is necessary to establish criteria for determining the effectiveness of IT in supporting the users of IT, and measuring the degree of success.

IT EFFECTIVENESS FROM A USER PERSPECTIVE

Establishing and maintaining high levels of user satisfaction has always been an important IT effectiveness factor. In the end, it is the user who determines whether IT is supporting the user role and the execution of business activities efficiently and effectively. Measuring user satisfaction is a way to understand users' requirements and needs for effective IT, by ascertaining the functional characteristics of IT, as well as by determining the need for user training and user support. In this respect, it should be noted that user satisfaction comprises two aspects: the user will only be satisfied if IT can be used easily and if it produces useful results. Users will only be satisfied if the return on the time they invest in learning IT capabilities is commensurate with the benefits obtained from using it.

IT effectiveness criteria, from a users perspective, were defined by Boehm and Gorry and Scott Morton, among others, more than 20 years ago, as follows:

- *Reliability of IT applications*: degree to which IT applications are available when needed, output is received according to schedule, and availability problems are quickly corrected.
- *Reliability of information*: degree of correctness and integrity of the data provided by IT applications, and the degree to which output and data captured in applications keeps pace with actual events.
- *Accessibility of information*: promptness with which information requested from IT applications is received.
- *Security of information*: degree, to which data in applications is protected from unauthorized access.
- *Ease of use*: simplicity in using IT applications, and the adequacy of outputs in any form, e.g., screen layouts, report formats, etc.

Since then, many companies changed their business processes incrementally or more radically and transformed much of the way work is performed; thus much about the jobs of people has changed. Many activities have changed or have been repackaged into new, broader roles for employees. Less complex activities have been eliminated to a great extent through IT, so that work has become more

Figure 5.3: New Models of Work and IT Effectiveness Requirements

New Models of Work	IT Effectiveness Requirements
Working on a fast clock • Short cycles, great intensity • Rapid recognition of consequences of actions • Hardly downtime, limited relaxation	**High availability, high "intelligence"** • Sub-second response times • On-line, real-time processing of everything • Automation of low-value work
Working with an eye on the customer • Close and intensive customer contact • Broad insight in customer requirements • Focus on world-class service	**Open-ended, informative** • Access to ubiquitous information bases • Access to ubiquitous transaction history • Decision support and office automation aids
Working in the open • Performance directly measurable • Work-in-process clearly visible • Shared work with team members	**Workflow-oriented, team-supportive** • Automated performance tracking • Workflow management support • Groupware support
Working for oneself • Decision making as well as doing • Emphasis on results, not on process persé • End-to-end responsibility, limited hand-offs	**Flexible, user friendly** • Minimizing hassle, reflecting personal style • Easy-to-configure processing capabilities • Consistent foolproof integration of systems
Working anywhere, anytime • From the office • At the client, in the field • At home, from a hotel	**Reliable, connective, secure** • Information synchronization all the time • Compatibility of tools • Easy upload, download and output facilities

substantive in terms of greater emphasis on knowledge and information sharing and a greater diversity of tasks. Also, downsizing, as the flattening of the hierarchical organizational structure is called, has removed several layers of management in a good number of today's organizations, and at the same time has pushed responsibilities to the operational level. Employees in today's information-based organizations have become "empowered," meaning that companies more and more rely on extensive employee "self-management."

Such drastic changes have seriously impacted the role and requirements of IT, supporting and often enabling "new models of work." These models and associated effectiveness requirements for IT are illustrated in Figure 5.3, inspired by Hammer, among others.

To support these new models of work and thus to enable employee effectiveness, the IT effectiveness attributes defined more than 20 years ago are still valid. What is different is the augmented level of requirements IT capabilities must meet, albeit along the same dimensions. Besides, IT effectiveness characteristics are defined for all available IT capabilities, rather than for individual IT applications.

Reliability characteristics of individual IT applications have been replaced by reliability characteristics of the whole set of IT capabilities; reliability of data provided by IT applications and their security requirements are broadened to the reliability and security characteristics of complete sets of databases; the degree of accessibility of information is no longer defined by individual IT applications but rather by the whole set of company-wide as well as designated external databases; ease of use no longer deals with the user-friendliness of individual IT applications but rather with flexible, yet homogeneous, access to heterogeneous databases and IT applications, etc.

What is different is the fact that IT applications as such are no longer the only objects of effectiveness criteria *perse*. Hence, the demand for functional flexibility of easy-to-configure processing and informational IT capabilities requires effectiveness criteria for modular IT components and flexible, logical flows of information streams between application building blocks, customized user interfaces, and networked databases. All together, IT effectiveness criteria have been broadened from individual IT applications and the data captured in these applications to include what today is known as the IT infrastructure.

IT effectiveness measurement from a user perspective is focused on the satisfaction of actual users of IT, as mentioned. These individuals, however, do not share the same background, nor do they perform the same business activities all the time, nor do they require the same information content or processing capabilities of IT. Following Juran's "quality is the fitness for use–the extent to which the product successfully serves the purpose of the user during usage," IT effectiveness measurement must allow for assessment of IT effectiveness in relation to actual users' needs. In other words: IT effectiveness scores, when measured, usually using interval scales, should not always be a 9 on a scale of 0 to 9, since the requirements stemming from the users' job might be not higher than, say, a 5. Mathematically expressed, user satisfaction can be defined as the score for the actual effectiveness of an IT capability divided by the score for effectiveness that the specific user really needs to perform his or her work with support of the given IT capability. Any score lower than 1 demonstrates lower IT effectiveness than required; everything higher than 1 would mean over-delivery of IT effectiveness for that specific user and his or her work.

Appropriate IT effectiveness measures must reflect users' perceptions of effectiveness rather than that being stated in technical terms. For example, the reliability of an application should be measured in terms of failures per hundred hours of operation, rather than in terms of faults per thousand lines of programming code or per number of Function Points that comprise an IT application. The flexibility of IT should be specified in terms of the time it takes to configure a change in functionality or the time it takes to act on a request to change, say, calculation rules in an IT application, rather than in terms of the total number of Function Points or programming lines changed. Defects should be classified by the impact they have on users rather than by the type of design or coding fault that caused them, etc.

IT EFFECTIVENESS FROM AN IT SUPPLY PERSPECTIVE

IT effectiveness from an IT supply perspective stems from operational- and maintenance-related interests of the people responsible for effective and efficient IT supply, as well as from overall architectural requirements, rather than from the usage of IT capabilities by business people.

Operational Aspects

Operations-related effectiveness criteria focus on the ability to support the day-to-day supply of IT services without problems. They refer to the ease of operation of IT capabilities, including incident handling, problem resolution, outages repair, investigation into malfunctioning, etc., and include aspects of IT infrastructure management, extensively described by Looijen and others.

Maintenance Aspects

Maintenance-related effectiveness criteria characterize the suitability of IT capabilities for use over time. Maintenance-related criteria are:

- *Maintainability*: the ease with which corrective maintenance can be carried out, influenced by complexity, quality of documentation, etc. Corrective maintenance relates to the correction of design, programming, or parameter setting errors. Maintainability of the IT infrastructure in particular is of the utmost importance to quickly repair failures and solve availability problems, because a very high reliability of operation is required.
- *Flexibility*: the ease with which perfective and adaptive maintenance can be done. Perfective maintenance is changing the IT capability to improve its performance and maintainability; adaptive maintenance is concerned with enhancing and extending IT to incorporate the evolving needs of the user and the evolving technological capabilities.
- *Testability*: the ease with which IT can be tested to ensure that it performs its intended function, and the availability of test data.
- *Re-usability*: the extent to which all or parts of the IT capability can be re-used in other capabilities.

Architectural Aspects

Architectural issues deal with important criteria such as ensuring longer term durability and reliability of IT capabilities, yet offering the required flexibility to cope with continuous business change and technological renewal, while at the same time protecting existing IT investments in IT capabilities as much as possible. Architectural effectiveness indicators are contingent on requirements specific to an IT application, a class of IT applications, or the IT infrastructure as a whole, e.g., some IT capabilities need to obey more stringent security rules than others because of specific business reasons.

Architectural effectiveness indicators are:

- *Portability*: ease with which an IT capability can be transferred from one computing environment to another,
- *Connectivity or interoperability*: ease with which an IT capability can be interlinked with other capabilities; linking a workstation-based spreadsheet with a mainframe database, for example,
- *Security*: from an IT supply perspective, the extent to which security and safety requirements can be met effectively and efficiently.

In the case of IT infrastructure, the maintenance-related indicator of *flexibility* might be regarded as an architectural indicator as well. Since an IT infrastructure in the sense of a "core competence" of the business must be continuously updated and improved to meet changing demands (as described in Chapter 2), it must be flexible enough to incorporate emerging new technologies such as extensive communication facilities, accessibility of distributed databases and smart, software-enabled workstations. The combination of flexibility and portability requirements of IT infrastructure is reflected in the increasingly used term *scalability*.

Scalability of the IT Infrastructure

As the numbers of IT applications, resource requirements, and users grow, an IT infrastructure should be able to satisfy these increasing demands on its resources (i.e., should provide scalable performance). Scalability, according to Berson, does not mean that an overcapacity of IT infrastructure components should be bought at extra cost as a "safety stock" to allow for possible, but currently unknown future capacity requirements. On the contrary, the IT infrastructure should satisfy current requirements and, at the same time, be easy to expand. A less attractive alternative to scalability is replacement of major parts of the IT infrastructure every time it reaches capacity limits. Much can be learned from operations management and production control, including capacity planning systems and cost accounting systems in the manufacturing industry.

According to Berson, the degree of scalability improves when the IT infrastructure is developed on the basis of emerging open-system standards, such as applied in the Internet environments. The ultimate goal of open computing environments (hence, IT infrastructure), accommodating open-system standards to support the users of IT applications throughout the organization and to extend the infrastructure to other companies in the business network, is to make truly distributed networks possible where:

- computing and internal and external information sharing can occur transparently across networks;
- information bases, IT applications, resources, functionality, and CPU power can be shared seamlessly throughout the environment;
- users will be provided with the greatest possible portability, interoperability, and scalability of applications.

Tradeoffs

When evaluating the effectiveness of IT, it must be understood that it is not always possible to meet all effectiveness requirements of both users and IT supply. There are two main reasons for this. First, a high level of effectiveness in one factor may imply a low level of effectiveness in other factors. For example, a high level of security might impact the ease of use and the ease of connectivity, and vice versa. Second, tradeoffs have to be made between high-effectiveness levels and the associated costs to attain and maintain them. The choice will depend on many factors, such as number of internal and external users of the IT application; degree of business dependency on the IT application or its mission criticality; costs to realize a desired level of an effectiveness criterion; and the nature of the IT application in question, for example:

- IT applications with a long life, and IT infrastructure capabilities in particular, require high levels of maintainability, flexibility, and portability.
- Publicly accessed IT capabilities require high levels of reliability of operation, security, and ease of use.
- IT capabilities that can cause damage to property or lives if they go wrong require high levels of reliability of information and testability.
- IT capabilities based on advanced technology or on technology supplied by suppliers facing continuity problems require high levels of portability.

CONCLUSION

The effectiveness of IT is related firstly to the role of IT in supporting and enabling the effective and efficient execution of business processes and business activities. Secondly, it is related to the availability and characteristics of IT as perceived by the people who use it. Thirdly, effectiveness of IT is related to more technical aspects, stemming from architectural and infrastructure requirements, as well as from the people who support and supply IT. Therefore, IT effectiveness measures are based on the requirements of three perspectives:

- *Business products, services, processes, and business activities:* IT coverage can be measured for each product and service, business process, and business activity, including the links to other companies (suppliers, customers, complementors) in the business network, by mapping different types of IT against the management and operational processes and activities. This results in the measure actual application of IT as a percentage of potential application of IT.
- *Users of IT:* Reliability of IT applications, reliability of information, accessibility of information, security of information, and ease of use are the categories of measures to determine user satisfaction with IT, which in turn should enable overall effectiveness of users.
- *IT supply:* Operations-related effectiveness measures focus on ease of operation of IT capabilities (incident handling, problem resolution, outages repair,

Figure 5.4: Measures of IT Effectiveness

Effectiveness Requirement stemming from:	Effectiveness Criteria	Sample Measures (not limitative)
Business Processes and Business Activities	IT coverage of management processes and activities	Per types of IT: actual application of IT as % of potential
	IT coverage of operational processes and activities	Per type of IT: actual application of IT as % of potential
Users of IT	Reliability of IT applications	Mean times between failures and to repair
	Reliability of Information	Correct data as % of total data available
	Accessibility of Information	Mean response time, batch turnaround time
	Security of Information	Number of secured data sets as % of total
	Ease of use	User-friendliness, rated on a ratio scale
IT Architecture and IT Supply	Operational criteria, e.g. • Handling • Problem solving • Outages repair	Number of outages, file recoveries, incidents, etc. per month; ease of operation, rated on a ratio scale; mean time to repair outages
	Maintenance related criteria: • Maintainability • Flexibility • Testability • Reusability	Mean effort/time to repair/adapt/test; number of reused components as % of total; quality of documentation rated on a ratio scale
	Architectural criteria: • Portability • Connectivity • Security • Scalability	Mean time/effort to transfer IT components, to connect IT components; number of IT components not adhering to standards as % of total, secured data sets of % of total

investigation into malfunctioning, etc.); maintenance-related effectiveness measures refer to maintainability (complexity, quality of documentation, etc.), flexibility, testability, and reusability; architectural effectiveness is measured in portability, connectivity, and security (the combination of flexibility and portability of the IT infrastructure is reflected in the term scalability).

An overview of the classes of IT effectiveness measures in the context of the BTRIPLEE framework is given in Figure 5.4, complemented by examples of appropriate measures.

REFERENCES

Anthony, R.N. (1965). *Planning and Control Systems, A Framework for Analysis.* Boston, MA: Harvard University.

Berson, A. (1992). *Client/Server Architecture.* New York: McGraw-Hill.

Boehm, B.W. et al. (1978). *Characteristics of Software Quality.* Amsterdam, NL: North Holland Publishing Company.

Davenport, T. H. (1993). *Process Innovation: Reengineering Work through Information Technology.* Boston, MA: Harvard Business School Press.

Garvin, D.A. (1988). *Managing Quality.* New York: The Free Press.

Gorry, G.A. and Morton, S. (1971). A framework for management information systems. *Sloan Management Review,* Fall, 13(1).

Hammer, M. (1992). *The Impact of Inforation Technology on Jobs and Work: Models, Themes, and Principles for System Design and Implementation, or, Answering Richard Scarry's Question.* PRISM Conference, Zürich, Switzerland, September.

In 't Veld, J. (1989). *Manager en Informatie, Informatiesystemen Met of Zonder Computer.* Leiden, NL: Stenfert Kroese.

Juran, J.M. (1974). *Quality Control Handbook.* New York: McGraw-Hill.

Kaplan, R.S. (Ed.). (1990). *Measures for Manufacturing Excellence.* Boston, MA: Harvard Business School Press.

Looijen, M. (1995). *Beheer van Informatiesystemen.* Deventer, NL: Kluwer Bedrijfswetenschappen.

Porter, M.E. (1985), *Competitive Advantage: Creating and Sustaining Superior Performance.* New York: The Free Press. Van der Zee, J.T.M. and W. J.D.

Koot (1989). I/T assessment, een kwalititatieve en kwantitatieve evaluatie van de informatieverzorging vanuit een strategisch perspectief. *Informatie,* (12), 837-851.

Truijens, J. et al. (1990). *Informatie-Infrastructuur, een Instrument voor het Management.* Deventer, NL: Kluwer Bedrijfswetenschappen.

Van der Zee, J.T.M. and Koot, W.J.D.(1989). IT assessment, een kwalititatieve en kwantitatieve evaluatie van de informatieverzorging vanuit een strategisch perspectief. *Informatie,* 12, 837-851.

Weill, P. and Olson, M. (1989). Managing investments in information technology: Mini case examples and implications. *MIS Quarterly,* March, 3-17.

Chapter VI

Measures of the Effectiveness and Efficiency of IT Supply

As discussed in Chapter 2, IT supply can be structured and organized in many different ways. IT supply activities can be positioned where business planning takes place (often in business units) or in shared service supply units. Three types of IT supply activities are distinguished:

- *Managing the IT infrastructure and operations* can take place at the business unit level, but because of the benefits of economies-of-scale and easier corporate control of architectural standardization and consistency, many organizations opt for sharing these activities. In that case, a central service unit or an outside IT supplier acts as service provider to the business units.
- *Developing, implementing, and maintaining IT applications* might also take place at the business level, or are performed by a central, shared service provider, or by outside suppliers, or by a mix of all three options. Although applications development might actually be executed at physically distributed locations close to the business (and future users), development and maintenance activities still can be managed centrally by a service provider.
- *Supporting IT users* can be performed either as a devolved activity to business units or as shared service provision.

The majority of companies, in both the U.S. and Europe, have adopted some kind of federal IT management structure. The federal IT management structure features devolved responsibility for IT to business units; the development of IT architectures for the business unit and derivation of business unit IT plans is an activity of each business unit. However, some form of corporate functional leadership for IT strategy and guidance of business units is held centralized to enable group-wide coherence in corporate information systems (e.g., financial reporting), data, computers, networks, operating software, etc. This is essential for internal coordination and communication within the corporation and, increasingly, with suppliers and customers. Corporate standards ensure this coherence and prevent

Figure 6.1: Corporate IT Management and Supply Activities

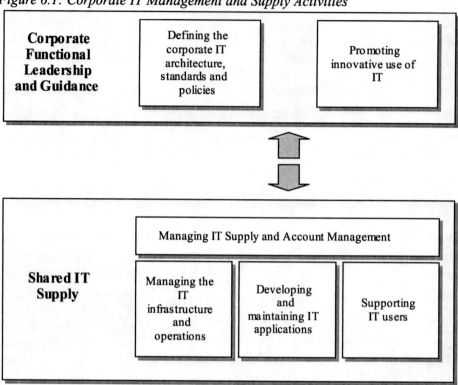

technology from becoming a constraint on organizational change. Also in this structure, the promotion of innovative use of IT and research into new, emerging technologies is often held centralized because of its corporate and strategic importance and benefits of economies-of-scale and -expertise. This federal IT management structure leads to six sets of interrelated, corporate IT management and supply activities, as depicted in Figure 6.1.

Both the functional leadership and guidance function, and the promotion of innovative use of IT, are regarded as IT management rather than IT supply activities; they are therefore not included in the further discussion.

The supply of shared, central IT services can be organized in different ways. In principle, companies choose from a range of six options, listed here in increasing order of competitiveness:

- in-house service unit, as a sole supplier and working only for the business, functioning as a cost center;
- in-house service unit, chartered to seek external business, functioning as a profit center;
- partnership with external service supplier;
- joint venture with external service supplier;
- in-house unit transferred to outsourcing supplier;
- all IT services purchased competitively from external suppliers.

As the level of competitiveness of IT supply increases, IT suppliers (including those in-house) are more often asked to demonstrate and quantify their performance levels, increasingly through benchmarking against other IT suppliers and including direct competitors. Unless the in-house unit can provide a better and cheaper service, IT services might be outsourced to external IT suppliers.

In any case, the challenge in managing the supply of IT services is to put in place the practices to run IT supply as a business. These practices must be aimed at maximizing customer value, operational excellence, innovation, and shareholder value: the four perspectives of the Balanced Scorecard concept of Kaplan and Norton distinguishing customer, internal, innovation and learning, and financial perspectives respectively.

A Balanced Scorecard will be developed for the three IT supply processes. The process view is taken because processes can be measured and compared independently from the organization of activities. On top of that, to address the measurement issues of IT supply as a business, the three IT supply processes of IT infrastructure and operations management, IT development and maintenance management, and client support must be complemented by two additional Scorecards. These are a Scorecard for "marketing and sales" activities (called "Account Management"), which are, as in any business, critical to survival; and a Scorecard for the aggregate management level of IT supply (IT supply management). Appropriate performance measures will be attached to these five Scorecards to determine the effectiveness and efficiency levels of IT supply as a whole:

- IT Supply Management,
- Account Management,
- IT Development Management,
- IT Infrastructure Management,
- Client Support.

This will complete the third and final layer of the BTRIPLEE framework.

MEASURES OF IT SUPPLY MANAGEMENT

The concept of running IT supply as a business means adopting the practices a professional service organization must use to be competitive and to survive. The concept does not only apply to commercial organizations. In particular it applies to in-house service centers (not-for-profit, but no loss) and profit centers (expected to make a profit).

As Maister confirms, a professional service firm must focus on "outstanding client service, professional satisfaction for employees, and financial success" if it is to survive. With the help of the Balance Scorecard concept, we've added the future orientation to these three goals by including innovation and learning. The management of IT supply, as a professional service firm, requires a delicate balancing act between the demands of the client marketplace, the realities of the people marketplace (the labor market for staff), the organizations' economic ambitions, and the sustainability of all these aspects in the future. The consequence of the concept of running IT supply as a professional business and adopting appropriate professional practices is therefore to focus on the answers to four simple questions, related to the measurement of overall performance of IT supply at the management level:

- Is IT supply effective? (Customer perspective)
- Is IT supply efficient? (Ultimately the customer and shareholder perspective, initially the Internal perspective)
- Will the IT supplier maintain its full potential in the future? (Innovation and learning perspective)
- Does IT supply deliver shareholder value? (Financial perspective).

The first question, "Is IT supply effective," asks whether IT supply is focused on doing the right things. Answers to this question may be found by measuring the extent to which pre-defined goals, derived from customer expectations, are realized. These goals are not stable but constantly evolving, as customers become more IT literate and more experienced in applying IT. Also, customer expectations rise as a result of comparisons with competitive and IT products and services, such as standard software packages, popular off-the-shelf plug-and-play PC tools, and outsourcing services.

The second question, "Is IT supply efficient," asks whether IT supply is focused on doing the right things right. Answers to this question may firstly be found by investigating overall IT supply-efficiency factors such as:

- Too much bureaucracy, measured by the number of management layers in place.
- Too much overhead, measured by the amount of indirect IT supply activities in relation to direct activities. Overhead might be reduced by combining, for example, accounting activities performed in each IT supply process into one single accounting function.
- Redundancy of similar activities performed in different IT supply processes, e.g., customer service performed in each IT supply process might be more efficient in a combined customer-service function representing all IT supply processes.

Secondly, answers to the efficiency question may be found by looking at the efficiency indicators of each of the IT supply processes of IT infrastructure management, IT development management, and client support. The answer is derived from the measures included in the related Scorecards of IT supply, ideally supported by external comparisons (benchmarks) and historical trends.

The third question, "Will IT supply maintain its full potential in the future," asks whether the IT supplier is doing as well as it possibly can to stay current with new developments so that its full potential will be maintained. Answers also come from selected performance indicators, aimed at the innovative capability of IT supply, and are derived from the Scorecards of the remaining IT supply processes and supported by external comparisons and historical trends.

The overall level of innovation of IT supply is an important performance criterion to determine the overall value of IT to an organization. Sethi, Hwang and Pegels, who took a detailed look at the ranking criteria and the overall effectiveness index developed by Computerworld, found strong positive relations between IT budget spent on IT staff, IT staff training, IT equipment value, and an organization's economic performance. They found that the more successful companies, measured by financial performance, have newer, more current technology and spend greater amounts on staff salaries and other benefits, and staff training. It can be reasoned that managing more state-of-the-art technology requires employees with higher qualifications and more experience, and therefore, employee salaries are higher. Alternatively, staff costs may be higher just because the management and maintenance of more current and up-to-date equipment requires a larger (or more expensive) staff.

The answer to the final question, "Does IT supply deliver shareholder value" relates to whether IT supply is in financial control, and, if appropriate, whether IT supply is profitable. Answers to the financial control question deal with the budget versus realization relationship, etc., while answers on the financial health question come from the performance indicators that are commonly used to measure the health of any business, such as profit as a percentage of turnover, profit per employee, ROS, ROA, etc.

Figure 6.2: Positioning the IT Supplier

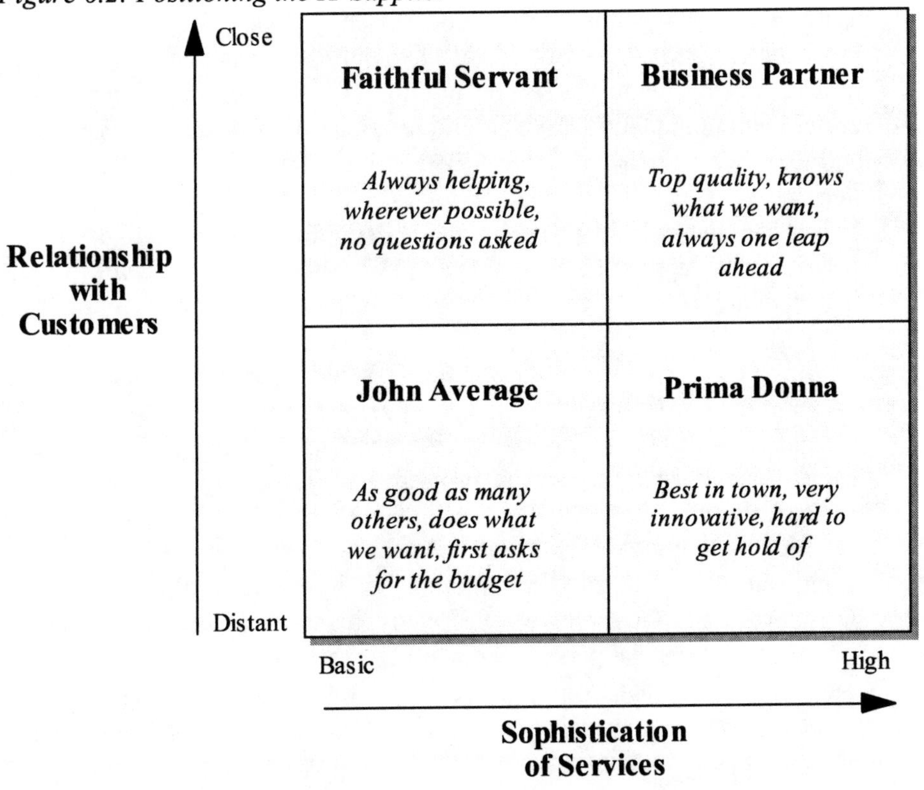

For IT supply management, the four stated questions offer a straightforward way to organize and rationalize the variety of otherwise disconnected indicators available, resulting in a Balanced Scorecard for IT supply management. Measurement, focused on the overall performance of IT supply, is an important approach to improving and safeguarding its performance. Measures themselves are, hopefully, the essential signs that IT supply is in good shape and likely to remain so.

The appropriate measures to be used should be derived from pre-defined goals, to be determined through the use of Service Level Agreements, through external comparisons (benchmarks), or by applying the framework of Figure 6.2.

This framework is based on proven and seasoned ideas derived from the classical Goal-Question-Metric framework of Basili and Rombach for systems development, the thinking of Von Simson on centralization and decentralization of IT services supply, and the work of Hamilton and Chervany on efficiency-orientation versus effectiveness-orientation. It can be used to derive a mission and role(s) of IT supply by elaborating on the answers to two basic questions:

- What are the services required by our customers, ranging from "basic" to "advanced"?
- How close is the customer relationship, ranging from "distant" to "close"?

The answers to these two questions lead to four possible service/customer relationship combinations:

- *Basic service, distant customer*: The IT supplier is regarded as an IT services and facilities supplier, delivering commodity services that are not discriminating by any standard, while fierce competition might exist from other suppliers.
- *Basic service, close customer*: The IT supplier is regarded as a "faithful servant," always helping wherever possible. Delivering reliable data center services and maintaining large corporate information systems are generally the most important parts of the total service, often offered as an internal supplier.
- *Advanced service, distant customer*: the IT supplier is seen as a high-quality consultant and supplier of state-of-the art IT services, able to draw from well-respected internal or external centers of expertise, but sometimes living in an "ivory tower",
- *Advanced service, close customer*: the IT supplier performs as a business partner: designing, building, integrating, operating, and supporting IT applications and an IT infrastructure that meet the highest professional and business standards, and which are fully aligned with the company's requirements.

What measures should be selected in a specific situation is contingent on the mission and roles of the IT supplier at hand. For instance, if the IT supplier is supposed to take on a "John Average" role, relatively more measures of the internal perspective and the financial perspective would be included. On the other hand, if the IT supplier is expected to play predominantly the "Business Partner" role, measures of the customer perspective and the innovation and learning perspective must dominate. Appendix C introduces a menu of appropriate measures in the form of Scorecards, reflecting the customer perspective, the internal perspective, the innovation and learning perspective, and the financial perspective, respectively.

MEASURES OF ACCOUNT MANAGEMENT

Account management becomes increasingly important in today's IT supply organizations. Many internal IT suppliers might not have achieved the best relationship with their clients in the past, and as a result, there is a danger that the traditional, internal IT organization is squeezed out of existence. For the sake of survival, both internal and external IT suppliers must market their products and services aggressively, since IT users have become more demanding, more IT aware, and more self-sufficient, while competition from various other suppliers is fierce.

IT suppliers, especially the internal ones, can no longer afford to keep a low (corporate) profile. The IT supplier must work hard to stay involved and help align IT for maximum usage and value throughout the organization. It should be the aim of account management to establish top-class customer relationships and to make sure that customers are satisfied and remain so. The primary purpose of account management is therefore to maintain and improve external relations. Adequate measures are therefore predominantly found in the area of customer orientation, above the other three perspectives of the Balanced Scorecard.

To define the measures of success in account management, the question arises "What constitutes good account management?" One might think that the successful application of the ingredients of the traditional marketing mix (**P**roduct, **P**rice, **P**romotion, and **P**lace) should reflect good account management. Kotler, however, believes an account manager should master the "marketing concept"–determining the needs and wants of target markets and delivering the desired satisfactions more effectively and efficiently than competitors. He confirms the importance of the four marketing Ps, but places them in the context of customer requirements and competitive pressure. Lauterborn goes further, rejecting the traditional marketing mix: he claims the four Ps are obsolete and replaces them by four Cs. Product is replaced by **C**ustomer wants and needs; Price is replaced by **C**ost to satisfy those needs (drawing on the notion that full lifecycle cost of ownership is more significant than initial acquisition price); Place is replaced by **C**onvenience to buy; and Promotion is replaced by **C**ommunication.

The ability to apply the four marketing Cs is a key success factor for account management. Ouellette adds to these generic marketing skills a set of marketing skills for IT services: an IT account manager needs technical, business, and interpersonal skill sets. Technical skills are the knowledge of the IT that the IT supplier brings to the job. In addition, the account manager must understand the evolution of this technology. Business skills encompass an understanding of business fundamentals, both knowledge of the specific organization and an awareness of trends in the organization's industry. Interpersonal skills involve the ability to interact well with other people in both one-on-one and group situations, and, above all, the ability to listen.

Listening to customers and arriving at customer-oriented performance measures means introducing and supporting instruments such as customer satisfaction surveys, focus group discussions, personal interviews, and detailed case study examination. Different groups of IT users, such as senior management, middle management, and operational employees, require different measurement instruments and approaches. Because the satisfaction of senior management is so important, and because the satisfaction issues involved may be complex, the most appropriate means for this "survey" might be a personal interview. The focus group approach can be used for a small number of key users and user managers, who are more likely to have complex opinions about IT services that cannot easily be expressed by answering a questionnaire. The concept of focus groups is familiar in, for example, the software packages industry; focus groups discuss and criticize the quality of the delivery of specific IT services.

Written questionnaires are usually the appropriate tool for middle management and operational users of IT to measure customer satisfaction. While the customer is probably not always right, his or her opinion is always important. It is also important to understand how the components of customer satisfaction change over time. There may even be seasonal elements in customer satisfaction, which for example could indicate service problems during vacation periods, or at the closing of the fiscal year.

The numbers of complaints, incidents, even compliments about operational services are, if well-registered, a good source of information. Other information that account managers gather could supplement or confirm findings from direct satisfaction measures, including indirect indicators of customer (dis) satisfaction, such as the number of IT personnel hired by other functions within the organization, or the level of payments to outside IT service vendors (this measure also reflects market share of the IT supplier, which indirectly might be an indicator of customer satisfaction).

Through these instruments, account managers gather the information they need to analyze customer satisfaction and to provide feedback to the responsible managers of IT development, IT infrastructure, and client support, to optimize customer satisfaction. Following up the measurement of customer satisfaction and customer service levels with measurements of market share and competitive positioning, a perceptive effectiveness assessment approach emerges.

Account managers also help customers make buying decisions, and often they close contracts. To improve the financial performance of the IT supplier, measured by indicators of the financial perspective of the Balanced Scorecard, account management is held responsible for increasing revenues. To increase revenues, account managers can decide to either sell the same amount of units of service at higher prices, or sell more units of existing services at the same selling price, or sell additional services. The IT supplier can only obtain high prices, however, if the IT service has unique features, since commodity IT services are, as any other commodity product, in most cases subject to fierce competition, selling price erosion, and small profit margins. Of course, selling more units of existing services at the same selling price, and selling additional services, requires a market of buyers, either within the organization or outside.

In Appendix C, a menu of appropriate measures of account management is introduced in the shape of Scorecards. It is only natural that there is some overlap with the aggregate IT Supply Management Scorecards, since IT supply management is in the end also responsible for customer satisfaction and commercial success. Specific customer-oriented measures for each of the three IT supply processes of IT development management, IT infrastructure management, and client support, which complement the account management measures, are discussed below.

MEASURES OF IT DEVELOPMENT MANAGEMENT

Although a lot has been done in the past to optimize performance levels of IT system development and maintenance activities, both through research and practical application, there is still plenty of room for improvement in most organizations. The concept of running IT supply as a professional business is equally valid for IT development and maintenance activities; again, finding adequate measures of the

Figure 6.3: Roles of IT Development and Maintenance Functions

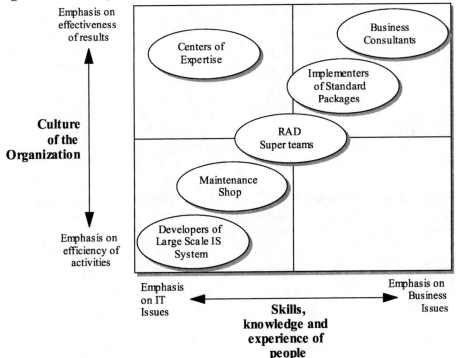

customer perspective, the internal perspective, the innovation and learning perspective, and the financial perspective must be guided by first reviewing the expectations of IT development and maintenance in a particular situation. Answers to performance questions may be found by measuring to which extent pre-defined goals, derived from customer expectations, are realized. Goals might be set through the elaboration of expected roles of IT development and maintenance according to the framework illustrated in Figure 6.3, and the derivation of the appropriate measures to determine IT development and maintenance effectiveness, efficiency, innovation, and financial control.

Figure 6.3 illustrates the spectrum of development and maintenance roles. In this figure, the Y-axis represents the difference in focus between effectiveness and efficiency, often embedded in the culture of the organization, as Hamilton and Chervany have indicated, while the X-axis shows the scale of the different skill sets required to bring results.

For IT developers whose role it is to mainly focus on the efficient delivery and maintenance of large-scale IT applications, the majority of appropriate performance measures are to be found in the internal perspective and customer perspective Scorecards. If the role of IT developers is expected to be found in the upper right quadrant, the majority of appropriate performance measures are obviously to be found in the customer perspective and innovation and learning Scorecards.

Development and Maintenance of Large-Scale Systems

In the lower-left quadrant of the matrix are traditional, activity-oriented approaches to application development and maintenance, appropriate for the development of large applications. For projects focused on the development of new IT, or the redevelopment of existing IT, the IT developer typically estimates the resources required to develop the necessary functionality and to implement the application, and estimates the corresponding costs. For the IT in place, often first installed years ago, IT development effort is directed at maintenance or enhancements, to keep this IT technologically current and aligned with the changing needs of the business.

For such activities, the effectiveness of IT development can be measured using indicators related to three principal categories of requirements:

*   *Responsiveness to customers' and business needs*: The IT supplier must be able to deliver reliable and user-friendly applications that correspond to the business and customers' needs, before plans and requirements change. The IT supplier must also be able to maintain these applications and act upon change requests when needed. This means that the IT supplier must be able to react quickly which, in turn, means setting resource priorities and managing staff effectively. The IT supplier must also meet professional quality standards in terms of user friendliness of delivered IT applications and "zero defect" software.
*   *Effective and reliable project management*: Effective management of development projects and maintenance activities means identifying and agreeing on

requirements specifications as precisely as possible at the outset, often restricting the size of a project, following a clearly defined and agreed-upon development methodology, and applying effective project management. Effective project management means setting target dates and costs before work begins, and delivering accordingly.

- *Adherence to IT architecture standards*: A further effectiveness factor deals with satisfying the need to use and share consistent information amongst multifunctional and company-wide business processes. This means adhering to corporate standards for data, user interfaces, report formats, infrastructure components, etc.

The efficiency of development and maintenance activities relates to "the extent to which effective IT is supplied at minimum costs," as previously defined. To derive appropriate measures of "effective IT" and "minimum costs," we need to take a closer look at both.

In the context of IT development and maintenance, "effective IT" supplied by developing and maintaining a system could be represented by the total number of lines of code (LOC) created, tested, and maintained. However, much work is carried out in IT development and maintenance projects which is not directly concerned with the creation or testing of code, such as specification, design, documentation, and project management; these activities have their own kinds of product which are all vital to the success of the project. Measuring these items in some appropriate way is certainly feasible, but it would be very difficult then to produce a readily understood single measure of the amount of work, taking all of these diverse kinds of products into account. Instead, the measure LOC is generally used as a "surrogate measure" representing the total amount of work carried out on the project.

When using LOC as a measure, consistency is vital; many LOC definitions have been cited (Jones lists 12), and inconsistent use of definitions can be very misleading about the size of products and, hence, about the levels of efficiency achieved.

LOC was the popular measure of size in the 1970s and 1980s. A more useful and now more popular perspective on size, Function Point Analysis (FPA), is concerned with the delivery of useful function to users; that is, the focus is on the utility of the delivered system, rather than on the amount of code which had to be written to create the system. FPA provides the best available solution to the problem of measuring the potential utility of an IT application to the user; actual utility depends on what the user does with the system, as well as on the capability of the system. Albrecht specifically designed Function Points to give an implementation-independent view of system size, and subsequent developments of Function Points, such as Symons' Mark II Function Points, have preserved this property. When considering efficiency, the number of Function Points is used as a surrogate measure for the utility to the user, in the same way that LOC is used as a surrogate for useful work performed by the developer. Although a number of slightly different approaches to Function Point Analysis have been introduced over the years by different organizations (IFPUG, NEFPUG, MARK II, and others), Function Points are generally accepted as a better size measure than LOC. FPA has become quite popular during the 1990s.

Staff months of effort (or its monetary equivalent), the predominant cost involved, is used as a measurement of the energy expended, the "cost or effort" part of the definition of efficiency. Once more, a consistent approach to this definition is vital, as there are many opportunities for error.

Another efficiency measure for development, called the Productivity Index (PI), is used by Putnam's SLIM (Software Lifecycle Management) model, based on a mathematical, non-linear relationship between the size of a project and the time and effort needed to complete it. The PI is used together with the Manpower Build-up Index (MBI), a mathematical calculation that allows for time pressure effects when measuring efficiency. The use of both, however, is not widespread, so efficiency can be best expressed in the number of Function Points produced per staff month. For the measurement of maintenance efficiency, this translates to the number of Function Points maintained or modified per staff month.

Finally, complementary and commonly used efficiency measures for maintenance activities are the number of staff months spent on maintenance as a percentage of the cumulative staff months available for development (or costs of maintenance as a percentage of total development costs), or the costs of maintenance as a percentage of total costs of operations.

It is also important to measure how efficiency is achieved. This entails measurement of such factors as the way in which work is organized (e.g., size of team and span of communication), skills (e.g., knowledge and experience levels), and methods, techniques, and tools (e.g., which are used and degree of appropriateness). By analyzing data concerning such factors, it is possible to measure their effect on performance, as has been described by Jones in a detailed fashion, and by Humphrey, who takes a more conceptual view describing different maturity levels of the software engineering process, ultimately leading to what some call "the software factory approach."

Rapid Application Development, Package Implementation and Business Consultancy

Returning to the matrix of Figure 6.3, the upper-right quadrant depicts results-oriented IT supply approaches that reflect the need for the IT supplier to develop IT capabilities much more quickly compared to the IT in the lower-left quadrant. Due to strategic business requirements and driven by competition, modern themes of business process redesign and business network redesign rely heavily on (new) IT and fast alignment of business activities and IT capabilities. Because it is crucial to drastically reduce the time to develop new IT applications, as well as development costs, companies adopt contemporary approaches such as Rapid Application Development (RAD).

RAD is a development approach that incorporates state-of-the-art:

- development techniques, such as re-use of intermediate and final development deliverables, object orientation, prototyping;

- development tools, such as repository-based I-CASE tools;
- project management approaches, such as time-boxed project management.

RAD features joint development teams, with members drawn from both IT development staff and affected business processes, to establish the specifications of new IT applications in JAD (Joint Application Design) sessions. Prototypes are then developed so that IT requirements can be quickly tested, changed, and accepted by the business; much faster than otherwise. Although prototypes may have to be discarded, they also might form iterative versions, known as evolutionary prototypes of final systems.

Another approach to drastically reduce the time to develop new IT applications, as well as to reduce development costs, is to buy functionality (in fact, Function Points) in the form of a ready-to-use application package, delivering a large amount of "useful work" at once. While a good deal of today's IT applications still needs to be custom developed, packaged software is used increasingly, often leading to changes of business processes. The established software packages to support business functions, such as financial management, human resources management, etc., which have been around for some decades already, are not the only popular ones. Modern, integrated "application platforms" such as the SAP offering are considered more and more often to support key business processes because of their infrastructure and integrating character, their broad range of functionality, their flexible capabilities to tailor functionality to meet specific business requirements, and their relatively low cost of acquisition and maintenance. Packages will nearly always prove to be a better investment, provided they meet the essential requirements, since they are not only less expensive to acquire and maintain, but also because they can be implemented more quickly so that its benefits can be achieved earlier.

IT supply, and especially IT development staff, can help select and implement packaged software. This can be extended by providing broader consultancy services to the business and thus contributing to business change, by leveraging skills and experiences such as insight into technology and its potential business impact, business process knowledge, a thorough understanding of business rules already encoded in information systems, and experience and realism in large-scale implementation and business change.

Appropriate classes of measures for IT development activities of the upper right quadrant come from three principal categories of requirements:

- *Business process knowledge*: The ability to understand how the business works in terms of flow of business processes and their structure, and the analytical skills to find out how the business could work better.
- *Understanding and application of state-of-the-art IT*: The insight into modern IT applications and their potential impact on the business, since IT applications are often built on top of, and integrated with, existing business function-supporting systems. IT development staff should be able to determine the IT support adequate for newly designed business processes and be able to build prototype applications for experimentation and demonstration.

- *Rapid Application Development*: Prototyping techniques, Joint Application Design (JAD) techniques, evolutionary development methods, time-boxed project management, etc., have to be mastered to be effective as an IT supplier.
- *Effective communication and teamwork*: Joint development teams penetrate existing functional boundaries and question functional responsibilities. Business process and business network redesign raise further issues such as the re-arrangement of responsibilities and the improvement of the quality of interfaces between organizational units. These are all issues that have to be dealt with when functional barriers, in place for long periods of time, are removed. Team skills, leadership, persistence, communication, and interpersonal relations skills are crucial to working constructively in multi-disciplinary teams and to delivering results.

As the need for more results-oriented approaches to development and maintenance clearly exists, as opposed to the activity-oriented approaches of the 1970s and 1980s, as Rijsenbrij and others indicate, the tendency in many development organizations is to move from the lower-left quadrant to the upper-right corner of the matrix illustrated in Figure 6.3. This has, of course, implications for skills to be developed and measures to be selected. However, most IT development organizations perform many of the indicated activities concurrently, and therefore need to live with quite a broad range of measures. These measures, as a menu of possibilities to choose from, appear in Appendix C in the form of Scorecards.

Figure 6.4: Roles of IT Infrastructure Management Functions

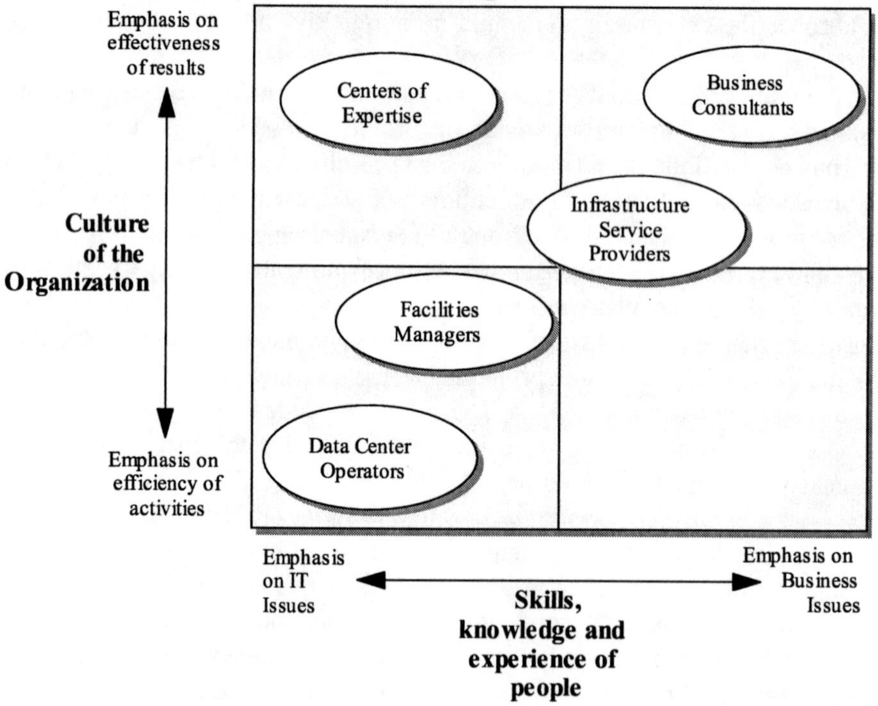

MEASURES OF IT INFRASTRUCTURE MANAGEMENT

Measurement of computer operations efficiency and data communications efficiency has the longest tradition of all five IT supply processes. Most organizations have extensive experience with formal measurement of data center operations, communications management, and related functions, often as an internal asset management tool providing voluminous reports of operating statistics. Technical measures such as CPU and DASD utilization, response time, and system availability are provided by the computers' accounting systems and sometimes used for external publication as well.

A traditional, yet very important aspect of infrastructure management is efficiency, mainly because of the large part of the IT budget consumed by infrastructure. Like IT development (see Figure 6.3), however, infrastructure management may cover a broad spectrum of roles and required skills, as depicted in Figure 6.4, and related performance measures, as will be discussed.

One of the conclusions of a study of the U.S. Department of Defense's Center for Information Management indicates, a data center's efficiency is mainly a function of its application portfolio. As a general rule, the study revealed, the newer the application portfolio, the more efficient the data center. Efficiency is also highly correlated with the size of the data center. Larger data centers can realize greater economies of scale and bigger payoffs from automation, particularly the use of hardware and software data center automation products. The study identified six rather obvious "keys to success" for efficiency:

- use economies of scale to reduce hardware and software costs;
- locate in a low-cost geographic area to reduce facility and staff costs;
- implement formal capacity planning and increase hardware utilization;
- establish standards and procedures to achieve a high degree of automation;
- optimize workflows to eliminate or reduce physical movement of items into and out of the data center and between workstations within the data center;
- implement organizational changes to promote quality, efficiency, and defect prevention.

Paans adds an important efficiency-improvement factor for many data centers: "Stick to only the core data center activities aimed at the delivery of a reliable IT infrastructure to operate information systems and data communication networks; eliminate all other ballast." From a theoretical point of view, this is of course a "motherhood and apple pie" statement, but Paans demonstrates the value of his advice by comparing actual data center staffing profiles with a best practice model, showing many inefficiencies that have "crept" into many data centers.

The evolution of infrastructure management measurement might offer lessons to be applied to the measurement of other IT supply activities. In particular, experience in data center measurement contains lessons regarding the different viewpoints from which measurements are taken (hence, the Balanced Scorecard) and the effective communication of measurement results. Infrastructure management measurement typically follows a historical progression in three stages to periodically assess its effectiveness and efficiency. This progression is consistent with the different roles and required skills of Figure 6.4, and associated perspectives of the Balanced Scorecard, as follows:

- first stage, the internal perspective;
- second stage, the customer perspective;
- third stage, the innovation and learning, and financial perspectives.

However, to evaluate the effectiveness and efficiency of IT infrastructure management, and to conduct specific, *ad-hoc* studies, all perspectives have to be taken into account.

First Stage of IT Infrastructure Measurement

In the first stage, IT suppliers begin to collect internal measures on data center operations. There are no real difficulties in measuring the performance of operations for purposes of internal management. Especially in large mainframe environments, where the investment is greatest and the need for efficiencies most pronounced, IT suppliers have tools and techniques for monitoring, tuning, and troubleshooting not only hardware, but also software, communications networks, operations procedures, and everyday support services. There is usually plenty of local history for comparison and trend analysis; in most large mainframe environments, there are software tools for performance monitoring and feedback, including a growing array of tools for communications management; there are external benchmarks against which to measure, often provided by hardware vendors; and operations measurement is largely automated, with technology monitoring and, increasingly, automatic fine-tuning.

There may exist two exceptions to this generally positive state of affairs in internal operations measurement:

- The most technically sophisticated and people-intensive functions within operations, systems programming, and technology planning resist routine measurement because of the variety and unpredictable nature of the tasks involved, and because they have little or no understanding of the broader perspective of measurement. These functions are more difficult to evaluate objectively, and an assessment of efficiency and effectiveness is based on management experience, observation, and intuition about what constitutes good performance.
- Extensive hardware monitoring facilities are not available in some environments, especially the non-mainframe, such as client-server environments. The relatively lower cost base of the IT supply side removes much of the imperative to fine-tune and maximize utilization. It is widely accepted that in the modern client-server environments, the majority of costs to manage these types of environments are increasingly found on the user side.

In this first stage, the IT supplier has been less successful measuring operations for purposes of external audiences (the customer perspective of the Balanced Scorecard), often because the measures reported to users recycle highly technical data appropriate for internal use only. Users often find that these technical performance statistics misrepresent their own experience with the service of the IT supplier. For example, the IT supplier publishes average system availability for the month of 99 percent; however, the one percent occurs during the last day of the month when Finance is trying to close the books.

Second Stage of IT Infrastructure Measurement

In the second stage, performance measurement reports result in terms more meaningful to management and users, hence the correlation to the customer perspective of the Balanced Scorecard. Measures assume the perspective of the business looking for service, not the machine providing it. This shift in measurement is often prompted by the realization that the statistical reports are not only not read, but also fail to improve the communications and relationships with management and users. The explicit purpose of a more business-oriented set of performance measures is to understand and respond to what constitutes good performance in the eyes of management and users. In this stage, performance measurement takes the form of a series of key indicators and of formal service level agreements (SLAs) negotiated with business management.

Business-oriented performance measures adopt the viewpoint and language of the business requiring service from the IT supplier. Many business-oriented measures are simply extensions of measures taken for purposes of internal management. They are distinguished from internal performance measures by two characteristics:

- They take an internal measure but reverse the viewpoint. For example, a common internal performance measure is average availability of the CPU. A corresponding business-oriented measure is the availability of a specific IT application or Local Area Network, perhaps linked to prime-time usage schedules. Similarly, the internal measure of batch job success rate corresponds to the business-oriented measure of on-time availability of key output. Similarly, response time becomes an external measure when measured at the terminal rather than within the CPU. Many such internal measures have business-oriented counterparts, discovered by asking how much the activity being measured matters to the user.

- They track discrete, user-visible events rather than averages over time. What sticks in the user's mind is not the long-term performance level, but rather the most recent problem and how it was resolved. Instead of publishing average availability for a month, a business-oriented approach tracks how many times the system was unavailable, how long the interruptions lasted, and how many users were affected. Similarly, more meaningful than average response time is a count of how often response time exceeded a predetermined threshold level. Business-oriented measures also track unusual events, how they were resolved, and how responsive technical support people were in the resolution. This leads to the simple but informative aggregate performance measure "perfect days"–tracking how often absolutely nothing unusual or disruptive occurred.

Third Stage of IT Infrastructure Measurement

In the third stage, corresponding to the innovation and learning and financial perspectives, organizations only report operations performance annually, showing how formal SLAs have been met. Operations performance has reached levels of excellence and reliability that eliminate the need for regular reporting. Excellent service is taken for granted, and the IT supplier is left to set its own performance targets, usually with an eye to continuous improvement over past performance. The only regular reporting to the business is direct communication of operating exceptions to affected users, and exceptions to SLAs. Feedback and discussion between the IT supplier and users still occurs regularly, but does not need to be prompted by detailed performance reports or formal measurement programs. As long as the ground rules and expectations for exception reporting are agreed upon, this informal arrangement, in combination with annual SLAs, is quite sufficient. Neither side is taken by surprise by unusual events, and the lack of detailed formal reporting does not serve as an excuse to avoid communicating unfavorable news.

This third approach represents a desirable condition: performance and user relationships are strong (comparable with the joint development of IT capabilities, as discussed) and the overhead of external reporting is dramatically reduced.

The combined measures for IT infrastructure management, as a menu of possibilities to choose from, appear in Appendix C as Scorecards.

MEASURES OF CLIENT SUPPORT

Finally, measures of client support effectiveness and efficiency reflect the importance of the operational relationships between customers and the IT supplier in today's competitive and highly demanding environments. Client support is the overall label for activities normally found in functions such as end-user computing (EUC) services, information centers (IC), call centers, user education and training departments, data center help desks, and other on-demand user services.

The critical role of client support is emphasized by Guimaraes and Igbaria's research, which demonstrates a strong and positive correlation between Information Center performance and payoffs that companies derive from end-user computing. Their research is based on a framework developed by Venkatraman and Ramanujam which conceptualizes the dimensions of IT capabilities to support management along 12 dimensions (ranging from anticipating surprises and crises, identifying key problems, etc., to fostering management control, fostering organizational learning, and enhancing innovation) and business objectives along the six dimensions of enhancement of management development, predicting future trends, evaluating alternatives, improving short- and long-term performance, and avoiding problem areas. The main conclusion of their research is that the Information Center's important areas of activities are strongly related to the level of company payoffs from end-user computing.

To further stress the importance of client support, Schlesinger and Heskett quote research into the economics of problem resolution and service recovery, which highlights the critical role of customer-contact employees, especially in the Internet era in which data centers directly communicate with end customers. Data collected by Technical Assistance Research Programs for the U.S. Department of Consumer Affairs show a close link between resolving a customer's problem on the spot and the customer's intent to repurchase. When customers experience minor problems, 95 percent say they will repurchase if the complaint is resolved speedily. If the resolution process takes even a little time, however, the number drops to 70 percent. A spread of 25 percent points can easily mean the difference between spectacular and mediocre operating performance. The comparison of in-company client support with individual customer buying decisions may not be 100 percent viable, since the individual user in an organization generally does not have the freedom to choose among different suppliers every day. But the correlation between service delivered by client support staff and customer satisfaction is very clear, and ultimately, it is the user of IT services who determines the quality of delivered services by the IT supplier.

Some authors claim that "spending money on customer service activities to improve effectiveness should be the goal rather than measuring efficiency." This implies that effectiveness is the foremost evaluation criterion for these activities, over efficiency. This also implies that the customer perspective measures of the Balanced Scorecard should prevail, compared to the other perspectives, when assembling a set of appropriate measures for client support.

This does not mean that the other perspectives are unimportant. Schlesinger and Heskett, for example, describe the logic of paying attention to the internal and innovation perspectives of client support as well: "Capable workers who are well trained and fairly compensated provide better service, need less supervision, and are more likely to stay on the job. As a result, their customers are likely to be more satisfied, return more often, and perhaps purchase more than they otherwise would. For organizations, this means enhanced competitiveness."

Schlesinger and Heskett's classification of "capable workers" calls for a review of the key qualities of client support personnel. A survey of the Help Desk Institute reveals the top 10 qualities as follows:

- good communication skills–oral, listening, written;
- technical skills–computer, software and systems knowledge;
- people, service and customer oriented;
- patient, relaxed, even-tempered;
- work well under stress/pressure;
- good phone skills;
- intelligent, able to learn and think logically;
- problem-solving skills, decisive;
- good analytical, questioning skills;
- friendly, personable, outgoing.

These skills are hard to measure objectively and precisely. To develop measures of the internal perspective, they rather include process-related aspects, such as:

- tracking activity levels, such as tracking calls and repeat calls, number of problems, incidents, cases or projects handled, education days provided, problems resolved, etc.;
- analyzing activity and work patterns, e.g., how many calls concerned a particular technology, or how many calls came from a specific user group;
- measuring responsiveness, for example, tracking the percentage of user problems that get resolved within an hour.

Process-related measures allow for target setting and trend analysis, indirectly indicate the staff's skill proficiency, and strengthen an appropriate customer service mentality.

Finally, the financial perspective mainly deals with the measures of performance to budget and recovery of costs. These indicators gauge management's ability to work within financial constraints rather than the group's ability to perform well.

To measure the performance of client support, a combination of measures of the customer, innovation and learning, internal, and financial perspectives must be selected. The combined measures, as a menu of possibilities to choose from, are included in Appendix C.

CONCLUSION

To address effectiveness and efficiency measurement issues of IT supply, the four perspectives of the Balanced Scorecard concept of Kaplan and Norton have been introduced: the customer, internal, innovation and learning, and financial perspectives respectively. For each of the three most important IT supply processes (IT infrastructure management, IT development management, and client support), Scorecards of appropriate measures have been developed. If IT supply is run as a business, which is the case if the IT organization is managed as a profit center, these Scorecards can be complemented by two additionally defined Scorecards: one for "Account Management" and one for the aggregate management level of IT supply (IT supply management).

Appendix C shows the 20 developed Scorecards (four Scorecards for five IT supply processes). Collectively, they help to answer the following questions:

- Is IT supply effective? (Customer perspective)
- Is IT supply efficient? (Ultimately the Customer and Shareholder perspective, initially the internal perspective)
- Will the IT supplier maintain its full potential in the future? (Innovation and learning perspective)
- does IT supply deliver shareholder value? (Financial perspective)

When applying the Balanced Scorecard concept, the actual measures to be used have to be selected from these Scorecards. Choices are contingent on the goals, roles, relative strengths, and weaknesses of the IT supplier in question. A large part of Chapter 7 is devoted to this selection process.

REFERENCES

Albrecht, A.J. (1979). Measuring application development productivity. *Proceedings of the IBM Applications Development Symposium*, GUIDE/SHARE, October.

Albrecht, A.J. and Gaffney, J. (1983). Software function, source lines of code, and development effort prediction. *IEEE Transactions on Software Engineering*, SE-9(6), 639-647.

Aldershof-Eikelenboom, A. and de Vroed, M.A. (1992). Betere informatiesystemen tegen lagere kosten? Prototyping!. *Informatie*, (11).

August, J.H. (1991). *Joint Application Design: the Group Session Approach to System Design*. Englewood Cliffs, NJ: Yourdon Press.

Basili, V.R. and Rombach, D. (1988). The TAME project: Towards improvement-oriented software environments. *IEEE Transactions on Software Engineering*, 14(6), 758-773.

Best Data Center Practices. (1994). *Capacity Management Review,* January, 5-6.

Boehm, B.W. (1981). *Software Engineering Economics*. Englewoods Cliffs, NJ: Prentice-Hall.

Butler Cox. (1991). The benefits of CASE: Myths and reality. *PEP Paper 20*. London: Butler Cox.

Computer Finance. (1994), "Client Server-An Expensive Way of Saving Money ?. 5(7).

Firnstahl, T.W. (1989). My employees are my service guarantee. *Harvard Business Review*, July-August, 28-34.

Guimaraes, T. and Igbaria, M. (1994). Exploring the relationship between IC success and company performance. *Information & Management*, 26, 133-141.

Hamilton, S. and Chervany, N.L. (1981). Evaluation information system effectiveness-Part 1: Comparing evaluation approaches. *MIS Quarterly*, September, 55-69.

Help Desk Institute. (1991). *Survey of Member Practices*. Colorado Springs.

Humphrey, W.S. (1989). *Managing the Software Process*. Reading, MA: Addison-Wesley Publishing Company.

Jones, C. (1986). *Programming Productivity*. New York: McGraw Hill.

Jones, T. C. (1986). Steps towards establishing normal rules for software cost, schedule, and productivity estimating. In Skwirzynski, J.K. (Ed.). *Software System Design Methods*, NATO ASI Series, F22, 567-575.

Kotler, P. (1984). *Marketing Essentials*. Englewoods Cliffs, NJ: Prentice-Hall.

Lauterborn, R. (1994). *Speech for Flem Marketing Services*, Gouda, NL.

Lubars, M.D. (1991). Reusing designs for application development. *IEEE Software*, March.

Maister, D.H. (1993). *Managing the Professional Service Firm*. New York: The Free Press.

Martin, J. (1991). *Rapid Application Development*. New York: Macmillan Publishing Company.

Ouellette, L.P. (1992). *How to Market the I/S Department Internally*. New York: AMACOM.

Paans, R. Rekencentra: Normen voor menskracht. *Compact*, 21(1).

Putnam, L. H. (1978). A general empirical solution to the macro software sizing and estimation problem. *IEEE Transactions on Software Engineering*, SE-4(4), 345-61.

Rijsenbrij, D.B.B. (1993). Basisconcepten in systeemontwikkeling. *Informatie*, (10).

Schlesinger, L.A. and Heskett, J.L. (1991). The service-driven service company. *Harvard Business Review*, September-October, 71-81.

Sethi, V., Hwang, K.T. and Pegels, C. (1993). Information technology and organizational performance, A critical evaluation of Computerworld's index of information systems effectiveness. *Information & Management*, 25, 193-205.

Symons, C. R. (1991). *Software Sizing and Estimating*. Chichester UK: Wiley.

Tomasko, R.M. (1987). *Downsizing: Reshaping the Corporation for the Future*. New York: American Management Association.

Van der Zee, J.T.M. (1989). Produktiviteit van de systeemontwikkeling. *Informatie en Informatiebeleid*, 7(3).

Van der Zee, J.T.M. (1994). Rapid application development. *Informatie*, (1), 40-48.

Venkatraman, N. and Ramanujam, V. (1987). Planning system success: A conceptualization and an operational model. *Management Science*, June, 33(6), 687-705.

Von Simson, E.M. (1990). The centrally decentralized IS organization. *Harvard Business Review*, July-August.

Chapter VII

An IT Measurement Program

In many ways, as has been become clear from the previous sections, IT measurement is a state of mind, and accomplishes little unless it drives improvement programs. An IT measurement program, structured in terms that all stakeholders are comfortable with, helps bridge the communication gap between the worlds of the business and IT, and helps manage the complexity of IT in an organization. It is therefore aimed at all stakeholders; it replaces opinion with fact; and it directs towards substantial, measurable improvements.

Based on the lessons from measurement in other disciplines, and from companies' experiences with IT measurement programs in the past, it is well known that measurement accomplishes nothing unless it indeed drives improvement programs. Also, those activities should be measured where the need for improvement is greatest, and the needs of different audiences or stakeholders must be taken into account (in Chapter 2, the main stakeholders were identified, being the shareholders, customers, and employees of the organizational entity being measured). In practice, senior and IT management tend to violate this common sense. As Rubin asserts, lack of focus on the important issues, as perceived by the stakeholders, is one of the reasons for his observed IT metrics program failure rate of 80 percent, together with too strong a focus on individual measures unrelated to specific organizational goals.

Examples of managerial "violations" include:

- Lack of measurement in general, rationalized by the perhaps mistaken assertion that everybody is happy and everything in control. The measurement philosophy is more or less "Hear no evil, see no evil, speak no evil."
- Measuring too little, gaining insufficient insight to take necessary actions.
- Measuring the wrong things, or measuring what is already done very well, so deluding management.

- Measuring too much, so being overwhelmed by an exhaustive amount of data that is put to no use.
- Producing lengthy performance reports which, because of technical content and vocabulary, go unread by the intended audience.

Many IT supply managers have developed some form of a performance management system and a series of internal performance indicators for their organizations. Good performance judged by these measures, however, does not necessarily mean that the IT supplier's customers are satisfied with the services and systems they are getting, nor that the systems are contributing to the performance of the business. To enable focus on the issues relevant to each level of management of the BTRIPLEE framework, a series of steps to follow is recommended. They are described in this chapter.

First, a number of important attributes of IT measurement programs will be reviewed in the first section. Then, it is argued that stakeholders should be able to define a well-balanced set of performance measures and associated targets, matching the goals of the organization and the application and supply of IT, on the basis of the BTRIPLEE framework. The second section deals with the process to select the appropriate set of IT measures from the ones proposed in Chapters 4, 5, and 6, and assign target values to them.

Further, an organization must have the ability and must be prepared to provide, collect, analyze, and report performance data. The introduction of a measurement program takes time and effort, both of which must be committed. The implementation of an IT measurement program, taking these factors into account, is described in the third section.

Organizations must be able to interpret the measures wisely, to attain the benefits that derive from having a measurement program, and to adapt the measures, the style, and the frequency of reporting the results to suit the different stakeholders. Organizations must also be able to direct positively the effects of a measurement program on people's behavior. Indeed, the aim of a measurement program is improvement (what gets measured, gets done), so it is important to control the reactions of people and translate them into positive energy. These management aspects are covered in the fourth section.

Finally, a real-life case of defining and implementing an IT measurement program is described in the last section.

THE ATTRIBUTES OF AN IT MEASUREMENT PROGRAM

To determine the attributes of an adequate IT measurement program, lessons can be learned from traditional management accounting systems. For example, in order to consistently and systematically assemble accounting data, organizations use accounting systems comprising agreed upon accounting rules and definitions, information systems, and reporting standards, at different levels in the organization.

In line with management accounting systems, the development of an IT measurement program should be aimed at a consistent attempt to systematically bring together different indicators of business performance and IT performance, at the three levels of the BTRIPLEE framework.

In Chapter 3 it was defended that measurement of IT value must be based on two key attributes: an overall management framework and a set of key measures for IT value. Both attributes were developed throughout the previous chapters. Additionally, a systematic IT measurement program requires performance targets associated with selected measures, and an underlying information and reporting system. Altogether, an IT measurement program should thus be based on the following attributes:

- *An overall management framework*: IT performance measurement must be woven into a broader management framework to be successful. Performance measurement should be related to strategic, organizational, and economic objectives. In other words, IT performance measurement is only the tip of the iceberg and has no intrinsic value in itself. Its value is determined by its use in a broader management framework that enables stakeholders to apply and provide the IT that meets business needs. The BTRIPLEE framework is designed to provide such an overall management framework.

- *A set of key measures and associated targets for performance*: A set of IT performance measures and associated targets for performance is the next attribute. A spectrum of performance measures must be applied, and the specific measures to be used vary according to the objectives of the organization and the level in the organization for which the measures are constructed. The performance measures to assess the business value of IT, the effectiveness of IT and the effectiveness and efficiency of IT supply have been discussed on the basis of the BTRIPLEE framework in the previous chapters. The associated targets for performance and performance improvement should be established for each measure, for example by benchmarking the company's performance against others, or by using relevant statistics published by industry and trade organizations, or by setting them as a result of negotiations between stakeholders.

- *Underlying information systems and reporting tools*: The ability to measure performance on a continuing basis assumes the existence of fundamental information systems such as project accounting, operating statistics, management information systems, and financial systems. By requesting performance measurement data, management ensures that these fundamental systems are in place and working. To provide continuous feedback, a routine reporting scheme should be in place, and periodic performance reviews must interpret measures and underlying individual performance.

These attributes of a measurement program are confirmed by many consulting engagements related to the development and implementation of measurement programs. Nusenoff and Bunde, who disclose their insights in measurement with 14 guidelines for the development and implementation of a measurement program, also confirm them.

THE DEFINITION OF AN IT MEASUREMENT PROGRAM

Analogizing with the functions and attributes of management accounting systems, the definition of an IT measurement program can thus be expressed as: the combination of an overall management framework, appropriate measures and

Figure 7.1: Definition of an IT Measurement Program

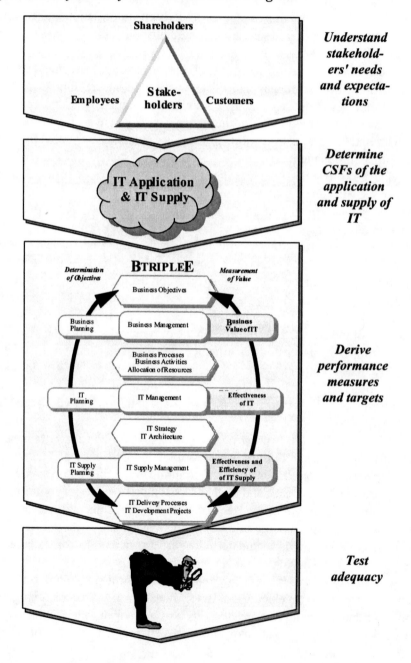

Understand stakehold-ers' needs and expecta-tions

Determine CSFs of the application and supply of IT

Derive performance measures and targets

Test adequacy

associated target values, informational sources, and tools, to systematically and consistently assess the application of IT, and the performance of IT supply, aimed at improvements in both.

Given the range of measures available to include in an IT measurement program, there is a clear need for a systematic approach to the selection process. To define a measurement program, a few structured techniques can be used to derive appropriate measures at each level of the BTRIPLEE framework. They are certainly not new nor experimental; the Goal-Question-Metric (GQM) technique of Basili and Rombach, the Critical Success Factors (CSF) approach, described by Rockart and successfully applied in case studies into IT performance measurement by Slevin, Stieman, and Boone, and the Miller-Doyle instrument, among others, might be well known.

There are no substantial differences amongst the GQM, CSF or Miller-Doyle techniques. They all explicitly connect business purposes and CSFs with IT requirements, from which appropriate measures for IT performance evaluation can be derived. Proper application of these techniques to the measurement of IT will help to ensure that measures are selected for the right reasons and that measure proliferation will be avoided; the necessary investment for measurement will thus be much more likely to pay off.

To derive an appropriate set of IT performance measures, four activities must be carried out, as illustrated in Figure 7.1:

- understand stakeholders' needs and expectations;
- define the Critical Success Factors (CSFs) of both the application and supply of IT;
- derive from both the appropriate measures and associated target values to measure the business value and effectiveness of IT (layers one and two of the BTRIPLEE framework), and the effectiveness and efficiency IT supply (layer three of the BTRIPLEE framework);
- test the adequacy of the set of measures and associated target values.

Understand Stakeholders' Needs and Expectations

In Chapter 2, we called the major constituents who directly influence a company's performance the stakeholders of the company; they include the owners (shareholders) represented by top management, customers, and employees. As Curtice and Kastner described, at one level is the need to balance the give-and-take between the business and each stakeholder, recognizing that stakeholders expect things from the business just as the business expects things from them. If either party gives or receives too little, the relationship suffers. At another level, in order to sustain high business performance, the organization must meet the expectations of the various stakeholder groups in a balanced fashion. Satisfying owners at the expense of employees, or even satisfying customers at the expenses of owners, will in the long run inhibit sustained high performance.

The company's strategic decisions should reflect the relative importance of stakeholders' needs and expectations (the planning side of the first layer of the

BTRIPLEE framework), and impact the decisions about the application and the supply of IT. Understanding the needs and expectations of stakeholders at different levels in and outside an organization takes account of organization-specific issues, such as the nature of the business; the competitive environment within which it operates; and the culture, procedures, and regulations which govern relationships between stakeholders.

The analysis of stakeholders' needs and expectations must be objective, based on facts, not on preconceptions. It should use techniques and tools like interviews, surveys, questionnaires, focus group discussions, and workshop sessions, in which all stakeholders participate in one way or another.

Define CSFs for IT Application and Supply

Based on the results of the previous step, organizations must determine the critical things that have to be done well in relation to the application of IT, in order to be able to measure the business value of IT, as discussed in Chapter 4. It is important to first understand what stakeholders expect from the application of IT, before any measure can be included in a measurement program. This involves classification of required IT support (as described in Chapters 2 and 5). Following classification of the different types of IT, CSFs for application of IT can be defined, and guiding IT principles and implications determined. Both the classification of required IT support and guiding IT principles should be derivable from an IT architecture and an IT strategy, and are included in the planning side of the second layer of the BTRIPLEE framework.

Organizations must also determine the critical things that have to be done well in relation to the supply of IT. IT supply organizations need to align their mission and possible delivery roles(s) (see Chapter 6) to be able to respond to expectations of their stakeholders, as is reflected in the planning side of the third layer of the BTRIPLEE framework.

Derive Performance Measures and Associated Target Values

The next step is to determine which measures should be monitored at each level of the BTRIPLEE framework. The focus of measurement must be on the defined CSFs, because what gets measured gets done. Measuring CSFs by applying aligned measures focuses attention on the important issues. For each defined CSF, at least one performance measure, and preferably a few more, must be defined to allow for a well-balanced set of measures. Measures that are not related to CSFs are at best superfluous and at worst wasteful and tending to divert attention.

When selecting performance indicators, it is critical to focus attention on the future. Since past performance is history, and measurement accomplishes nothing unless it drives improvement programs, history is important only if it contributes to future success as well, as Kaplan and Norton assert.

The business value measures of the first BTRIPLEE layer should be defined with top management. An initial set of IT effectiveness measures (second BTRIPLEE layer) is best identified with a select and attentive group of stakeholders from the business and IT supply side, and, if possible, from the customer community. One starting point for defining IT effectiveness measures is to discuss with the actual users of IT already in place and in use, with the CSFs in mind and based on the IT architecture, what they think (based on their experience) constitutes successful application of IT, and how that might be measured with help of the proposed measures in Chapter 5. Another, complementary approach is to select customer-oriented measures from among those commonly found in Service Level Agreements, system development project plans, and customer satisfaction surveys.

IT supply effectiveness measures (third BTRIPLEE layer) can also be derived from among those found in Service Level Agreements, system development project plans, and customer satisfaction surveys, while both IT supply effectiveness and efficiency measures might initially be based on established measures. As the art and science of IT supply performance is relatively well developed, and comparative data is publicly available, another starting point would be to include some of the relevant measures discussed in Chapter 6 and Appendix C.

Many performance data are associated with and originated by people who perform work in the IT area. Because the commitment and acceptance of a program by the people whose performance is subject of measurement are key to sustained success, the 'human side' of measurement has to be somewhat further explored. As said, it is very important that all stakeholders, including the people whose work and performance are measured, commit themselves to the measurement program. They only will commit themselves, however, if they perceive the program to be fair, focused on the right issues, correct in its measures and measurements, and conducted in a structured and traceable manner. Measurement of people can imply both negative and positive behavioral effects, and both have to be dealt with in a different way. Therefore, the people whose work and performance are going to be measured, and who are part of the group of all stakeholders, should participate in the definition and implementation of a measurement program.

When measures have been selected, appropriate target values are associated with each of them. This is often a very sensitive subject, since comparing actual, measured performance with target values will often result in discrepancies. Once observed, much discussion might arise whether the metrics have been well defined, whether measurement itself has been performed accurately, whether the target values have been set at an acceptable level, and so on.

One of the problems of performance measurement is the relative lack of agreed-upon industry standards and accepted target values for performance. As stated, some help in setting realistic performance targets may be obtained from the comparison of actual performance against established Service Level Agreements, the comparison of performance-to-plan data for system development projects, and the results of customer satisfaction surveys. Many organizations, however, rely on external benchmarking data (see next chapter) because of the lack of appropriate internal data. As long as no internal history has been built up, this external data could be used (with care) as temporary target values for the measures based on ratio scales. It is not appropriate for measures based on interval scales, however.

Test the Adequacy of the Measures and Associated Targets

The results of a first measurement should be used as a basis to determine the first target values for these measures. No doubt that errors in the definitions of measures and associated target values (and flaws in the applied measurement techniques, bugs in supporting tools, etc.) will be uncovered in a first period of usage of the measurement program. However, a first round of measurement allows the designers and audiences of the measurement program to review the usefulness and the practical application of certain measures and associated target values. For this purpose, an appropriate sub-set of measures for the different BTRIPLEE layers of business value, IT effectiveness, and effectiveness and efficiency of IT supply is selected and put to work. This sub-set can be used to test the adequacy of the measures, associated target values, collection of information, and reporting mechanisms, in a controlled environment, before implementing the complete program.

In testing the set of performance measures and associated target values, it is important to present at least some of the results. Stakeholders expect to see some follow-through, in the form of both improvement actions and feedback. This feedback might be provided in a brief summary report, or even better, in a presentation to all stakeholders. The presentation of test results should be a key means of informing all stakeholders about the progress in the development of an IT measurement program. If there is bad news to report, information about the steps to be taken to address the associated problems should also be included.

Adjust Measures and Targets Over Time

Designing an IT measurement program and identifying the appropriate performance measures and associated targets, matching the goals of the organization at different levels, is not a one-off project. Rather, it is a recurring and iterative process. Performance measures might be added to the program because of their increasing importance, while others could be dropped because they have lost relevance. Over time, the associated targets for performance might be adjusted, because of improved (or decreased) established performance or changing conditions and requirements, either within or outside the organization. Because it is so "organic," the process, as well as its results, can never be thoroughly objective, precise, and complete.

Gold, manager of the Information Processing Measurement Program at IBM, experienced this when starting a measurement program in IBM. He said: "Many people want to wait until they have the 'perfect measure.' Not only is there no such thing as a perfect measure, but also the importance of each measure changes over time. So a measure that looks great today may have little usefulness in three years. When our group was trying to devise a set of measures for the information systems activities at IBM, we wanted about one dozen indices. But our measurement team seemed to be continually dissatisfied with the measure. Finally, we realized we

Figure 7.2: Evolving IT Measurement Program

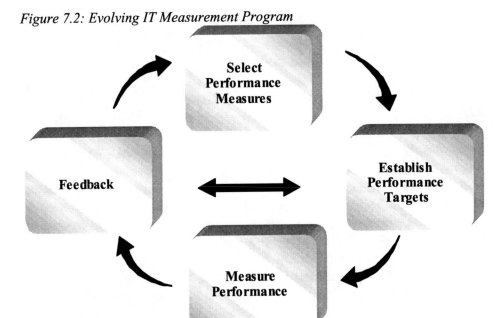

would never find 12 perfect measures. The publication deadline forced the group to decide which measures were viable at that time, and which were not. They tested those measures at a few locations and reported the results. That was the way the measurement program got started. Now that the measurement program at IBM has been going for several years, it has become obvious that the needs of the business, and the things that management wants to measure, are changing. Some of the original measures are no longer pertinent. Four years ago the company was focusing on cost. Today it is focusing on leading-edge opportunities. The measurement program has to tie the benefits of information processing to the current business concerns, and they change. IBM revises their measures every year, after asking for ideas from others throughout the firm."

The recurring and iterative process of designing an IT measurement program and identifying the appropriate performance measures and associated targets is illustrated in Figure 7.2.

In any case, it is vitally important that the program is, right from the start, credible, understandable (although not necessarily overly simplistic), and resistant to abuse (e.g., by backdoor approaches to changing the score without changing the real performance produced). The program and set of selected measures must be stable to some degree, so that results are consistent, reproducible, and performance can be tracked over time (e.g., year by year) producing useful trend lines. Altogether, a measurement program must be dynamic and evolutionary; not revolutionary, chaotic, or static.

THE IMPLEMENTATION OF AN IT MEASUREMENT PROGRAM

If the definition and verification of a measurement program has been carried out, which means that real activities are measured using a set of selected performance measures, associated targets, measurement techniques, and tools, the next step is to weave the measurement program into the organization and existing management practices. Having discussed the What of measurement program design, it is the How of putting the program into practice that is now of interest.

The implementation of an IT measurement program should not be different from any other implementation. In fact, there are striking similarities between the implementation of information systems in an organization, and the implementation of an IT measurement program. Therefore, some reference is made in this section to the implementation of IT itself, and the associated management issues, when they also apply to the subject of IT measurement programs. In particular, an interesting section of Walton's *Up and Running* is devoted to implementation aspects of IT systems, and it is a slightly modified version of his "phase-by-phase development of key ingredients for effective IT implementation" which is used here as an overall framework to discuss implementation issues of IT measurement programs. The framework is based on the development of three conditions essential for effective implementation:

- alignment of business, organizational, and technology strategies, in relation to IT and IT measurement;
- commitment of stakeholders to IT measurement;
- competence of stakeholders.

These conditions become increasingly specific as implementation progresses. Ultimately, in the introduction and operation phase of an IT measurement program, they take the form of:

- *Operational alignment*: The program in practice is consistent with the company's technology, organization, and business strategies, which are themselves aligned.
- *Stakeholder ownership*: Strongly committed stakeholders own the program in place.
- *Stakeholder mastery*: Stakeholders, who master the program in place and continue to learn influence the program's further evolution.

Figure 7.3 shows these conditions in the different phases.

Deficiencies in any of the key ingredients can be harmful. Without alignment, energy generated by program ownership and mastery can be misdirected and wasted, as was discussed in the previous section. Without ownership, positive conditions of mastery and alignment may achieve incomplete utilization, leading to fewer improvements (the ultimate goal of an IT measurement program) than desired. Without mastery, strong ownership and alignment may lead stakeholders to engage the program with enthusiasm and for the right purpose, but ineffectively.

Figure 7.3: Key Ingredients for Implementation

Key Ingredients	**Phase One** Generating the Context for IT Measurement	**Phase Two** Designing an IT Measurement Program	**Phase Three** Putting the IT Measurement Program into Practice
Alignment	Vision aligned with business, organization, and technology strategies	IT measurement program design aligned with vision	Operational use of IT measurement program aligned with vision
Commitment / Support / Ownership	High organizational commitment, stakeholder support for IT measurement	IT measurement program designed to tap and promote stakeholder ownership	Stakeholders feel strong ownership for IT measurement program
Competence / Mastery	Competence in IT and IT measurement literacy	IT measurement program designed to use and promote mastery of IT measurement	Stakeholders mastering the IT measurement program

Gill, a U.S.-based consultant on measurement programs, stresses the importance of mastery. She says: "Harnessing the appropriate level and amount of people skills when implementing measurement and quality programs in the organization is very important. People-skill deficiencies account for most of the failures that occur when implementing such programs. Whereas IT staff members have little difficulty in understanding technology and change, failure in implementation efforts is brought on by an absence of skills such as selling, persuading, and leading."

With these last words, she assumes that IT people are in the driving seat of the implementation wagon of IT measurement programs, which, in my experience, is seldom the case. Of course they participate as important stakeholders, and they should, as we will see; leadership for implementation, however, lies most often in the hands of top management.

Several key issues cut across alignment, commitment, and competence in the implementation phase. They are:

- *Timing*: Should the program be put in practice as a whole, or is a phased approach more desirable?
- *Leadership*: What should be the role of upper management throughout the implementation process?
- *Participation*: Who should be involved, at what stages of the process, and for what purposes?

- *Organization*: What organizational aspects have to be dealt with?
- *Communication*: How should results be made public?

These issues are briefly discussed below.

Timing-Full-Blown Versus Phased Implementation

When implementing anything, including an IT measurement program, basically two strategies exist. The choice of a full-blown (all-at-once, or big-bang) implementation versus a phased approach depends on the organization (is it able to absorb full implementation at once?) in relation to the size and complexity of the designed measurement program. In fact, implementation of an IT measurement program is a matter of managing the initial gaps between the expectations of stakeholders of an IT measurement program and the results of measurement and performance improvement once stakeholders master the program.

The first scenario is to implement the entire set of measures and associated instruments for all levels of the BTRIPLEE framework (business value of IT, IT effectiveness, IT supply effectiveness and efficiency) throughout all affected organizational units. In such a scenario, the purposes of measurement can be optimally aligned with the designed program. It also has the advantage that the program and its implementation are taken more seriously by all stakeholders, because they understand the impact of the program on performance improvement.

This scenario should be selected if the measurement program is not overly large and complex. It also should be chosen if the organization is under great pressure to make significant improvements in a short time in all or part of the areas of the application and supply of IT. In this case, risks of not succeeding have to be managed well, to avoid counter productivity and cynicism.

The second scenario for the implementation of an IT measurement program is to follow a phased introduction. A phased approach makes managing the gaps between existing and required levels of knowledge and skills, available tools, developed procedures, etc. easier. A phased process might increase the smoothness of implementation, in terms of alignment, commitment, and competence. It enables new measurement capabilities to be owned and mastered, before the next set is added. It also yields a series of small successes that may gain the confidence of the people involved, and those who will be involved in later phases. It is this phased approach that has been applied in most measurement programs in which I have participated.

A phased approach for the implementation of an IT measurement program might be compared, from a managerial perspective, to the evolutionary and iterative development and implementation of information systems. As has been learned from such a development approach, it is important to define the number and size(s) of the partitions and iterations to be implemented as releases or versions at the start of the implementation program. This is important from a planning and preparation point of view, and also to maintain control of the total program to be implemented. The size of each release of an IT measurement program will depend on the priorities attached to the sub-set of measures of each release, the organizational units involved and their organizational readiness, and the total length of elapsed time that is acceptable to implement the whole program. In general, each of the releases should be large enough to be non-trivial and small enough to be implementable without too many risks.

There are basically two ways to segment IT measurement program releases:

- By *depth* of measurement: For each level of measurement from the BTRIPLEE framework, a sub-selection is made from the total set of selected measures to be put into place; for each layer, at least some measures are chosen and implemented. In the next release, for each of the layers measures are added, and so on, so that the phased implementation of the program will reach its full depth step-by-step.
- By *breadth* of measurement: A choice is made to implement either the complete set of selected measures for business value of IT, or for effectiveness of IT, or for effectiveness and efficiency of IT supply. Within the domain of effectiveness and efficiency of IT supply, a further segmentation could be selected, e.g., start with the implementation of measures for the activities of 'IT Infrastructure Management,' or start with the implementation of the full set of measures for 'Development Management.' In subsequent phases, the remaining areas and BTRIPLEE levels of IT measurement are adopted.

Figure 7.4 represents these two approaches for a phased implementation of an IT measurement program.

Figure 7.4: Phased Implementation of an IT Measurement Program

Segmentation by Breadth

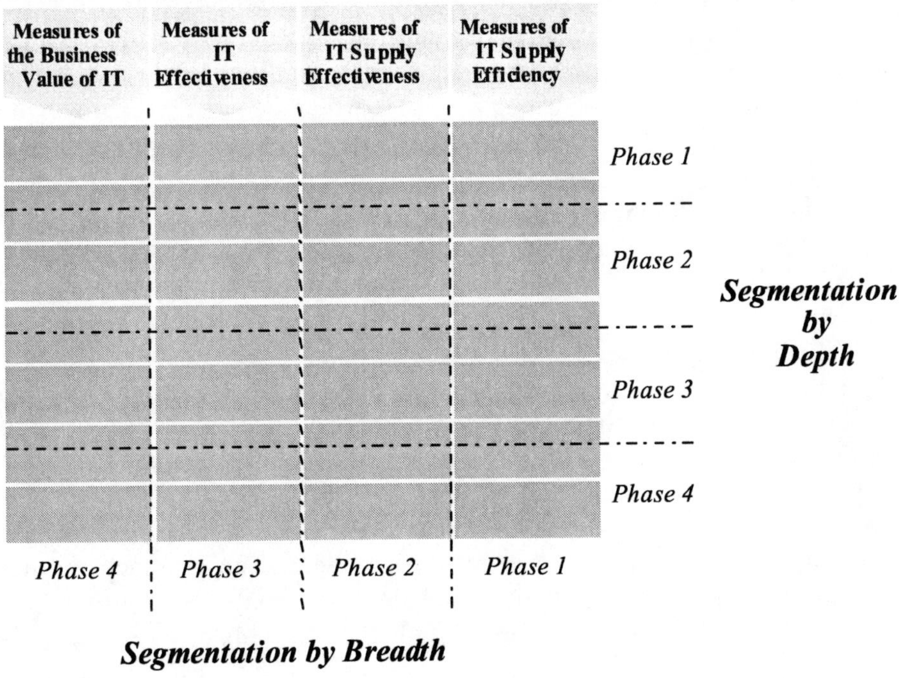

In the segmenting by breadth example, Phase 1 could be called the measurement of efficiency of IT supply, Phase 2 the measurement of the effectiveness of IT supply, etc. The order of phases given in the figure is illustrative, but in practice, this is the sequence in which the organizations who measure the value of IT have started their measurement endeavors.

Leadership-The Role of Top Management

The importance of top management's leadership to the implementation of any sort of performance measurement program is well known, and for many years. For example, Peters and Waterman already refer to it in their *In Search of Excellence* (1982): "There is no way that such a [performance measurement] program will ever take hold without the unstinting support of the whole top management team." And Gold of IBM declared: "The support of management was critical; it was achieved through numerous presentations and training courses which spanned the entire management structure of the company."

Three major tasks for management can be identified when it comes to implementation of an IT performance measurement program, consistent with Figure 7.3: ensure alignment, strengthen stakeholder support and ownership, and develop stakeholder mastery.

Participation-A Taskforce for Measurement

Participation of all stakeholders is important to address issues on the levels of alignment, commitment / ownership, and competence / mastery early on, rather than having to fix too many flaws in the program later, with the risks of losing commitment and ownership as a result of that. Based on my experience with implementing measurement programs, I would like to stress that it would be a severe mistake not to thoroughly involve the people whose work and whose performance will be measured when implementing a measurement program. Early participation of these important categories of stakeholders (IT users and IT supply employees) is extremely important. Early participation allows for the anticipation of resistance and doubt, and it offers the opportunity to deal with such issues when they still are in their infancy. As Peters and Waterman confirm, "People like to perform against standards; if the standard is achievable, and especially if it is one they played a role in setting."

Not everybody is likely to be able to participate, and it would be neither efficient nor effective because of the size of the total group of stakeholders. A pragmatic solution has to be found for participation, for example the formation of a taskforce, representing the organizational units that constitute the total group of stakeholders. In my experience, a taskforce is best staffed with both individuals that are already favorable to the idea of measuring and being measured, as well as criticasters of measurement. The presence of these different attitudes in one team, if well balanced among the team members, increases the likelihood of a realistic and achievable implementation. It also helps enormously to bridge the different worlds of stakeholders (reflected by the different perceptions about the application and supply of IT), which increases the level of ownership of all.

Organization-The Requisites for Measurement

The organization of the implementation of a designed IT measurement program requires setting up the aforementioned taskforce, allocating a budget for it, preparing a project plan, and getting started. It further requires the fulfillment of organizational requirements, such as the:
- production and dissemination of a measurement guidebook, comparable with the well-known accounting manual for financial measurement-a publication containing the set of measures, associated target values, and procedures for collection and analysis of measurement data;
- production, dissemination, and organizational implementation of (automated) support tools;
- development of appropriate education and training sessions, as well as coaching skills and capabilities, all tailored to the different classes of stakeholders;
- definition of different reporting schemes, suiting the needs of different stakeholders in terms of content and reporting style and frequency;
- integration with other management control and reporting mechanisms;
- actual collection of measurement data on a continuous basis, as much as possible interwoven with the more standard and regular activities that are already performed.

Communication-Report Results

To a certain extent, it requires an act of faith to launch an IT measurement program because it is very difficult to demonstrate the benefits to those who are questioning what such a program can deliver to them. Stakeholders' expectations therefore need to be carefully managed, and proper communication to them is a very important vehicle to maintain the sustained cooperation, commitment, and support.

Gill, in her primer on advice for measurement programs, lists a few attention points for proper communication in relation to IT measurement:
- Make data and results visible, and avoid mystery or secrecy in the interpretation of results.
- Be receptive to any and all questions. Questions and observations may prove to be sources for additional measurement and reporting opportunity.
- Anticipate resistance and doubt, and formulate answers for dealing with them in advance.
- Develop a consistent measurement terminology throughout the organization to minimize misunderstandings and misinterpretations.

The communication of measurement results needs further attention, since results are normally what "everybody is waiting for." First, not all of the information that has been captured should necessarily be reported; stakeholders are probably not that interested in all of the details. Furthermore, there should be a mix of positive and negative results reported. All positive results will give an appearance that the measurement program is self-serving; all negative results are obviously demoralizing to everybody involved.

As said, the content and style of reports and presentations will vary depending on the audience. When it comes to content, top management is probably most interested in the results of measurement of the business value of IT; user management, IT users, and IT supply management will be more interested in the effectiveness of IT and the "customer perspective" measures of the Balanced Scorecard of IT supply; the IT suppliers' employees and management will probably be most interested in the results of the other perspectives of the Balanced Scorecards that have been developed for them (see Chapter 6).

In relation to style, there is much literature around on how to present measurement and statistical data in the most attractive and insightful way. Bar charts, column charts, Kiviat charts, pie charts, bubble charts--they all have their advantages for particular types of measures and purposes of presentation. It is important to think through how the measurement results should be presented for each type of measure and to each category of stakeholders since, in my experience, "the medium makes the message."

Over time, experience can be gained in reporting results. IT measurement is not "a one-shot deal" so the first reports might be considered as prototypes. With the reporting system in place, numerous reasons for making modifications will arise and have to be dealt with anyway.

THE MANAGEMENT OF THE IT MEASUREMENT PROGRAM

Although the design and implementation of an IT measurement program might not be easy, the operation of it (consistently and systematically collecting, analyzing, and reporting performance data) requires the sustained commitment of an organization and its stakeholders to exploit such a program to its full potential. This commitment is important, in particular since IT measurement is a long-term undertaking and its benefits might not be manifest in the short term.

When an IT measurement program is implemented well, the program and its components are aligned with the overall business, organization, and technology strategies, and they are well supported, owned, and mastered by their stakeholders. The same factors that enable the successful implementation of a measurement program must continuously be addressed when managing it over time, such as leadership, participation, organization, and communication. To maintain these conditions, and to ensure that business change and IT performance changes are continuously reflected in the program, it has to be managed accordingly.

The continuous participation of stakeholders should be guaranteed over time, to ensure that reliable measurement results are obtained. In addition to that, there's a number of "caveats" that might occur if the management of a measurement program does not pay sufficient attention to human factors, possibly hindering the successful application of measurement:

- perception of measurement being a-cultural,
- bureaucratism,
- cynicism,
- impatience,
- stagnation,
- perfectionism,
- internal professionalism,
- deteriorated management attention.

Although some of them are symptoms and some of them are root causes, they all might lead to undesired effects, although in certain cases, some listed caveats are not necessarily negative effects. Perfectionism, for example, might be a desired effect, as well as internal professionalism. It all depends on the mission, roles, and CSFs that apply to the measured phenomena in a given situation and a given context, whether these would be negative effects.

The combined energy of all stakeholders of the measurement program has to be channeled in the same direction, by taking advantage of the positive effects of measurement on the behavior of people. This channeling has to be actively managed, in a number of ways. Firstly, the prevention of negative effects is by taking action to reverse root causes and make them effective. Secondly, actions should be taken to channel energy in a positive direction. By paying attention to the linkage of positive trends, learning aspects, and the avoidance of "Black Peters" to the aspects of alignment, stakeholder commitment, stakeholder mastery, fusion of measurement with other management controls, and communication. Positive effects of measurement on human behavior are related with root causes and ground rules such as:

- Focus of measurement on the critical issues, and the meaningfulness of actual measurement and reporting, underpin the importance of the measurement program and encourages stakeholders to continue with it.
- Measuring results, rather than the means to obtain the results, motivates people to focus on satisfying stakeholders.
- Measuring trends should lead to improvements, since it is only natural for people to try to perform better than last month and last year,
- Benchmarking performance against other organizations improves the collective moral to "beat the others" together.
- Consistent and systematic collection and reporting of performance data improves the common belief that measurement is valuable as a management tool.
- Open and continuous communication about measurement results and improvement actions obtain and maintain belief in it, and leads to sustained commitment and participation.

Collecting and Analyzing Performance Data

As mentioned earlier, the ability to measure performance on a continuing basis assumes the existence of fundamental information systems (preferably automated), such as project accounting, operating statistics, management information systems, and financial systems. These fundamental systems must be in place and working. Procedures and databases link disparate pieces of existing operational measures so they can be used for analysis purposes. Once such links are available, timely performance data can be received and consistently and systematically analyzed. Periodic performance reviews must interpret measures and determine gaps between the real performance produced and targets set.

In general, the more measurement data is available, the better an analysis can be performed. This, however, is contradictory to the assumption that a measurement program should be limited to a relatively small number of key performance measures to keep a measurement program manageable and practical. As a result, the core set of measures of a measurement program should be kept to a meaningful set of key performance measures, but at times, a more detailed set of measures can be used to further dig into the specifics of a particular aspect of interest. This can be temporarily, as a one-off action, or more continuously when applicable. In the latter case, more measures should structurally be added to the measurement program and its set of measures.

Once measurements are performed, and deficiencies of required performance are detected, root causes of these deficiencies have to be identified in order to turn them into improvement actions. There can be many root causes, and it is seldom straightforward to find clear and obvious connections between low performance and the reasons for it. With help of relevant expertise and experience in measurement, analysis techniques, the business, its business processes, and IT supply processes, correlations can be found between measures of the different BTRIPLEE layers. Each may be subject to further investigation and discussion when analyzing measurement results. At each level, the need may arise to measure at a more detailed level in order to learn more about a particular process or performance aspect.

Analysis of performance data and finding correlations can be very difficult and complex; it is probably still an art rather than a science and at times, management judgment has to take over from theory. The challenge is to interpret performance data and find correlations in relation to possible norms, benchmarks, history, experience, assumptions, and the like. Although the BTRIPLEE framework is helpful in ordering and classifying the main issues, possible causal relationships between its layers are either not yet known to the common knowledge base of research, or not yet widespread among the business community.

Reporting Results and Managing Improvement Actions

To demonstrate the purpose for which the program is originally envisioned, measurement results must be seen to be used to fuel sustainable improvement actions. Developed improvement actions justify the need for the measurement program itself, and demonstrate the seriousness of management that drives the program. Measurement results and improvement actions therefore must be communicated, and above all, managed.

To provide continuous feedback, a routine reporting scheme should be in place. There is no hard and fast rule for how often reporting measurement results should be published. In general, it is the type of measures and type of stakeholders to report to that determine the frequencies of different measurement reports. For example, measurement results of the business value and the effectiveness of IT is probably best reported annually, while IT supply effectiveness and efficiency could be published more frequent, e.g., quarterly. The IT suppliers' employees will probably be most interested in the results of the "internal perspectives" of the Balanced Scorecards every month, while project-oriented progress measures may be reported weekly because of the necessary direct control of projects.

It is important to prioritize and balance improvement actions across the associated organizational units and management levels of the BTRIPLEE framework. This balancing act is necessary in order not to overstress one organizational unit with many improvement actions and leave others untouched. Too many improvement actions for one organizational unit and none for another makes the program suspicious; it will be perceived as not being fair or not well balanced. The psychological effects on people, and their perception of the measurement program as a whole that would result from doing so, might be disastrous.

Likewise, it would be a bad idea to only define, say, efficiency improvements for IT supply and leave effectiveness improvements for IT supply untouched. The effect of developing such unbalanced improvement actions might be (in this case) that people will focus on efficiency improvement alone, forgetting the importance of effectiveness. As a result, efficiency might improve, but at the undesired cost of effectiveness.

The key message is to balance improvement actions, just as the measures themselves have been balanced at the design of the measurement program. Once a balanced set of improvements have been defined, priorities are determined on the basis of relevant criteria. The allocation of priorities for improvement at the business value and IT effectiveness levels of the BTRIPLEE framework in fact relates to the planning side of the BTRIPLEE framework, so that criteria of the Information Economics approach of Parker and Benson could be applied. For the prioritization of IT supply effectiveness and efficiency improvements, reference is made to the CSF, GQM, and Miller-Doyle approaches that have been mentioned earlier. Planned improvements must be non-trivial and unreachable, in other words: ambitious but attainable.

The prioritized improvement actions must also be linked to the desired results by reviewing the relevant IT performance measures and associated target values. In some cases, the target values might be adapted to cope with new insights, derived from the actual measurements.

In this way, the planning and control loop of the BTRIPLEE framework is closed: new plans are made, many of them as a result of the outcomes of the control

Figure 7.5: The Management Agenda for Improvement

Action	Measures	Measured Value	Target Value	Difference		Revised Value	Deadline	Responsible

(measurement) activities. Just as with all other planning activities, the improvement actions are linked with the common planning elements such as cost, time and planning milestones, responsibilities for execution, etc., resulting in a one-page "*management-agenda*" for improvement. (see Figure 7.5)

CASE STUDY-THE IT MEASUREMENT PROGRAM AT ANWB

Let's have a closer look at how an IT measurement program can be designed, implemented, and managed, by reviewing ANWB's IT measurement program set up. The Royal Dutch Touring Club ANWB is an autonomous, commercially run membership association with more than three million members. It was established in 1883 to encourage bicycle riding (at that time, an important means of transportation in The Netherlands), organize competitions for amateurs, print maps, and protect the rights of bicyclists. Since then, ANWB has evolved substantially into a full-service profit organization for "people on the move," and offers products and services in the main areas of recreation, tourism, mobility, traffic, and public transportation. In fact, ANWB's mission is to assist members and other interested parties (private and corporate customers) in attaining convenience with all kinds of leisure and travel products, travel information, books, insurance products, the provision of road assistance for car breakdowns, and personal, medical, and legal assistance for travelers abroad. Membership has penetrated 45 percent of Dutch households and approximately 65 percent of households owning at least one car. More than 3,000 employees provide a broad range of services to members and other customers from the head office in The Hague, from 50 regional shops, from about 30 other agencies, and from call centers and through the Internet. The core range of services of ANWB is managed by a number of relatively autonomous Business Units.

IT at ANWB is strategic in and of itself. Information is an integrated part of most ANWB's products and services, while its distribution channels are made possible through technology (e.g., the Internet). Furthermore, ANWB employs a host of IT systems that directly support its primary processes. IT also enables ANWB to develop products and services effectively, disseminate products and services efficiently, and provide customer service through databases and multimedia distribution systems, including intranets, extranets, and the Internet.

To manage IT, ANWB adopted the federal IT management structure in 1992, featuring:
- responsibility for IT planning and control devolved to business units where decentralized information managers (DIMs) are in charge of IT management;
- governance of ANWB's overall IT strategy through a small corporate information management (CIM) function;
- a shared, central unit acting as IT services provider.

The shared, central IT services provider, called ACS (ANWB Computer Services) delivers IT products and services to the business units of ANWB. It operates as a profit center and is run as an autonomous organizational entity. ACS is expected to be competitive and to survive on its own, meanwhile delivering high quality IT products and services. To periodically and consistently evaluate competitiveness and quality of service supply, the need arose to put a coherent measurement program in place and systematically track the performance of ACS. This program is aimed at making ACS's performance visible, tangible, measurable, and controllable, on behalf of the three groups of stakeholders: ANWB management ("shareholders"), business units ("customers"), management and personnel of ACS ("employees"). In other words, an IT measurement program was developed at ANWB-ACS for the third layer of the BTRIPLEE framework: the effectiveness and efficiency of IT supply. The program is not aimed at measuring all activities, but rather at those where the need for improvement appears to be greatest. Besides, it is supposed to include real improvement programs, as will be illustrated below.

Defining the Measurement Program

The IT performance measurement program, as it is called at ANWB, incorporates jointly developed and accepted performance indicators, targets, and reporting formats. Figure 7.6 depicts the process used to build and implement the performance measurement program. It can be characterized as a very intensive and interactive, sometimes confrontational, yet result-oriented approach for developing an IT performance measurement program. It included many workshops, aimed at establishing consensus amongst stakeholders on the different aspects of performance management, as illustrated in Figure 7.6.

Prior to the stakeholder workshops, the relevant expectations vis-à-vis IT supply of each category of stakeholders needed to be surveyed, with the help of the matrices of Figure 3.8 (Effectiveness versus efficiency of IT supply), Figure 6.2 (Distance and sophistication of IT supply), Figure 6.3 (Roles of IT development and maintenance), and Figure 6.4 (Roles of IT infrastructure management functions).

Figure 7.6: Defining the Performance Measurement Program

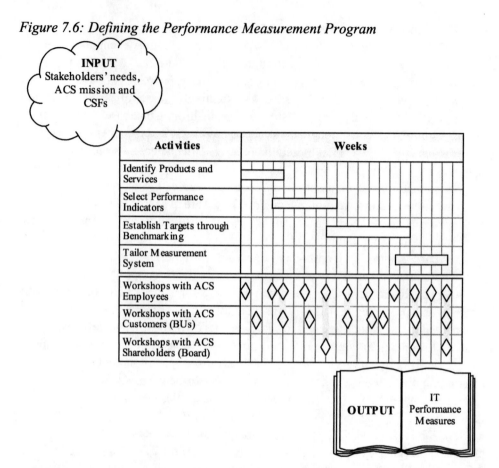

The board and the BU representatives expressed their needs as "hassle-free, competitively priced IT services." Then, based on this input, representatives of ACS defined the employee needs and expectations, leading to the "mission statement" and CSFs for IT supply, as shown in Figure 7.7.

To better understand customer expectations, and to arrive at a limited set of appropriate performance indicators, ACS employees and their customers reviewed the product and services portfolio of ACS. The products and services, as delivered by ACS, were defined in broad terms, such as "providing end-user-computing support" or "executing project management." In total, 32 products and services were defined. With the help of a simple questionnaire, stating the definitions of each product and service, each workshop participant had to rate these products and services in terms of relative, perceived importance, and its perceived quality, on an interval scale from 1 to 5.

Figure 7.8 shows the average ratings of the two categories of stakeholders on different axes. If ACS's customers would have rated the quality of products and services exactly the same as ACS, the circles would have been positioned on the diagonal line. The circles appearing above the diagonal line represent the products that received lower quality ratings from customers than from ACS.

Figure 7.7: Mission Statement and CSFs

ACS's Mission Statement

ACS wants to contribute to the continuity of ANWB through the support of effective and efficient use of IT

Critical Success Factors

Partnership	Good business relations, preferred supplier, business knowledge, P.R.
Quality Services	High service quality levels, reliable project plans, SLAs
Quality Products	Focus on core business, competitive prices, modest innovation
Financially Sound	Recover all costs, apply fair charge back mechanism

Figure 7.8: Rating of Products and Services

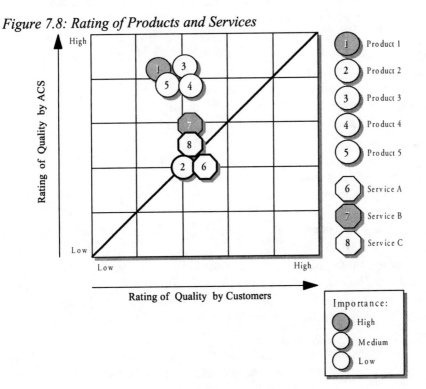

This matrix, derived from the Miller-Doyle instrument, proved to be very valuable to focus attention on the most important products and services, discrepancies in quality perception, and later on the selection of a limited number of relevant performance indicators.

Firstly, the important products and services with relatively low quality were included in the set of products and services to be tracked by the performance measurement program. Also, products and services rated "high" by ACS, but only "medium" or "low" by the customers, were included in the set of products and services to be tracked, because of the discrepancy in the perceived quality level. In total, 12 products and services were selected out of the 32 initially listed.

For each product or service, one or more performance indicators were selected from the lists of measures in Appendix C. On a more aggregate level of ACS management, indicators of the IT supply management scorecard were selected to cover aspects such as partnership, financial performance, innovation, and internal efficiency. The selection of appropriate measures didn't raise a lot of discussion; agreement on a set of 32 measures in total was soon established.

The next step, benchmarking of ACS's performance on the basis of the selected performance indicators to find out about the acceptability of ACS's performance, proved to be possible for 24 of the 32 selected measures. Eight measures, all expressing user satisfaction aspects with IT services, were defined on an interval scale from 1 to 7 because this scale was either perceived to be more realistic than cumbersome measures on ratio scales, or meaningful measures on ratio scales just were not available to our collective knowledge. Unfortunately, measures on the 1-7 interval scales cannot be benchmarked against other companies, because of differences in definitions. Since trend analysis of performance actually becomes really meaningful only after some years of internal history build-up, management initially had to live with current scores. Later on, history had indeed built up at ANWB, so that trends are managed and acted upon.

The products and services that could be benchmarked against other companies were first measured at ACS, using the agreed-upon measures, consuming an elapsed time of eight weeks. Benchmarks were retrieved from:
- public sources, such as the Helpdesk Institute Survey, Function Points databases, research reports, library reports, etc.;
- private sources, such as the databases of our consulting organization, and the Gartner Group;
- specific research (literature search, telephone interviews, actual measuring at other companies) for this matter.

Based on this comparison, competitive and ambitious targets were set for ACS for each measure. For each of the products and services of which the performance level could not be compared (measures at interval scales), a target was set as a result of a series of discussion and negotiation between ACS employees and their customers.

As a consultant to this process of defining a measurement program, I had different roles to play in the process of target setting. First of all, there's the process-facilitating role, of course. Besides, roles included playing devils' advocate (when targets at too high levels were requested), playing "the man from Missouri" (when targets were not ambitious enough), and playing the referee (when ACS employees and their customers could not agree on targets). The many, sometimes tough discussions proved to be very fruitful, ultimately resulting in commonly accepted performance targets for IT supply.

Implementing the Measurement Program

The choice for either a full-blown or a phased implementation was not difficult: the size and complexity of the designed measurement program were manageable in relation to the capabilities of the organization. These capabilities were (to a large extent) developed through the involvement of employees during the definition process of the measurement program. The definition phase in fact had sent clear signals about what was important and valued by top management, IT users, and IT supply management, so people had already become acquainted with what were perceived to be the most important products and services, associated measures, and accepted target values.

The implementation included:

- The production and dissemination of the measurement guidebook, containing the set of measures and their definitions, appropriate method for collection of measurement data, and in most cases the associated target values.
- Definition of different reporting schemes, suiting the needs of different stakeholders. Basically, two different types of reports were introduced: the annual report, classifying measures according to the Balanced Scorecard concept; and the post-mortum project review, reporting the most relevant data of the project reviewed.
- Start of the actual collection of measurement data on a continuous basis.

Since its birth, the program has been managed by a dedicated, so-called "Quality and Performance Engineer," who is staying on top and who constantly ensures that the program is alive and evolving, or in other words, performing well.

Conclusion from the Case Study

From the start, the business relevance of developing an IT measurement program at ANWB was obvious: all categories of stakeholders requested the program to be put into place, and all participated in designing and implementing it. The IT measurement program and its components have been successfully incorporated into both the interface between ACS and its customers, and the interface between ACS and ANWB management. As the program continues to be in full use at ANWB, the successful manageability of the IT measurement program has been proven as well. Altogether, the measurement program for IT has been fulfilling a necessary function at ANWB, and comparable programs for other, non-IT-related disciplines and activities have been implemented as a result.

The program consists of an overall management framework (the mission statement of ACS and associated Critical Success Factors), a set of key measures for performance and associated performance targets, and an underlying information and reporting system. Some measures have been added over time, while none have been rejected so far. Some targets associated to performance measures have been adjusted to appreciate changes in actual performance, to cope with increasing customer demands, and to provide the necessary carrots for ambitious performance seekers.

CONCLUSION

The application and supply of IT must be measured continuously and systematically where the need for improvement is greatest, taking the needs of the main stakeholders (shareholders, customers, and employees of the organizational entity being measured) into account. Effective IT measurement requires a well-accepted performance measurement and management program encompassing several elements:

- an overall management framework (e.g., the BTRIPLEE framework);
- a set of key measures for performance, and associated performance targets;
- an underlying information and reporting system;

A systematic approach to select the appropriate measures is vital. To derive a complete set of relevant IT performance measures and associated targets, four activities must be carried out:

- understand stakeholders' needs and expectations;
- define the Critical Success Factors (CSFs) of both the application and supply of IT;
- derive from both the appropriate measures and associated target values to measure the business value and effectiveness of IT (layers one and two of the BTRIPLEE framework); and the effectiveness and efficiency of IT supply (layer three of the BTRIPLEE framework);
- test the adequacy of the set of measures and associated target values.

The next step, the successful introduction of an IT measurement program, enables and ensures three important aspects:

- operational alignment, so that the program is consistent with the company's organization and business strategies;
- stakeholder ownership, so that the program is owned by strongly committed stakeholders;
- stakeholder mastery, so that the program is mastered by its stakeholders who continue to learn and who, ideally, influence the program's further evolution.

This step requires strong management leadership, stakeholder participation, operational organization, and communication of results. Finally, a measurement program (and measurement results) must be seen to be used to fuel sustainable, balanced improvement actions. Improvement actions therefore must be clearly communicated, and above all, managed.

REFERENCES

Basili, V.R. and Rombach, D. (1988). The TAME project: Towards improvement-oriented software environments. *IEEE Transactions on Software Engineering*, 14(6), 758-773.

Carlson, W.M. and McNurlin, B.C. (1989). Measuring the value of information systems. *I/S Analyzer Special Report*. Bethesda, MD: United Communications Group.

Curtice, R.M. and Kastner, G.T. (1995). Balanced performance measures: Tracking the pathway to high performance. *Arthur D. Little's PRISM* (second quarter), 57-69.

Gill, P. (1991). A primer on advice for measurement programs. *System Development*, June, 5.

Kaplan, R.S and Norton, D.P. (1992). The balanced scorecard-Measures that drive performance. *Harvard Business Review*, January-February, 71-79.

Miller, J. (1993). Measuring and aligning information systems with the organization. *Information & Management,* (25), 217-228.

Nusenoff, R.E. and Bunde, D.C. (1993). A guidebook and a spreadsheet tool for a corporate metrics program. *Journal for Systems Software*, 23, 245-255.

Parker, M.M., Benson, R.J. and Trainor, H.E. (1988). *Information Economics: Linking Business Performance to Information Technology.* Englewoods Cliffs, NJ: Prentice-Hall.

Peters, T.J. and Waterman, R.H. Jr. (1982). *In Search of Excellence, Lessons from America's Best-run Companies.* New York: Harper & Row.

Rockart, J.F. (1979). Chief executives define their own data needs. *Harvard Business Review*, March-April, 81-93.

Rubin, H. (1991). *Measurement in the 1990s: Shifting the Focus to Business Value.* European Function Point User Group Conference, November 21-22, Sheffield UK.

Slevin, D.P., Stieman, P.A. and Boone, L.W. (1991). Critical success factor analysis for information systems performance measurement-A case study in the university environment. *Information & Management*, 21, 161-174.

Van der Zee, J.T.M. (1994). Rapid application development. *Informatie,* (1), 40-48.

Van der Zee, J.T.M. (1997) *In Search of the Value of Information Technology.* Tilburg, The Netherlands: Tilburg University Press.

Walton, R. E. (1989). *Up and Running, Integrating Information Technology and the Organization.* Boston, MA: Harvard Business School Press.

Chapter VIII

Benchmarking IT

One key ingredient of IT measurement is the establishment of a frame of reference, consisting of expectations, standards, or yardsticks for the various aspects of the application and supply of IT. Clearly, there is a lack of generally accepted, quantified norms for the application and supply of IT, and many of the measures defined throughout the previous chapters and Appendix C. One way of establishing norms is to measure current performance and define future expectations based on these outcomes, thus relying on internal data, historical trends, internal or external expertise, and negotiation between IT supplier and IT customer in the case of IT supply. This may, in fact, be the only practical approach available in many instances.

A second way to establish performance targets is to engage in comparative analysis, comparing performance levels to those of business and technology peers. A relatively passive form of such a benchmarking approach is to use public data and information gathered from entities outside the organization, for example, published research outcomes, information from trade groups, IT suppliers, governmental bureaus of statistics, and so on. This might be complemented with a more active benchmarking approach, aimed at the gathering of information from other organizations (benchmark partners) through the exchange of details on the application and supply of IT. Both a passive and a more active benchmarking approach are an acceptable and often more effective alternative for organizations to find out about their performance as long as generally accepted and objective measures do not exist and as long as no appropriate internal history has been built up yet.

Measurement and benchmarking can be used to analyze either real or perceived problems with the application and supply of IT, in order to improve control. On the basis of comparison with others, it can be revealed whether atypical patterns in IT usage and supply are present. The case study at ANWB, described in Chapter 7, is an example of this benchmarking purpose. With the help of the BTRIPLEE framework and its associated measures at different layers, the application and supply of IT was analyzed, and with the help of comparative benchmark data, conclusions could be drawn as a result.

Measurement and benchmarking can also be used more systematically and continuously. Organizations may use benchmarking data to arrive at acceptable performance targets or to calibrate performance targets included in an IT measurement program. For example, it might be important to continuously determine how the organization performs competitively, and to adjust its performance targets accordingly. This, for example, happens at ANWB's ACS (see previous chapter). It should be noted that target values assigned to performance measures may differ from benchmark data, either positively or negatively, since they must reflect the specifics of the organization at hand.

Finally, benchmarking of IT can help organizations in exposing people to different approaches, ideas, insights, and mechanisms for the application and supply IT. Benchmarking, in this case, is used to learn from best practices of other, leading organizations, and to stimulate the transfer of those into their own.

In any case, the BTRIPLEE framework can be used to order and categorize, and to measure the different aspects of the application and supply of IT. Benchmarking enriches the application and applicability of the BTRIPLEE framework and it helps broaden management's frame of reference. The best "return on investment" in measurement and benchmarking" is realized if they are systematically, consistently, and periodically used to act as a key lever for structural improvement of performance in the application and supply of IT, and ultimately, the overall performance of the organization.

In this chapter, apparent benchmarking characteristics and the main conditions for success will be reviewed, followed by a description of the process of IT benchmarking. Also, the execution of the benchmarking process will be illustrated in three case studies, each demonstrating the practical application of benchmarking for different purposes and answering different management questions about specific aspects of the application and supply of IT.

BENCHMARKING CHARACTERISTICS AND CONDITIONS FOR SUCCESS

The term "benchmark" comes from the discipline of geodesy. If an area of land is surveyed to make a map, a certain point in the surroundings serves as a benchmark. Within the area the distance is measured between every object and the benchmark. A benchmark actually is a reference with which other values can be compared.

Spendolini collected 49 business definitions of benchmarking in a business context and ran into problems when he tried to develop a single definition that could serve as a generic baseline for the term. After many attempts he gave up and developed the "benchmarking menu" which is illustrated in Figure 8.1.

Figure 8.1: Benchmarking Characteristics and Conditions for Success

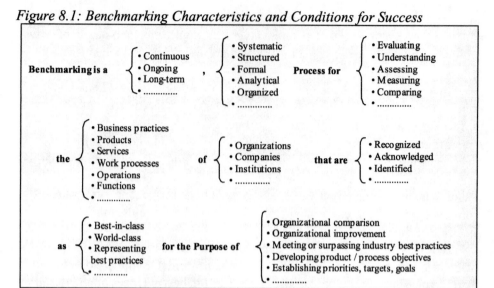

Source: M.J. Spendolini, The Benchmarking Book

In business terms, benchmarking can be defined as the search for ways to improve performance by means of measurement and comparison. In any definition, by comparing quantified performance of a function, or a process, with other, leading organizations, it is possible to identify which aspects of performance differ, to what extent they differ, and also, after analysis, why these performances differ. The size of observed differences in performance might be an indicator of the size of necessary or potential improvements. With the help of an analysis of acknowledged performance differences, tangible opportunities can be defined, and quantified performance targets can be set. Thus, a number of benchmarking characteristics can be identified:

- Benchmarking means a systematic comparison with other, leading-edge organizations. With this, benchmarking implicates an external focus, as well as a structured approach.
- Benchmarking is based on measuring and comparing. To achieve credible results, measuring and comparing require precise descriptions, definitions and explanations of the products, services, processes, and other phenomena that are to be measured and compared.
- Benchmarking is aimed at establishing quantified targets for improvement. Improvements can only be achieved if the necessary organizational commitment is present. This implies, as discussed in the previous chapter, that the quantification of the phenomena that are to be benchmarked has to be done together with the people directly involved, in order to create such an organizational commitment for improvement in an early stage.

Although the measurements made, the indicators employed, the benchmarking process executed, and the possible actions derived may vary widely, a number of universal conditions for success still applies:

- *Top management commitment*: The board has to believe in the value of benchmarking; top management must be open to new ideas and willing to learn from better ways to approach certain problems. If the "not invented here" syndrome is a characteristic of the culture of the organization, benchmarking will probably have little or no effect,
- *Benchmarking must be dictated by strategic purposes or purposes of improved control, and not just because of the trendy image of benchmarking*. To give benchmarking a chance, sufficient attention, time and budget has to be made available,
- *Benchmarking has to be followed up by the implementation of recommended improvement actions*. The feasibility of suggested improvement actions, in the present situation, and under the present circumstances, should have been tested during the benchmarking process; they are not recommended by just copying other organizations. Implementing improvement actions means integrating them into the planning, budgeting, financial, and other applicable processes.

Just like the more general application of benchmarking, benchmarking of the application and supply of IT is a process performed to achieve improved application of IT and to obtain better performance of the IT supplying function. Based on comparison, IT benchmarking offers the opportunity to improve by learning from organizations that excel in the application and supply of IT. The purpose is to identify exactly what the causes of differences between their and our performance are. The search for these causes leads to insight into other, apparently better methods and techniques, procedures, technical resources, human resources and their knowledge levels and skills, prevailing culture, and other factors underlying the better application and supply of IT. This insight must be turned into concrete improvement actions and improvement targets for the application and supply of IT, either as part of an established, ongoing IT measurement program, or as a one-off exercise.

THE IT BENCHMARKING PROCESS

In the preceding text, the term "IT benchmarking" is mentioned many times. In this section, the process of IT benchmarking at one or more levels of the BTRIPLEE framework will be further elucidated.

Most researchers who have published approaches to benchmarking identify different process stages. Spendolini says there are five, Camp identified 10, Bemowski quotes AT&T who uses a process of 12 steps, Alcoa employs one of six, etc. In my experience, the nine-stage process described below works very well in practice, because each stage is small enough to be manageable and large enough to be non-trivial. The benchmarking process is presented in Figure 8.2.

In this model, the benchmarking process is drawn as a timeline. It might, however, also be drawn as a circular model, as Spendolini does, acknowledging the fact that benchmarking is a process, in the true sense of the word. Unlike a project,

Figure 8.2: The IT benchmarking process

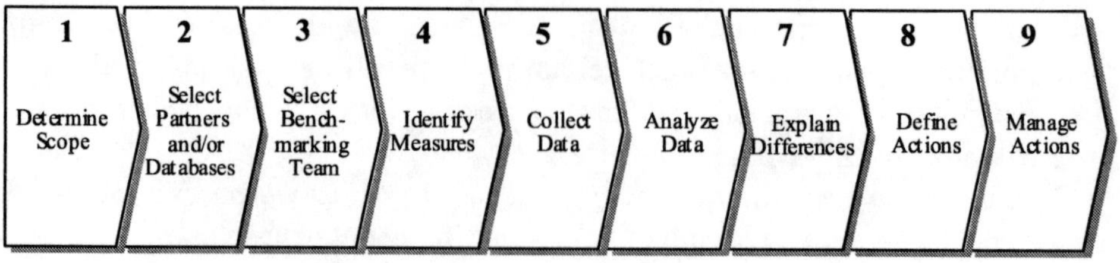

1	2	3	4	5	6	7	8	9
Determine Scope	Select Partners and/or Databases	Select Benchmarking Team	Identify Measures	Collect Data	Analyze Data	Explain Differences	Define Actions	Manage Actions

which has a start and an end, IT benchmarking often becomes a repetitive and continuous activity because of the satisfactory results, and gets included in the IT measurement program as illustrated in the previous chapter. Of course, the objectives, the measures, and the resulting improvement actions will change as time and improvement progress.

Determine the Scope

Firstly, what is going to be benchmarked, and what is not going to be benchmarked, is exactly and explicitly determined. If the scope is too broadly defined, it will be practically impossible to achieve reasonably thoroughly investigated results. It would turn out to be impossible to explore the real causes of differences in performance between benchmark partners, because the subject of benchmarking would cover too many aspects and benchmarkers would get bogged down in endless details. On the other hand, sufficient range should be taken into account, to avoid coming up with improvements leading to sub-optimization of a limited activity, department, or sub-process. Besides, if the scope is too narrow, investments made in benchmarking are not paying off, while the initiation of a benchmarking process generally raises high expectations.

The scope can be defined on the basis of geography (a branch, a country, a location, etc.), or on the basis of business boundaries (a business unit). These kinds of scope definitions have the advantage of being clear for one's own organization, but could have the possible disadvantage of a more complex basis of comparison with other organizations. The organizational structures of organizations might be quite different for many reasons. Processes, in contrast, are more similar and therefore much easier to compare. As much as possible, complete processes must be benchmarked rather than organizational units.

Select Benchmark Partners and Databases

The next step in the benchmarking process is finding benchmark partners and other sources of information. In many cases, both information from benchmark partners and information from other sources are used to complement each other.

Scanning management literature, press articles, and periodicals for success stories, special award winners, etc. can identify possible benchmark partners. Other sources of information are IT suppliers, professional associations, and independent management consultants. Above all, personal networks of relationships can be very useful.

Benchmark partners can also be found outside one's own type of industry or outside one's home country. This proves to be very helpful in practice: in many industries, and in small countries in particular, it is easier to find organizations that are willing to participate in benchmarking studies if the environment and benchmark partners are non-competitive. Moreover, benchmarking of processes or activities can be extremely useful if comparisons are made with organizations that make money by performing these activities as their core business. For example: Xerox, for many years a benchmarker of almost all its business processes, did not use another supplier of photocopiers to benchmark the activities of the Logistics and Distribution department, but singled out L.L. Bean, Inc., the outdoor sporting goods and mail-order house, as the best candidate for benchmarking. The reason is obvious: it is of vital importance for a mail-order house to have perfect warehousing and distribution operations in place. Besides, both companies had to develop warehousing and distribution systems to handle products diverse in size, shape, and weight. Although active in quite different industries, the similarity of the benchmarked activities appeared to be striking. As an analogy, in the case of benchmarking the performance of an IT organization, IT supply activities can very well be compared with those of a professional IT supplier, a software house, or a facilities management supplier of which IT service supply is a core business.

Passive benchmark information can be selected from private and representative public databases that contain comparative data. Databases maintained by consultancy firms are generally not public, but data provided by governmental bodies, academic institutions, IT manufacturers and suppliers, trade associations, market research firms, and professional research associations, are. In any of these cases, one should make an effort to find out which definitions are used for applied measures, in order to be sure that apples are being compared with apples, rather than with oranges.

Select the Benchmarking Team

Once it is known what to benchmark, and against whom, a benchmarking team can be formed under the leadership of a benchmarking sponsor. This is ideally the person who is responsible for the activities that are being benchmarked. If not, it may appear to be difficult or impossible to implement the necessary improvements, as the required commitment is not adequately present.

A benchmarking team should collectively have sufficient functional and technical knowledge and expertise in the areas of interest, including adequate IT knowledge, as well as a profound knowledge of the organization as a whole. Such a diverse, multi-disciplinary team limits the danger of imposing limited normative judgment on measurement results, drawing conclusions too quickly.

Members of the team need to have superb communication skills, such as interviewing, presentation, meeting, and writing skills. This is especially important since much communication with benchmark partners is involved. Furthermore, team members need to be analytically skilled, because many data have to be processed and analyzed.

Although it might be desirable to have an experienced consultant facilitate the benchmarking process, it is the benchmarking team of the organization itself that must execute the process, in order to achieve adequate in-depth knowledge and to develop a strong commitment to implement improvements in the future.

Identify Measures

Before the actual collection of benchmarking data can start, it is necessary to exactly define what to collect and how measure, with help of the BTRIPLEE framework and the associated measures at each level. What will be collected and compared depends on the motives and objectives of the benchmarking process, as said. It is very important to make proper agreements about these objectives and related definitions, types, and formats of indicators, ratios, etc. The better these agreements are made and fixed, the faster it is possible to perform the next phase (the actual collection of data) and the more reliable the results will be.

It is necessary to establish practical definitions and descriptions of measures, in particular if benchmark partners are involved; if multiple team members make comparisons; and if comparisons are made over time. When defining IT benchmarking measures based on the BTRIPLEE framework and the associated measures discussed in Chapters 4, 5, and 6, only some of the typical questions to be answered include:

IT financials
- How is IT equipment depreciated?
- How to deal with taxes (VAT)?
- Where are the boundaries between system development and maintenance activities and, consequently, costs?
- How to deal with recharged costs?
- Are the efforts of users included in IT costs?
- Which business measures should be used to relate IT costs?

Business processes
- Are both managerial and operational activities included in processes?
- Are inter-organizational processes/business links included?

Users' involvement and satisfaction about IT
- How many users should be surveyed to establish representative results?
- Should a classification be made with respect to "users" (for instance administrative versus technical, management versus non-management, etc.)

Information systems (application portfolio)
- Are all types of IT applications assessed and benchmarked? For example, are 'physical' IT applications such as cash dispensers, robotics, and process automation also included? Is infrastructure IT such as office automation and E-mail also included? Are customer-related Internet applications involved?

- What other criteria are applied to decide whether an IT application should be included in a benchmark study (number of users, relative importance, etc.)?

Human and technical IT supply resources
- Are (categories of) decentralized/distributed IT functions included?
- Should distinct job families, job descriptions, knowledge levels, classes of experience, and skills categories be distinguished to rate personnel?
- Which categories of hardware do we include to benchmark "technology "?

Collect Data

The next step of the benchmarking process is the collection of benchmarking data, on the basis of the measures that were identified during the previous stage of the benchmarking process. Before information from benchmark partners is assembled, information about the own organization and operations should be collected first. The advantages are clear: the understanding of internal operations and potential improvement areas become more accurate, and the team is much better prepared to discuss issues with benchmark partners, if the internal operation is better understood. Besides, if flaws in measures and definitions of measures become apparent, they can be solved easier if only internal data has been collected. Corrections can take place without too many problems and without loosing credibility with benchmark partners.

Analyze Data

After the data gathering stage follows an analysis of benchmarking data and the interpretation of differences between benchmark partners. During this stage, it may appear from the analyses and discussions that misinterpretations of the measures' definitions have occurred, or that measurement errors have crept into the data set, so that rechecking or recollection of data will be necessary. As soon as it is believed that the data are reliable, it can be compared and patterns or trends noticed. Generally, a "top ten" of striking facts can be drawn and reported. This top ten will in its turn be the input for the next stage.

Explain Differences

The objective of this stage is to draw reasonable and logical conclusions from the collected and analyzed benchmarking data in terms of best practices, strengths, and weaknesses of benchmark partners. Furthermore, any performance gap that exists between the benchmarking organization and its benchmark partners must be identified and explained. Special attention is paid to finding relationships between cause and effects. Symptoms are represented by the collected and analyzed benchmarking data, but the root causes of differences in performance levels still have to be identified. For that purpose the first step is to take a closer look at the business processes (or IT supply processes, depending on the level of benchmarking interest). This step is followed by a review of differences in cultural, organizational, personal, technical, and economical aspects. In the example of IT supply, one should look at issues such as allocated knowledge and skills; methods, techniques, and tools used; the users' role; organizational and technical risks; effectiveness of the management processes, quality assurance procedures, etc.

This stage of the benchmarking process is probably the most difficult, complex, and fuzziest, of all. At this stage, measurement ends and judgment of the benchmark team must take over. The interpretation of benchmark data, and the validation of assumptions and hypotheses rely on the collective body of knowledge and experience of the benchmark team and possibly some outside experts. A series of creative workshops often suits the need to involve a mix of qualitative and quantitative analysis, to find patterns that reveal trends, and to draw meaningful inferences and conclusions.

Define Concrete Actions

As soon as the causes of performance gaps and their effects are made clear, actions are to be defined. Actions are dependent on the objectives of benchmarking. For example, if benchmarking is aimed at assigning targets to the BTRIPLEE measures of an IT measurement program, the appropriate action would be to incorporate targets into that program based on the benchmarking results. If the prime purpose of benchmarking is to reveal sustainable improvement opportunities and actions, decisions have to be made with respect to impact, dependencies, costs/benefits, feasibility, etc. In that case plans--including milestones, required investments in terms of money and effort, responsibilities for execution, etc.--have to be defined and managed (see also Chapter 7).

Manage the Actions in Projects

Sometimes change can take place immediately, but most often a phased approach for the implementation of improvement actions is the best solution. This is not different from any other improvement plan. In any case, improvement actions are best managed as projects, as illustrated in Chapter 7, under the banner of a proper project structure and regular progress reviews.

BENCHMARK CASE STUDIES

The benchmarking process presented in the previous section provides the basic guidelines for IT benchmarking. The benchmarking process is structured and follows a logical sequence of activities, and at the same time allows for flexibility to accommodate some level of variation. The execution of the benchmarking process in practice, on three occasions as case studies, indeed needed such a rigid structure, and also the flexibility to vary according to the situation at hand, as is demonstrated below.

In contrast to the case studies presented before, which are predominantly explanatory case studies focusing on "how" and "why" questions, the cases studies described here also deal with the "what" question. The "why," "what," and "how" questions are addressed as follows.

The three possible, specific purposes of benchmarking mentioned in the introduction of this chapter relate to the "why" question. Why do organizations engage in a benchmarking process? Is it to:

- apply benchmarking as part of a control system, e.g., an IT measurement program to arrive at or calibrate performance targets?
- solve either real or perceived problems with the application or supply of IT, and improve control?
- generate new ideas for the application or supply of IT through the exposure to IT-based products, services, and practices of others?

The purpose of IT benchmarking was different in each case. The benchmarking process carried out in the first case study was aimed at developing new ideas for the application of effective IT. Benchmarking in the second case focused on arriving at performance targets as part of an IT measurement program, while benchmarking in the third case was meant to improve control.

Secondly, the "what" question relates to the boundaries and the exploratory nature of each case study. Each case study has a different scope: the first case study focused on the effectiveness of IT (the second layer of the BTRIPLEE framework), the second case study dealt with the effectiveness and efficiency of IT supply (the third layer of the BTRIPLEE framework), while the third case study was aimed at an investigation into one aspect of IT supply: maintenance of information systems.

Finally, the "how" question relates to the correctness of the IT benchmarking process as it has been described, and to its practical applicability in real life. In each case, the execution of the benchmarking process needed the strict process structure described before, as well as the flexibility to deviate in order to cope with the requirements resulting from the different "why" and "what" questions. The first case study followed exactly the process described. The process used in the second case study, aimed at performance target setting, was woven into the process of defining an IT measurement program, and therefore executed slightly differently.

Figure 8.3: Overview of Three Benchmarking Case Studies

	Why	**What**	**How**
Case Study 1	Develop New Ideas	Effectiveness of IT	Straight Forward
Case Study 2	Set Targets	Effectiveness & Efficiency of IT Supply	Part of Defining an IT Measurement Program
Case Study 3	Improve Control	Performance of Maintenance of IT	Phased Approach

The third case study was aimed at attaining improved quantitative handles for control. The situation, or rather the cautious management of the commissioning organization, required a phased approach, which still followed the basic benchmarking process described before, as will be demonstrated.

As an overview, the "whys," "whats," and "hows" of the three benchmarking processes are shown in Figure 8.3. The case studies are further elaborated on below, followed by an evaluation and the drawing of an overall conclusion.

Case 1: Benchmarking the Effectiveness of IT

A large Dutch service organization considered reorganizing many activities related to "Customer Service." Customer service activities include information supply, settlement of complaints, sales by phone, etc. To substantially improve the effectiveness and efficiency of customer service, a redesign of existing business processes was suggested in such a way that IT would be a key enabler of efficiency and effectiveness improvements. Therefore the study was aimed at learning, through benchmarking against service organizations being known for excellent performing customer service organizations, especially in terms of the design of business processes and the application of IT.

Apart from these aspects, other phenomena like the organizational structure, the quality and productivity of employees, the quality of the communication with the customer, the effectiveness of housing and accommodation, overall levels of effectiveness and efficiency of services supply, etc., were also included in the study. The benchmarking specifics of these aspects are not described here in order to stay within the scope of the subject.

Determine the scope

The organization in question supplies a broad range of services to an extensive and varied audience. The scope of the benchmarking study included all customer service activities, but only as far as these activities were related to telephone service through (generic) "0/1-800 numbers." Service through other (dedicated) phone numbers, and service activities that were handled in writing (for example the settlement of complaints by letter), were left out. This way the scope of the benchmarking study was limited to what is called the service through "call centers."

Select benchmark partners and databases

Benchmark partners were mainly found through my business contacts as a facilitating consultant. An initial list of domestic and foreign companies was composed, with an explanation of why each company was selected (for example because of its innovative IT solutions, its excellent customer service, an extraordinarily low personnel turnover, etc.). Each company had a large customer service organization, but they all came from different industries: a few insurance companies being part of the "direct writers" category, a mail-order house, manufacturers and importers of office supplies, organizations in the travel and tourism information supply industry, etc. Also a foreign company performing exactly the same activities in the same industry as the concerning organization was listed. Dutch direct competitors were not on the list, because it was considered unlikely that they would participate.

The board of the commissioning company made a choice from the list of 20 companies. Eventually, six organizations were involved in the benchmarking study, of which two were active practically only in the United States. Without exception, the selected organizations were all interested in cooperating in the benchmarking process, under the condition that they would obtain the results of the study in return. Of course, this promise was later redeemed, in the form of a report for the participants, who incidentally remained anonymous for privacy reasons.

In addition to identifying benchmark partners, essential literature and qualitative and quantitative data were selected to complement the basis and sources of reference of the benchmarking process, from three main sources:
- results of generic studies previously performed by the consultancy firm,
- quantitative studies regularly performed by specialized research firms and available on the basis of subscription,
- literature searches.

Select the benchmarking team

The benchmarking team consisted of two consultants and five employees from both the "business side" and the internal IT organization, chaired by the manager in charge of customer services. The employees were well integrated in the organization (they knew the right people to talk to), and they were aware of different developments in the organization. The employees of the organization and the consultants formed small teams and undertook the next steps together.

Identify measures

Before the measures to be used were identified, an overall, global business model was constructed, identifying the most important business processes. Next, measures were determined for the measurement of both process output and process execution. IT-related measures were selected from the IT effectiveness level of the BTRIPLEE framework (the other levels were excluded from the scope of the benchmark study), while business-oriented measures were derived from the literature and qualitative data assembled earlier. Process output in call centers appeared to be measurable in terms of waiting time for customers who wanted to communicate, satisfaction of customers about the answers to their questions and the settlement of their complaints, the number of times they were put through to other customer services representatives to answer the same question, etc. Process execution can be measured using a combination of measures, including IT-related measures such as number of employees per computer terminal, availability of databases, coverage and quality of IT support of led dialogues (the course of a telephone conversation), etc.

Collect data

At first, qualitative information was gathered through interviews with several employees of the benchmark partners. These interviews were followed up by the collection of quantitative data at each participating benchmark partner. The teams extracted the necessary quantitative data from different administrative systems and performed a limited number of additional data collections to acquire the information, which was not directly retrievable from administrative systems. Although it turned out to be impossible to actually assemble all information from every organization involved, about 85 percent of the desired information was collected overall. This appeared to be a good basis for an objective comparison and a clear analysis of the effectiveness and efficiency of the business processes and activities in the domain of customer service and the application of IT.

Analyze data

After the teams had produced their results in a format that was agreed upon beforehand, the resulting data were compared during a number of sessions. This led to a large spreadsheet, clearly demonstrating differences in performance (output). For each measure, averages and standard deviations were calculated. The purpose of this was to arrive at a kind of standard or target per measure, and to further map the differences in performance between the concerning organization and the other benchmark partners. In a few cases it appeared necessary to verify certain data, and sometimes estimates had to be made because the real data were not available or postulated. Also some "intelligent manipulations" turned out to be necessary to transform available data into useful figures, better corresponding with agreed-upon definitions. After these manipulations, the results still formed a good basis for an objective comparison of the quantitative data from benchmark partners and data from external sources (databases, literature).

Explain differences

For the explanation of differences in performance between the benchmark partners, the team discussed possible relations between performance (effects) and performance driving factors (root causes). Differences, explicable by organization-specific circumstances were as much as possible distinguished from differences not explicable by these factors.

In particular, the constructed business model and business knowledge of team members proved to be very useful at this stage. The lively discussions, the brainstorming, and the formulation and rejection of hypotheses brought about a better understanding of the subject and a deeper insight into the key performance factors of business processes and the applied IT.

This led to the definition of "standards of performance": for each performance aspect, quantified targets were set, on the basis of the benchmarking results. To some measures the average measurement results were assigned as target value; for several others the averages were adjusted to meet the specific situation. Target values for some measures were set at the "best-of-breed" level, to align them with specific ambitious goals, of which the team thought they were critical to the call centers' success.

Define concrete actions

On the basis of the benchmarking process, a series of related improvements to become an excellent customer service organization were defined. This resulted in an overall plan for the phased implementation of improvements over a period of three years. Suggestions were made for a new organizational structure, the implementation of modifications to the critical business processes, and improvements in IT. In particular, customer waiting time and customer satisfaction were designated as priority improvement actions; while the number of employees per computer terminal was going to be decreased to 1, the availability of customer information captured in databases was going to be made more accessible, and led dialogues were going to be improved. All changes were justified and planned on the basis of estimates of organizational impact, costs and benefits, timeliness, as well as estimates of possible impact on other initiatives already underway.

Manage the actions in projects

The improvement actions were converted into improvement projects. These were further implemented and managed by top management.

Conclusions

The business relevance of IT benchmarking is obvious in this case. It is demonstrated by the fact that the process was commissioned and chaired by the manager in charge of customer services. Management believed in the value of benchmarking, it was open to new ideas and willing to learn from other, both domestic and foreign service organizations. Sufficient management attention, time, internal budget, consultancy budget, and adequate resources were made available, underpinning managerial commitment and the business relevance of benchmarking. Most importantly, however, the organization was able to gain new insights, to adopt different ways of working, and to improve customer service activities through IT, as a result of the benchmarking process.

The benchmarking process could be carried out according to the steps described earlier in this chapter. It required an elapsed time of three months, excluding, of course, the actual implementation of improvement actions. In practical terms, the external focus and the structured approach proved to be key cornerstones of the whole process. The external focus excited participants enormously, while the structured approach kept things manageable. The measurement and comparison aspects of the process required the expected precise descriptions, definitions, and explanations of the products, services, and business processes measured and compared. This appeared to be crucial not only to achieve credible results, but also to demonstrate the seriousness of the benchmarking process to the external benchmark partners involved.

Case 2: Benchmarking the Effectiveness and Efficiency of IT Supply at ANWB

The measurement program that tracks the performance of ANWB's IT organization (ACS) is based (as mentioned in the previous chapter) on performance measures jointly developed and accepted by ACS's stakeholders: IT employees, users' representatives, and board members. Benchmarking against other organizations played an important role in the development of performance targets for competitive supply of IT products and services at ANWB. As the development of the IT measurement program has been discussed already in the previous chapter, the discussion in this section will be brief, and focused on the benchmarking aspects and their role in setting targets for the selected performance measures.

The starting point for the development of the measurement program was to monitor the performances of the IT supplying organization with the help of a limited number of measures from the BTRIPLEE level "Effectiveness and efficiency of IT supply." Based on the need of the board and the customers (the Business Units), and based on the vision and earlier defined success criteria of the IT organization, products and services were identified that needed monitoring through the measurement program. These products and services, together with relevant performance measures, were collectively identified by the IT organization, the users of IT products and services, and ANWB management (see Chapter 7). To identify associated performance targets (standards), the benchmarking approach described was applied.

In this case study, no benchmark partners in the true sense of the term were used. Rather, databases maintained by the facilitating consultant organization were used as reference. In the few cases that the databases were not sufficient, personal contacts were used to answer *ad-hoc* questions and to provide comparative snapshot information.

The benchmark team consisted of a core team (two consultants and five employees from the IT supply organization ACS) and a, what we called, "reference-team" (six key representatives of the different Business Units). The ACS employees, coming from different IT disciplines and from different hierarchical layers, worked side by side with the consultants on a daily basis on the project. The reference team met regularly to discuss user's expectations and related benchmarking issues. It turned out that, not surprisingly, the IT employees in the team, who work in everyday operations, had a clear insight in information sources necessary for data gathering. The consultants supplied the external benchmarking information and ensured that the right level of abstraction remained guaranteed: IT employees sometimes liked to discuss technical details that were actually less relevant, while users tended to oversimplify things from time to time.

As ACS is required to be competitive, and as ACS employees felt they themselves were almost personally measured and compared, precise descriptions, definitions and explanations of the IT products, IT services, and IT supply processes measured and compared were developed. During several intensive sessions, results from internal data collection were compared with information from external databases. Initially, this led to exhausting discussions and doubts about both the gathered facts and the reliability of external benchmarks. In spite of these discussions, consensus was reached about ACS's performance in relation to external benchmarks, and acceptable performance targets could be negotiated for each performance measure.

Conclusions

The business relevance of IT benchmarking is obvious: benchmarking against other organizations played an important role to determine competitive targets for supply of IT products and services at ANWB. In fact, to determine competitive performance targets, ANWB had virtually no choice but to benchmark, which indeed provided the targets sought for. All stakeholders committed to the performance measures and competitive performance targets developed during the benchmarking process, which underpins its business relevance.

The process slightly deviated from the one described in this chapter, as it was woven into the development of an IT measurement program. The actual benchmarking part took an elapsed time of two months. Sufficient management attention, time, internal budget, consultancy budget, and adequate resources were made available to make the benchmarking process (and in fact, the definition and implementation of the IT measurement program) a success.

Case 3: Benchmarking of Maintenance of Information Systems in the Financial Industry in The Netherlands

The management of one of the three largest Dutch banks questioned whether or not the regular maintenance of the core banking information systems was too expensive. Since no generally accepted standards or norms exist, it was suggested to answer this question by comparing the bank's maintenance activities with those of other large financial institutions in The Netherlands, and then arrive at an opinion about the many aspects of the answer to this "simple" question.

In the first instance, the bank's management was not overly optimistic about this proposal. It was not immediately believed that the information, necessary to compare and benchmark, would and could be supplied by potential benchmark candidates. Therefore a first phase of qualitative benchmarking was introduced, aimed at:

- a qualitative comparison of the benchmark partners' approaches to information systems maintenance;
- a comparison of these approaches with a "best practices" model, to be derived from current literature and expert opinions from scholars and consultants.

This first phase, if successful, would be followed by a second, quantitative benchmarking phase. In reality, this phase again was split in two parts, 2a and 2b. This was done because after finishing Phase 1, the management of the bank was still not fully convinced that either sufficient reliable benchmark partners could be

Figure 8.4: Benchmarking Process Used in Case 3

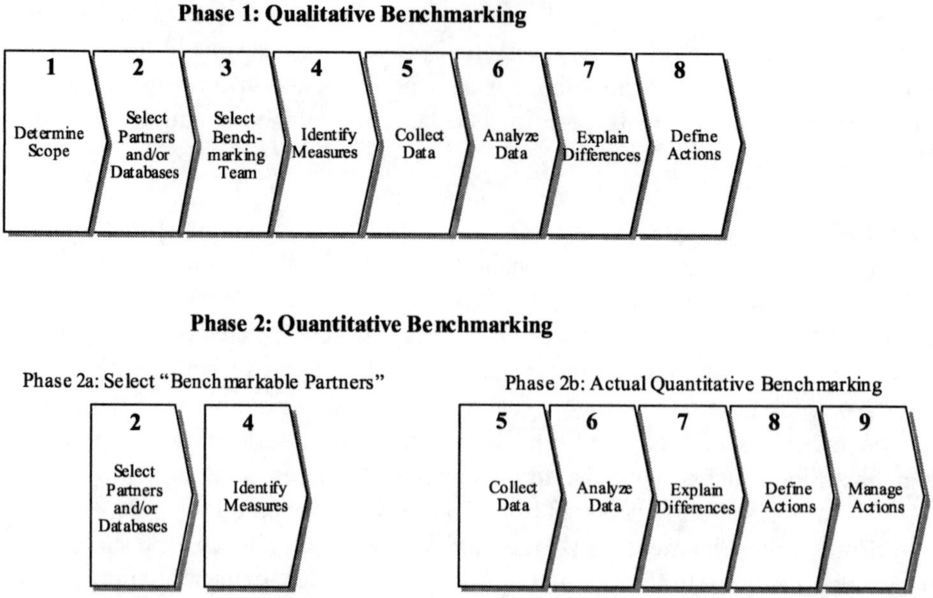

Phase 1: Qualitative Benchmarking

1	2	3	4	5	6	7	8
Determine Scope	Select Partners and/or Databases	Select Benchmarking Team	Identify Measures	Collect Data	Analyze Data	Explain Differences	Define Actions

Phase 2: Quantitative Benchmarking

Phase 2a: Select "Benchmarkable Partners"

2	4
Select Partners and/or Databases	Identify Measures

Phase 2b: Actual Quantitative Benchmarking

5	6	7	8	9
Collect Data	Analyze Data	Explain Differences	Define Actions	Manage Actions

found, or that they would be able to supply the necessary quantified information. Phase 2a was therefore devoted to clearly identifying which measures would be feasible to include in the quantitative benchmarking round, on the basis of a short study of the measurement systems and practices in place by the benchmarking partners. After assuring that reliable information about certain key measures could and would be collected with all benchmarking partners, Phase 2b could be carried out. This benchmarking process, as it was executed, is shown in Figure 8.4.

Phase 1-Qualitative Benchmarking

Phase 1-Determine the scope

To get started, the scope was defined by the commissioning bank together with the consultants, not in consultation with potential benchmark partners. The bank was going to fund the benchmarking study, and therefore its interests had to prevail. The scope was limited to finding improvements of the effectiveness and especially the efficiency of troubleshooting activities; small enhancements of application software; and the support of users, the data center, and other system development functions (answering their questions, basically).

Phase 1-Select benchmark partners and databases

The facilitating consultants, including myself as the project manager, approached benchmark partners. The list included seven Dutch-based, but predominantly multinational companies: two other large banks in The Netherlands, a pension fund, an insurance company (because they are all active in the financial industry), two large industrial companies (because of their large user base, and also because of our curiosity to find out whether differences would exist between different types of industries), and a manufacturer/supplier of packaged software (because maintenance and user support was a core business activity of this company). Without exception, all selected organizations were interested in cooperating in the benchmarking process, under the condition that they would obtain the results of the study in return.

The commissioning bank started to feel confident that benchmarking among a total sample of eight large and interesting companies would bring some results at least.

Phase 1-Select the benchmarking team

The core benchmarking team consisted of two consultants and an employee of the commissioning bank. During the execution of the benchmarking processes, this core team was supported by:

- a scholar from the Tilburg University in The Netherlands, who performed a thorough literature study on the subject to raise the important questions, and who participated in brainstorming sessions during the process;
- two consultants, who participated in the brainstorming sessions as well.

Phase 1-Identify measures

No real measures were used in the first, qualitative benchmarking round. Rather, areas of interest were defined, based on two important inputs:

- First, a conceptual input-process-output model of information system maintenance was constructed. This model, mainly based on current literature, describes the different aspects influencing effectiveness and efficiency levels of maintenance processes, within their business and application portfolio context.
- Secondly, important questions were derived from the (limited) research and literature available, to be answered by the benchmark partners, leading to a set of qualitative indicators needed for the data collection during the next phase of the study.

Phase 1-Collect data

Qualitative information was gathered through a series of structured interviews with several employees of both the bank and the other benchmark partners. These interviews were followed up by the collection of as much quantitative data as possible and the gathering of examples of best practices from each participating benchmark partner, not only to be better informed on behalf of this first phase, but also to test whether benchmark partners would qualify to participate during the second, quantitative benchmarking round.

Phase 1-Analyze data

No specific remarks can be made about this analysis phase-it went as smoothly as it could go. By drawing up schemes of the maintenance practices of benchmarking partners, and comparing them with a "best-of-breed" model, which was developed, the analysis resulted in apparent differences between organizations.

Phase 1-Explain differences

The differences in effectiveness and efficiency between the benchmark partners, and between the commissioning bank and the "best-of-breed" model, could be explained without too many difficulties, mainly because of the collective experience and expert views of the scholar, the consultants, and the bank's representative.

Phase 1-Define concrete actions

On the basis of the qualitative benchmarking process, a series of presentations was given to the banks' management teams, including a set of concluding hypotheses and issues to be dealt with during the next phase: quantitative benchmarking. On that basis, we were asked to continue with that next phase.

Phase 2A-Select Partners for Quantitative Benchmarking

After the first benchmarking round, it became clear that some benchmark partners would not be able to participate in the second, quantitative round. Different reasons were given: either they were not able, or they were not willing to supply the necessary data, or they were not interested in spending the necessary time on the study within the timeframe we gave them. One benchmarking partner (the software supply company) could not participate further because of a very sad reason: it had gone broke!

What remained was a set of five, highly interested companies: the commissioning bank, one other large bank, the pension fund, the insurance company, and one large industrial company.

The benchmarking team defined the measures for which data was going to be collected through a formal questionnaire. This was done by reviewing the measures in place with the commissioning bank, and by adding missing measures that were needed to cover the scope and depth of the maintenance activities and their business and application portfolio context that were researched and benchmarked.

Phase 2B-Actual Quantitative Benchmarking

Quantitative information was gathered through structured questionnaires and follow-up interviews. During the analysis phase, it became clear that two benchmark partners had supplied us with at least partly inconsistent information. The measures of one benchmarking partner in particular (the other bank-in other words: the direct competitor) gave us some headaches: their measured performance in some processes differed substantially from that of the commissioning bank. The difference was so substantial, that it was almost too hard to believe. Checking and rechecking taught us, however, that their actual performance indeed was not the same because of different objectives for information systems maintenance and because management focused on day-to-day problems, rather than on future goals.

After these discussions and re-checking with benchmark partners, the benchmark information became consistent enough to give the team the feeling it was working with a reliable set of data. The explanation of differences in effectiveness and efficiency between the benchmark partners, and between the commissioning bank and the "best-of-breed" model, was performed by combining results of the qualitative benchmarking phase with new insights from the quantitative benchmarking exercise. In fact, two-thirds of the performance shortages, explained as a result of the quantitative benchmarking, had already been identified by the first round of qualitative benchmarking. Of course, the quantified evidence came across much stronger than the qualitative, expert-based findings. The quantitative benchmarking revealed the remaining one-third of the total performance gaps and related improvement areas, which, as such, demonstrates the relevance of quantitative benchmarking over qualitative benchmarking only.

On the basis of the benchmarking process a series of substantive improvement areas and concrete actions for enhanced control could be defined. At the time of writing, the commissioning bank is preparing its decisions about our recommendations. It is a little early to convey what they have decided, and how they will manage it.

Conclusions

The benchmarking process carried out was aimed at improving control of the maintenance of core banking information systems and associated costs. The bank's management was unsure whether the cost level was "right," and as no other means were available, benchmarking appeared to be an appealing approach to tackle this issue. Despite the slight uncertainty of the bank's management at the start of the process, its readiness to benchmark, together with the benchmarking results, and its readiness to implement recommended improvement actions, confirms the business relevance of benchmarking.

The bank appeared to be most interested in performance data of comparable Dutch banks, more than in the performance of other, non-banking organizations. This can be explained by the competitive situation in the financial industry, and the fact that The Netherlands is a small country, where in the same industry, everybody knows everybody. The case also illustrated how benchmarking may lead to quantified targets for improvement, but only for the aspects of performance in which the bank showed worse than benchmark partners. For the maintenance aspects of which the bank's performance appeared to be lower than others, management was overly interested to know why and eager to improve. On the other hand, the bank's management felt satisfied when they saw they performed relatively better at specific aspects, and did not see any reasons to improve those.

Conclusions from the Case Studies

First of all, each case study demonstrates the value of benchmarking as a systematic, quantified comparison with other, leading-edge organizations, implicating an external focus and a structured approach.. The term "leading-edge" is sometimes troublesome, though. In practical terms, it is very difficult to demonstrate or prove what "leading-edge" really means. When selecting benchmark partners, it appears that the perception of companies being "leading-edge" is of higher importance than a thorough analysis of actual performance.

It also appears that when companies are compared with each other, they always hope to be the best. If the performance of an organization is compared with performance data of other companies contained in databases or assembled as part of the benchmarking process at hand, it will want to score in the upper league. Nobody wants to perform worse than his neighbor, so that performance and improvement targets are almost automatically set at the highest level.

To establish credible benchmarking results, measuring and comparing require precise descriptions, definitions, and explanations of the products, services, processes, and other phenomena that are measured and compared. In each case study, quite some time and many discussions were devoted to these aspects of benchmarking, especially in the banking case study.

As benchmarking is aimed at attaining real improvements, only to be achieved if the necessary organizational commitment is present, the benchmark teams in each case study consist of a mixture of consultants and people directly involved. In this way, organizational commitment for improvement in an early stage can be established. In all cases, benchmarking was followed up by the implementation of recommended improvement actions, while the results of the process also confirmed aspects of excellence in performance.

From the cases it is clear that a number of conditions for benchmarking success have to be applied. First of all, top management commitment is crucial, to be expressed by a board that believes in the value of benchmarking and which is open to new ideas and willing to learn from better ways to approach certain problems. Secondly, qualified employees of a commissioning organization have to be made available to form the benchmarking team. In each case, mixed teams of consultants and members of the commissioning organization performed the benchmark studies, and this appeared to be of crucial importance. Thirdly, in each case study, results could not be ignored; they were quite visible in the organizations of both the commissioning companies as well as the benchmarking partners, so they had to be followed-on. The combination of these three reasons appeared to be powerful enough for management to act upon the results in all three cases.

The best demonstration of the business relevance of benchmarking is to look at its results. The first case study delivered new insights and fresh ideas as a result of benchmarking, while the second case delivered the performance targets sought for. The third case delivered the qualitative and quantitative means to improve control.

CONCLUSION

Quantitative measurability and benchmarking of the application and supply of IT is of great importance. Comparing with and learning from the best can lead to establishing targets for selected BtripleE measures of IT performance based on ratio scales, and in a broader sense, to structural improvements of the application and supply of IT.

However, benchmarking is not the "silver bullet" to solve every problem or answer any question. At some point, management judgment must take over from measurement, while benchmarking serves a key role in supporting both. In any case, measurement and comparison must be interpreted wisely in relation to their business context.

Although benchmarking can be used as a successful management tool, some limitations exist. Because benchmarking means comparison with others, original and visionary ideas may suffer if benchmarking is applied as the " silver bullet." Many strategic, innovative products and services spring from the intuitive feeling for the market, seldom using market analysis, let alone a comparison with others. Such products, like the Apple Macintosh, the Sony Walkman, and the Chrysler Voyager became market leaders because the companies introducing these products completely followed their own course. Likewise, many organizations applied strategic IT without looking at others at all. Therefore, finding the right balance between benchmarking and other approaches such as putting emphasis on Core Competencies is recommended. Finding the right balance is contingent on the specifics of the organization and the needs of stakeholders at any given time. Doing this is feasible, however: Xerox, for example, can be considered a leading company in benchmarking of operational processes, and visionary in the field of product development at the same time.

The danger of treating benchmarking of the application and supply of IT as being merely a "numbers game" is particularly restricted if measuring and comparing are not perceived as goals in themselves, but rather as adding value to the successful application and supply of IT. The usefulness of benchmarking increases as it becomes more obvious to all stakeholders what is intended with benchmarking, and when specific improvement actions are initiated as a result.

From the case studies presented in this chapter, it is clear that the benchmarking process as such is very feasible and doable, providing the results sought. In my experience, and as has been demonstrated by the case studies, the technical aspects of benchmarking are not the issue. What is complicated is to get the different but necessary internal and external parties interested, involved, and committed; meanwhile seducing them to openly compare and discuss each other's performance levels and reasons why. What makes benchmarking processes complex, sometimes fuzzy, but always interesting, are the politics and tactics, rather than the technical execution of it.

REFERENCES

Bemowski, K. (1991). The benchmarking bandwagon. *Quality Progress*, January, 19-24.

Camp, R.C. (1989). *Benchmarking, the Search for Industry Best Practices that Lead to Superior Performance*. Milwaukee, Wisconsin: Quality Press.

Deschamps, J.P. and Nayak, P.R. (1995). *Product Juggernauts: How Companies Mobilize to Generate a Stream of Market Winners*. Boston, MA: Harvard Business School Press.

Melymuka, K. (1991). Peer pressure. *CIO, The Magazine for Information Executives,* June.

Pralahad, C.K. and Hamel, G. (1990). The core competence of the corporation. *Harvard Business Review*, May-June.

Pryor, L.S. (1989). Benchmarking: A self-improvement strategy. *The Journal of Business Strategy,* November-December.

Spendolini, M.J. (1992). *The Benchmarking Book*. New York: American Management Association.

Tucker, F.G., Zivan, S.M. and Camp, R.C. (1987), "How to Measure Yourself against the Best," *Harvard Business Review,* January - February.

Walleck, A.S., O'Halloran, J.D. and Leader, C.A. (1991). Benchmarking world-class performance. *The McKinsey Quarterly*, (1).

Appendix A

Attributes of Measures

In any situation, it is necessary to select the appropriate measures from the many measures that have been proposed and discussed, to evaluate IT and to interpret actual measurement results in the context of the specific situation and the company's ultimate business objectives and goals. In other words: the dashboard of IT value gauges has to be custom designed to reflect the specific internal and external issues at hand.

Measures are not all of the same kind. Different types of measures exist to support different purposes and sorts of measurements. Measures can be distinguished by their:
- applicability to support a type of measurement,
- type of scale,
- relationship to other measures,
- comparability.

Applicability of measures

Measurement in general serves different purposes, having consequences for the actual measures to be used. Three different purposes of measurement are:
- *Measuring process and activity levels*: The focus of this type of measurement is on periodic scores of the effectiveness and efficiency of processes, and deals with cost, timeliness, and quality of processes and activities. Associated measures track the process and the size of activities rather than the quality of the outcome of activities. An example is the development process of IT applications, for which the measure Function Points Per Staff Month indicates the level of activity, and Function Points Per Calendar Month indicates speed of the process.
- *Measuring results*: The focus here is on the measurement of cost and effectiveness of delivered products or services, or the post-mortem evaluation of just completed projects. In the example of application development, the level of user satisfaction and the number of defects during the first three months of operation would be appropriate result-oriented measures to evaluate some of the aspects of an IT application (the result of the development process).

- *Measuring performance to budget*: Associated indicators gauge either ad-hoc or in a more continuous way management's ability to match requirements to daily constraints, rather than the ability to perform activities at a certain efficiency level, or the effective results of efforts. For an application development project, the percentage of budget overrun (in money) and project plan slippage (in time) are good examples of associated measures.

Type of scale

Measures are either quantitative or qualitative. Four distinct sorts of measures can be distinguished: nominal (or categorical), ordinal, interval, and ratio measurement types, each with their own scales:

- *Nominal scales* are used to classify. An example would be either "yes" or "no," to questions like "Do you have experience with system ABC?" or "Are you generally happy with the services of the IT supplier?" etc. The nominal scale is qualitative.
- *Ordinal scales* are used to rank and compare, for example, Company A spends a little or a lot more on IT than Company B. The often-used rankings of 'better' versus 'worse,' or 'high' - 'medium' - 'low' fall into this category. The ordinal scale is qualitative.
- *Interval scales* are quantitative scales on which the difference between the numbers on the scale can be interpreted meaningfully. An example is the overall customer satisfaction rating of 6 on a scale from 1 to 9. Such a rating is in fact a quantitative representation of a rather subjective, qualitative assessment. However, when asking large, representative sample sizes for a subjective opinion, the average of these subjective opinions will probably be close to objectivity, in context. If, for example, the majority of IT users are unhappy about the service level of IT supplier ABC, an average customer satisfaction rate of 3.2 on a scale from 1 to 9 should be regarded as an objective score of the customer satisfaction measure of the client base of supplier ABC.
- Ratio scales are quantitative scales such that the numbers on this scale have meaning. An example of this scale would be the number of dollars a company spends on IT. The scale possesses the property that intervals between points on the scale are comparable. For example, the difference between 100 million dollars a year and 120 million dollars per year is the same as the difference between 150 million a year and 170 million per year. In addition, it might be meaningful to compare an IT cost of 150 million per year with an IT cost of 100 million dollars a year, by stating that the former IT cost is 1.5 times that of the latter.

Ideally, measurement implies quantified, objective measures on ratio scales. However, quantified measures of a qualitative and more subjective nature (measures on the interval scale) can also be useful and may, in fact, be the only practical measures available in many instances.

Relationship with other measures

Most measures do not stand alone but rather are linked to each other, one way or another. Within groups (e.g., the category of IT effectiveness measures, or the category of IT supply effectiveness measures), measures relate together to form a pyramid of rising (vertical) levels of abstraction under a single performance criterion, and have relationships horizontally, as illustrated in Figure A.1. These relationships might be either strong or weak, and either statistically proven or logically derived.

The idea of building pyramids has been developed by Minto for a different purpose (to write clear business documents), but the concept can be equally useful for structuring and ordering performance measures. According to Minto, "at higher levels, aggregate performance measures summarize the performance measures grouped below them (vertical linkage). Performance measures in each grouping must be part of the same logical set of measures, and they must be in strict logical order (horizontal linkage). The logical order can be formed either deductively or inductively. If the order is deductive, the second performance measure is a result of the first one, and the third measure follows from the first two measures. If the order is inductive, the measures are of the same kind and independent of each other."

Figure A.1 illustrates both the deductive and inductive relationships between measures. The measure "costs of IT" is broken down into three measures. "Costs of

Figure A.1: Pyramid of a Group of IT Performance Indicators

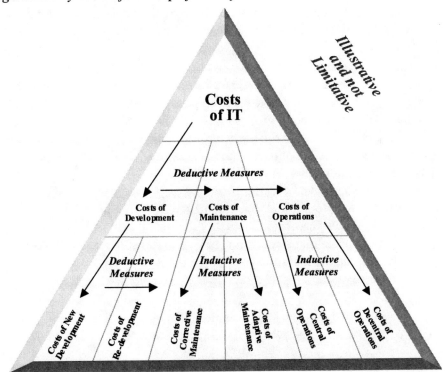

maintenance" is a consequence of the development of IT applications in the past, while the costs of IT operations are implied by both the costs of development and later adaptations and changes to the application. The three cost measures demonstrate a clear deductive relationship.

At the lower levels, the cost of development can be divided into new development and re-development of IT applications. The re-development of (parts of) IT applications cannot happen without the existence of previously developed IT applications. Re-development is thus an implication of (and thus deductively related to) the existing development of new IT applications.

The costs of maintenance, however, do not show a deductive relationship but, rather, an inductive one. Adaptive maintenance of IT applications is not implied by corrective maintenance; both types of maintenance exist side by side in their own right. Both are, however, maintenance activities, and therefore they are considered to have an inductive relationship. The same reasoning applies to different types of operations, in which the examples of centralized and decentralized operations are included.

Although the objectives, frequency, etc., of measurement at different levels might be different, the measures themselves do not need to be mutually exclusive. Some of the same measures at different organizational levels might complement each other. For example, for each completed application development project, it is possible to afterwards measure the efficiency of development in terms of delivered Function Points Per Staff Month. At the higher level, it is possible to measure the efficiency of the application development process by summing up the efficiency levels of the several projects that have been executed over a period of time, say a year, and compare the overall efficiency level with the performance of past years.

Comparability of measures

The final attribute of measures is associated with possible objectives of measurement. Choosing the appropriate, comparable measures is vital in reaching measurement objectives, both from an internal historical perspective (internal trends) or external comparative perspective (benchmarking). Both perspectives require consistency in terms of definitions of measures, and in terms of comparability of measurement results.

Measures can be tracked over time to build an aggregated picture of the subject of measurement, and to smooth out fluctuations of individual measures in a particular period. A few years is probably the minimum length of time needed to get a reliable picture of the main trends for many measures; the actual period is, of course, contingent on the measures used.

REFERENCES

Minto, B. (1987). *The Pyramid Principle: Logic in Writing and Thinking.* London, UK: Pitman Publishing.

Remenyi, D.R., Money, A. and Twite, A. (1993). *A Guide to Measuring and Managing IT Benefits.* Oxford, UK: NCC Blackwell Ltd.

Appendix B

Measuring the Value of IT at ANWB

The aggregated BTRIPLEE framework, its valuation layers, and their associated classes of measures as described in the first six chapters of this book have been developed to consistently and systematically assess the business value and effectiveness of IT, and the effectiveness and efficiency of the activities that are performed to make IT available. A demonstration of the applicability of the BTRIPLEE framework and associated classes of measures in a real-life situation is described in this appendix, as a case study.

First, a brief profile of the Royal Dutch Touring Club ANWB (Koninklijke Nederlandse Toeristenbond ANWB) is provided, followed by a summary of the broad range of IT applications used by ANWB to support its business, its members, and other customers. Secondly, the approach, techniques, and information sources used to apply the BTRIPLEE framework, its valuation layers, and their associated classes of measures are described. Finally, the results of the validation are analyzed and evaluated, resulting in a conclusion of this chapter.

ANWB

The Royal Dutch Touring Club ANWB is an autonomous, commercially run membership association with more than three million members. It was established in 1883 to encourage bicycle riding, organize competitions for amateurs, print maps, and protect the rights of bicyclists. Since then, ANWB has evolved substantially.

Many of ANWB's activities have celebrated their centenary. The club magazine, for example, has been published since 1885. Since 1893, when a campaign against the levying of tolls on Dutch roads began, the association has played an active role as an advocate for its members' interests with the government. When the government failed to react to the campaign, the association itself attended to matters. This was the case with the construction of cycle paths and the erection of warning signs. In 1894, the first signposts were put up. In that same year, members were able to insure themselves against the financial consequences of bicycle accidents, and thus ANWB moved into the field of insurance. With the ascent of motorcars and mass tourism, the provision of assistance developed into a core activity: assistance with breakdowns by "Road Services," and personal help and legal assistance from the "Emergency Center."

Today, membership has penetrated 45 percent of Dutch households and approximately 65 percent of households owning at least one car. More than 3,000 employees provide a broad range of services to members and other customers from the head office in The Hague, from 50 regional shops, from about 30 other agencies, and from a number of Internet and extranet sites.

Still serving the common interests of its members in the main areas of recreation, tourism, mobility, traffic, and public transportation, today's focus is to assist members and other interested parties in attaining convenience. The core range of services of ANWB are managed by a number of Business Units, and include the supply of access to many kinds of information (about road and trip conditions to prevent travelers having problems; about hotels, restaurants, camping sites, and cars to prevent members and tourists taking inappropriate decisions, etc.) over the telephone (voice-response), by computer (Videotext and Internet), in magazines, brochures, maps, guidebooks, CD-I, etc. It also includes car breakdown assistance in The Netherlands, diverse assistance in case of emergency abroad, and a broad array of private insurance policies. Recent new services include a credit card for members, "Cars-on-call" (a car subscription service for members), and "Datakluis" (a service offered to members storing the details of important documents and items such as passport, driving license, credit cards, insurance policies, etc., in a computerized "safe").

IT AT ANWB

ANWB is certainly an information-based organization: IT at ANWB is strategic in and of itself. To start with, almost all of the many ANWB products and services have huge information content. Moreover, IT supports all managerial business processes, with general ledger systems, accounts payable and accounts receivable systems, personnel information systems and payroll processing, inventory and logistics systems, etc. Next, ANWB employs a host of IT systems that directly support its primary processes. IT also enables ANWB to develop products and services effectively, disseminate products and services efficiently, and provide customer service through databases and multimedia distribution systems, including the Internet.

IT at ANWB includes the automated support and enabling of:
- membership administration;
- road assistance scheduling, tracing and tracking;
- emergency support and legal services scheduling, tracing and tracking;
- customized design and (electronic) publication of maps, guides, books, brochures, CD-Is, etc.,

- collection and dissemination of all kinds of tourist information through various media;
- direct marketing and brochure sales of products and services;
- real time information supply about road conditions, traffic jams, etc., through, amongst others, voice response systems and multimedia techniques;
- organization and administration of a variety of courses, training sessions, etc., for members;
- insurance policy administration and claims processing;
- tour operator activities, such as brochure preparation, trips reservation and administration, etc.;
- travel agency activities;
- signpost design and development through CAD/CAM.

MEASURING THE VALUE OF IT AT ANWB

Recently, ANWB was involved in at least five large, time- and money-consuming but strategic IT projects:

- development and expansion of touristic Information Data base Access (IDA);
- re-development / replacement of the membership administration system (CARPLUS);
- development of ANWB's logistics information systems (INFOLOG);
- implementation of a new IT infrastructure on behalf of the 50 ANWB regional shops;
- development of a new, state-of-the-art road assistance scheduling, tracing, and tracking information system (CIS).

Having experienced a large growth of IT costs over the past three years, two recently appointed board members decided to have several serious questions investigated and answered:

- Do we spend our money on the right IT?
- Does IT offer ANWB any strategic value?
- Are we able to effectively use our IT?
- Are we capable of managing and implementing our projects?

This situation clearly demonstrates the business relevance of applying the BtripleE framework, its valuation layers, and their associated classes of measures. The first two questions are related to the **B**usiness value of IT, since this level of the BtripleE framework links IT costs with the organization's financial, business, and strategic performance. The third question has to do with the **E**ffectiveness of IT, since this level explores the extent to which IT effectively supports business processes, activities, and employees. The fourth question deals with the **E**ffectiveness and **E**fficiency of IT supply. This means that all levels of the BtripleE framework, extensively discussed throughout the book, were relevant to answering all four questions.

Since this case study was performed as a consultancy engagement, and confidentiality has to be preserved, neither the specific findings nor specific recommendations to ANWB are made public in this book, except for some findings at the highest level to put things in context. Also, specific techniques and information such as questionnaires, workshop materials, and benchmark data are not published in order not to violate the professional, legal, and ethical obligations of the consultancy business and consultancy firms. Their characteristics are described, however, in order to be able to validate their relevance and applicability. Besides, as it is the intention of this case study to provide empirical evidence for the validity and business relevance of the BTRIPLEE framework, its valuation layers, and their associated classes of measures, rather than the validation of specific techniques, the absence of specific example of those should not be perceived as a shortcoming.

The application of the levels of the framework and associated measures are discussed in the same sequence of the first six chapters of this book, and in line with the execution of the case study.

Measuring the Business Value of IT

To determine the business value of IT, ANWB's IT costs had to be correlated with its performance on three related dimensions: financial, business, and strategic performance. ANWB's question "Do we spend our money on the right IT?" had therefore to be converted into three sub-questions:

- How much do we actually spend?
- On what is that money spent?
- Is IT and are IT costs positively related with financial, business, and strategic success?

Dynamics of IT costs

To answer these questions, total annual IT costs were collected for a number of years and segmented by activity and by resource to understand the dynamics of IT costs at ANWB, to perform trend analysis, and to benchmark IT spending against other companies. ANWB's centralized IT budget was easy to retrieve, since it was managed by the (centralized) IT department, but all business unit controllers had to be visited frequently to collect, check, and double-check information on decentralized IT spending. In order to make sure that all IT spending was collected, a standard chart of accounts was used to assist the controllers to reliably take stock of IT spending by activity (in this case: development, maintenance, operations, end-user computing support, and "other"), and by resource (in this case: hardware, personnel, outside services including software, and "other"). In total, it took an elapsed time of six weeks to build the aggregated picture of ANWB's IT spending over a period of three years.

Benchmarking was performed with the help of the consultant's database containing IT spending patterns of many companies around the world. We measured and compared overall IT costs as a percentage of revenue, annual growth rate of IT costs, IT costs by resource (hardware, personnel, outside services, and other), and IT costs by activity (development, maintenance, operations, end-user computing support, and other). These ratios were relatively easy to calculate and to compare, once all central and decentral IT spending figures were collected.

It appeared that over a period of three years, total IT spending had more than doubled in absolute terms and almost doubled as a percentage of revenue. However, when compared with data of other information-intensive organizations such as banks and insurance companies (available through the benchmark database), the total annual amount of money spent on IT as a percentage of revenue was not alarming. It seemed, based on these comparisons, that ANWB did not necessarily spend too much money on IT, but the growth of overall IT costs needed management attention--in particular because further growth had to be expected, since the systems under development at that time were going to be implemented and would consequently generate additional operational costs. Moreover, since analysis showed that especially decentralized IT spending had grown enormously (from 9 percent to 46 percent of centralized spending), our conclusion was that growth of decentralized IT costs needed improved control (46 percent is very high and far beyond the estimate of, for example, Gartners' prediction of user-controlled IT costs). This conclusion was supported by the fact that it had taken us quite some effort to collect information on decentralized spending, and to make the overall picture visible to management, which was shocked as a result! A discussion with management confirmed that a currently lacking, systematic approach to overall IT cost control was needed. The associated measures of this aspect of the BTRIPLEE framework were adopted for such a systematic control mechanism.

IT development costs appeared to have grown much faster than any other category of IT costs. In fact, IT development had grown tremendously, while maintenance of existing IT systems had been neglected. This meant that past investments in IT were insufficiently maintained, so that ANWB ran the risk that the IT capabilities in which it had invested so much would need to be replaced earlier than in the case of regular maintenance. To make this clear to ANWB management, the analogy of buying a car, and not having it maintained according to manufacturers' instructions, was used. Everyone is aware that such practices are risky; such is also the case with IT systems. As a result, ANWB management initiated the necessary actions to limit system development activities and spend more attention on the maintenance of existing applications.

In conclusion, by analyzing the dynamics of IT cost, the questions "How much do we actually spend?" and "On what is that money spent?" could be answered on the basis of the theory described in Chapter 4. The question "On what is that money spent?" was answered by analyzing IT expenditure by IT activities and resources, rather than by the application of IT by business function or process. This perspective of IT spending is dealt with in the next sections.

Measures of financial performance through IT

To determine the value of IT, measured by improved financial performance as discussed earlier, IT costs were related with financial performance measures. IT costs were first expressed as a percentage of revenue, as discussed, which helped us to compare ANWB's spending on IT with data of other companies.

The financial performance measures sales by employee, sales by total assets, ROI, ROA, and ROS, suggested in Chapter 4, were not all applicable at ANWB, since a part of total revenue is not generated by sales but rather by the annual membership fee and by interest income. We therefore replaced the denominator of sales by revenue, and two positive correlations between IT investment and financial performance ratios drawn in Chapter 4 were confirmed:

- *Revenue by employee* (surrogate measure for sales by employee) increased over the years, indicating that more business can be done per employee; while improved and more widespread IT (and, in particular, the number of PCs and computer terminals) has probably contributed to that economic advantage.
- *Profit as a percentage of revenue* (surrogate measure for ROS) increased over the years. IT might have helped in automating human tasks and as such decreased the costs of realized revenue, or prevented variable costs to increase while revenue (and the number of business transactions) grew.

As a general conclusion, the financial performance of ANWB appeared to be measurable, although not with all indicators suggested. In particular, we did not test the suggested measures Sales by total assets, nor ROA or ROI, since insufficient information was available.

Measures of business performance through IT

To evaluate the contribution of IT to improving ANWB's business performance, Chapter 4 suggests evaluation of the relation between IT costs and multiple (including non-financial) business measures for different categories of business performance. As many non-financial performance indicators are specific to sectors we didn't make comparisons with other organizations, but rather looked at historical trends.

This approach proved to be troublesome at ANWB. IT costs were related with a few non-financial business measures, all showing the same trend: IT costs per non-financial business measure had more or less doubled over the past three years. For example, IT costs per ANWB member nearly doubled because the growth of number of members was 2.6 percent per year, while IT costs had increased more than 100 percent over the past three years.

This misalignment of numbers was mainly caused by the fact that IT investments do not have an immediate impact; the benefits of IT can take several years to show results. An econometric study of Brynjolfsson found lags of two to three years before the strongest impacts of IT were felt. Especially the benefits of infrastructure, while potentially large, are indirect and often not immediate. Looking at the IT cost structure of ANWB, 45 percent of total IT costs were spent on the development of new, partly infrastructure IT systems (relative spending on IT development was about twice as high as in other organizations): the development and expansion of tourist information databases, the re-development of the membership administration system, the development of logistics information systems, the implementation of an IT infrastructure on behalf of the regional shops, and the development of a road assistance scheduling, tracing, and tracking information system. These development costs had been the major cause of the large jump in overall IT costs. Unfortunately, none of these systems was implemented (not in operational use) at the time of the study, so that business benefits could not have been reaped yet, neither could they be measured.

In conclusion, the valuation of the contribution of IT to improving ANWB's business performance could not be effectively performed because ANWB faced a lag time between incurring costs (at the time of measuring) and reaping the benefits (to be expected later than the moment of measuring). This is always the case, but the time lag problem was extreme at ANWB, since the enormous growth of IT expenditure troubled the analysis of relationships between IT expenditure and its benefits.

Measures of strategic performance through IT

The third dimension of business value of IT deals with the question to what extent IT costs are distributed over the areas in which results are expected to generate strategic success. As stated in Chapter 4, the key to determining strategic business value of IT is to first determine the areas that contribute most to ANWB's success.

We interviewed several members of ANWB's management to confirm ANWB's mission: to serve the common interests of its members in recreation, tourism, mobility, traffic, and public transportation. In order to do so, ANWB management believes it is of key importance to:

- maintain a large membership base, by keeping the annual membership fee as low as possible;
- satisfy members, by offering easy-to-acquire, superb products and services, either free of charge, or at relatively low prices;
- operate profitably, so as to be able to fund innovation and renewal, and achieve sustainable success.

In other words, those areas that contribute most to ANWB's success are those that increase its ability to create more value for more members, to launch new products and services, and to improve operating efficiencies.

It appeared that allocating annual IT costs of each of these critical business areas (as suggested in Chapter 4) would be too complex and alien, mainly because of the unusual high number of shared, infrastructure IT systems at ANWB. Instead, as a practical yet viable interpretation of the theory developed in Chapter 4, we assessed which groups of business functions were of highest strategic importance, relative to others, and in which groups of business functions IT was concentrated most. This approach is compatible with the theory, which includes "priority business functions" as one of the viable options to choose CSFs. In other words: this approach confirms the theory described, because it is in line with the intention of the theory and therefore assumed to be acceptable.

An assessment of the relative strategic importance of each group of business functions (called business area), judged by ANWB's management during a workshop, reflected the interpretation of "critical success factors." For each business area, we took a snapshot of the current degree of automation, measured by the level of actual automation as a percentage of potential for automation. We also constructed an imaginary picture-a projection of the near future-consisting of the current IT concentration complemented with the impact of the systems under development. This picture would provide a basis to answer the question whether ANWB would be gaining strategic business value through IT, after completion and implementation of the IT systems under development.

To create this picture, the current degree and the perceived quality of IT support for each of the seven defined business areas was estimated by ANWB's employees during a series of workshops. Then we included the potential effect of the systems under development (new initiatives), on the basis of discussions with the business area managers, and arrived at a future "IT concentration score" combining the IT in place and under development. If the IT concentration score of each business area were the same as the strategic importance of the business area itself, IT would be

Figure B.1: Strategic Impact of IT

Business Area	Strategic Importance	Degree of Automation	Quality	New Initiatives	IT Concentration Score
Membership Administration and Support	●●	●●	●	Yes	●●
Membership Representation	●●●	●●●	●●●	No	●●●
Sales of Products	●●●	●●	●●	Yes	●●●
Sales of Services	●●●	●	●	Yes	●●
Road Assistance and Emergency Center	●●●	●●	●●	Yes	●●●
Sign posting	●	●●●	●●	No	●●
Facilities & Support	●●	●●●	●●	Yes	●●●

●	= Low
●●	= Medium
●●●	= High

strategically aligned with ANWB's objectives. Figure B.1 shows the results of this exercise. The approach applied is consistent with the theory of Chapter 4 (and reflected in Figure 4.10) in terms of the philosophy to categorize different types of IT according to their strategic impact. It only differs slightly in terms of its practical implementation.

Figure B.1 tells us that ANWB's IT was only partly strategically aligned with its objectives:

- *Membership administration and support*, although important, was not considered to be of strategic relevance. Because the medium level of IT coverage (degree of automation) of a relatively low quality was not satisfactory, the decision to re-develop a new membership administration system seemed to be right. But as the business area was not very strategic (only a medium strategic score), abundant IT spending on a new membership administration system should not occur. As a result of this analysis, complemented with some further investigations, ANWB decided to stop the development project and start over again, aiming at a more functional system with fewer bells and whistles than the system under development, and much lower estimated annual costs of operations and usage.

- *Membership representation* scored as a strategic business area. IT coverage was sufficient, quality was fine, so the IT money spent in that area was well invested from a strategic point of view.

- *Sales of products* was a strategic business area as well. IT coverage was at the average level, and quality was marginal. Two initiatives were underway: the development of ANWB's logistics information systems, and the implementation of a new IT infrastructure on behalf of the regional shops. As such, these investments made sense from a strategic point of view.

- *Sales of services*, again, was strategic, while current IT support clearly was insufficient from coverage and quality perspectives. The development and expansion of tourist Information DataBase Access made sense from a strategic point of view.

- *Road assistance and Emergency Center*, one of ANWB's core businesses and thus strategic in itself, needed to upgrade the supporting IT, not only because the current IT was insufficient, but also because organizational changes caused the business area to work in a completely different way. The IT investments were of strategic significance.

- *Signposting* was of less strategic importance than other business areas. IT was quite well developed, probably an over-investment from a strategic point of view.

- *Facilities and support* include financial, human resources, facilities, and IT management. These are the business areas, which historically got most attention, and many of the business functions were well supported by IT. The logistics information systems under development, linking the sales locations with warehousing and purchasing functions, were new initiatives that caused the IT concentration score to be "high," not fully in line with the "medium" *strategic value of support processes.*

Reviewing this list, it can be argued that ANWB had invested and was investing in the right strategic areas, with the exception of over-investments in Membership administration and support, Signposting, and Facilities and support. As a result, the answers to the first two questions:

- Do we spend our money on the right IT?
- Does IT offer ANWB any strategic value

were found by applying measures linked to the first level of the BTRIPLEE framework. First of all, we concluded that overall IT cost was not abnormal, but that IT cost growth needed management attention. In particular, decentralized IT cost needed management control, and development costs had to be partly shifted to maintenance in order to protect earlier investments in IT. Secondly, a positive correlation between IT cost and financial performance was not rejected. Thirdly, it was simply too early to correlate IT cost with business performance improvement, caused by the fact that current IT costs do not yet have an immediate impact. Finally, the analysis of IT costs and strategic performance showed that ANWB's IT was fairly well aligned with its strategic objectives.

Measuring the Effectiveness of IT

The third question to be answered, "Are we able to effectively use our IT?" needs measurement at the IT effectiveness level of the BTRIPLEE framework. Measures are focused on the three perspectives of:

- business processes and business activities,
- users of IT,
- IT supply.

These three perspectives were included in the measurement of IT value at ANWB. At this level, we measured the availability of IT to business processes and activities (IT coverage), user satisfaction with IT, and effectiveness of IT from technical perspectives, as discussed in Chapter 5.

IT effectiveness from a business process and business activities perspective

To determine the effectiveness of IT, first the availability of IT--to support the 29 operational processes and 19 management processes that we collectively defined--was evaluated through the measurement of the level of current IT support and the exploration of remaining opportunities for further IT support. In fact, this was a more detailed analysis of the IT support in the business areas mentioned before, using the same approach, but in greater detail. As said, we also investigated the level of IT support in the near future, supposing that the systems under development were implemented and used. We measured:

- actual IT support, by firstly reviewing the output of processes, then estimating the amount of human work that would have been required to produce that output, and finally, estimating the human labor eliminated by IT,

- potential degree of IT support;
- actual IT support as a percentage of potential IT support (IT coverage).

The measurement was performed in a series of workshops, during which first the degree of actual IT support was discussed with users and business area management for each process and its underlying activities. With the help of examples depicting potential IT support opportunities, as illustrated in Figures 5.1 and 5.2, and examples of the application of IT at other companies supplied by us as knowledgeable consultants, we then brainstormed about the potential of further IT support. The resulting picture of actual IT support as a percentage of potential IT support showed a relatively high degree of coverage of existing IT in many of the management processes compared to operational processes. This was surprising, since most cases of IT effectiveness measurement that I experienced show that operational processes are further automated than management processes. When we completed the picture with the additional, projected level of IT support of the systems under development, and supposing that these were implemented and used, this difference of coverage disappeared. This analysis demonstrated to ANWB management that a balanced approach to IT coverage in both operational and managerial processes had been followed--to some extent unconsciously, but nevertheless successfully.

IT effectiveness from a user perspective

IT effectiveness from a user perspective was measured at ANWB in two ways:

- To measure the perceptions of ANWB employees of the overall effectiveness of IT, 120 employees were surveyed anonymously about their usage of IT; their experience and general satisfaction with IT; the effectiveness of the education, training, and support they got to use IT properly; their commitment to take on responsibility for implementation efforts; etc. Unfortunately, this survey was not as successful as we hoped it would be, primarily due to the response rate, which was only 24 percent (50 percent is generally considered a minimum to ensure that the opinions of IT enemies or friends are not over-represented).
- We measured in more detail the satisfaction of users of 21 identified IT applications by asking them to rate the performance of the IT application on the user satisfaction attributes discussed in Chapter 5: reliability of the IT application, reliability of information, accessibility of information, security of information, and ease of use. In this case, the response rate was very high, since the survey was not anonymous, and follow-up could be done (and had to be done) in letters and phone calls to non-respondents. Many of the selected applications can be considered to be "infrastructure applications," as they are shared by many different business areas and processes, so that the specific requirements of IT infrastructure, as defined in Chapter 5, were addressed.

The results of the first survey revealed a lack of interest in IT and IT applications in general, and a shortfall of commitment to take on responsibility for successful IT usage. This low commitment might also have been the reason for a low response rate of 24 percent of returned questionnaires, but this was not further investigated. As said, measurement results represented only 29 employees (out of 3,000), which is insufficient to draw reliable conclusions. ANWB management felt that the quantitative findings confirmed their expectations, however, so that management judgment took over from hard measurement in this case.

The results of the second survey successfully revealed the satisfaction levels of users of the 21 IT applications. Some of the applications were rated good, average or insufficient on all or most of the user satisfaction attributes; others received a more varied appraisal. In any case, the effectiveness of each application could be expressed successfully, and an extrapolation could be made to convey an overall effectiveness satisfaction rating for the whole. Two important applications in particular showed severe shortcomings, so that a more thorough audit was started to investigate causes and effects of the low effectiveness of these applications in question. Also, some satisfaction attributes were rated consistently poor for all applications, e.g., ease-of-use and availability of appropriate documentation, depicting a general dissatisfaction about these specific effectiveness attributes for the complete application portfolio.

In conclusion, effectiveness of IT in general, and of the most important IT applications in particular, could be measured successfully from a user perspective. Analysis revealed both the overall as well as the specific effectiveness of IT and its usage to ANWB management. As a result, a number of practical actions to be taken were recommended.

IT effectiveness from an IT supply perspective

We also looked at the operational- and maintenance-related effectiveness attributes of the 21 identified IT applications, as well as their architectural effectiveness attributes, as discussed in Chapter 5. Structured questionnaires, filled in by and later discussed with maintenance professionals, system managers, and operations management, asked them to rate several specific and relevant effectiveness aspects of maintainability, architecture, and operability. The answers successfully led to the determination of the more technical-related quality aspects of the individual IT applications, as well as to the common and therefore overall technical quality of the application portfolio, including aspects of flexibility and portability (and thus: scalability), reflected in the architectural aspects of the 21 applications.

As a result, the third question, "Are we able to effectively use our IT?" could successfully be answered through the use of measures of the three perspectives (business processes and business activities, users of IT, and IT supply) of the IT effectiveness level of the BTRIPLEE framework, as demonstrated.

Measuring the Effectiveness and Efficiency of IT Supply

The fourth question, "Are we capable of managing and implementing our projects?" was answered through the use of the concept of the Balanced Scorecards for IT supply and the associated measures of IT supply effectiveness and efficiency.

The effectiveness and efficiency of two important IT supply processes of ANWB's internal IT supply organization (ANWB-ACS) were measured: IT Development Management and IT Infrastructure Management. For both IT supply processes a number of measures were applied, reflecting the distinct perspectives of the Balanced Scorecard concept. The two (out of five possible) IT supply processes and their respective scorecards are perceived to be representative to reliably validate the concepts described in Chapter 6.

Effectiveness and efficiency of IT Development Management

IT development in general was measured using indicators of three perspectives of the IT Development Management Scorecard:

- *Customer perspective*: For seven recently developed IT applications, the costs per Function Point delivered (see Chapter 6) were measured and benchmarked against a database containing IT development measures of other organizations. Costs were expressed in the time spent per Function Point, rather than hard currency, since staff-months are more universal measures and easier to compare than are units of currency at a given moment. Similarly, the elapsed time to develop these applications was measured by Function Points delivered by calendar month, and benchmarked. These measurements were performed successfully, and deviations from averages were discussed with the project leaders involved. Some deviations could be explained, others not directly, causing follow-up investigations into cause and effect relationships.
- *Internal perspective*: A further break-down of quantified performance indicators by development phase demonstrated some interesting deviations from benchmarks, e.g., the feasibility study phase of an average project at ANWB took twice as long as at other companies, although ANWB did not spend more time on it; neither ANWB's IT department nor the users spent a lot of effort on testing and implementing IT applications, but it took them a relatively long time compared to other organizations. Also, performance to budget was measured and discussed, resulting in quite some discussion about the role of the users versus the IT professionals, scattered responsibility for budgets, freezing functional specifications during development, and the like. Finally, the existence and actual application of methods, procedures, techniques, rules, and other management controls were verified, using a series of measures on interval scales.
- *Innovation and learning perspective*: The number of training days per employee per year was measured and benchmarked, showing under-investment in that area.

The effectiveness of the projects under development was further and more specifically investigated by reviewing four of these projects:

- re-development/replacement of the membership administration system (CARPLUS),
- development of ANWB's logistics information systems (INFOLOG);

- implementation of the new IT infrastructure on behalf of the regional shops;
- development of the new road assistance scheduling, tracing, and tracking information system (CIS).

In workshops attended by both users and IT professionals, a series of effectiveness factors were discussed for each project. Measures were selected (with the help of the Scorecards in Appendix C) for effectiveness factors such as risk management, project management, availability of facilities and support, allocation of required skills, commitment and involvement of users, etc. The effectiveness measures were rated on an interval scale, so that projects could be compared with each other, and overall effectiveness expressed and reported to management.

The application of the Balanced Scorecard measures for IT development, in conjunction with the benchmarking of IT development performance against other organizations, appeared to be a successful approach for demonstrating the effectiveness and efficiency levels of IT development at ANWB. Not all measures were used (which is impossible anyway), but only those applicable to answer management's questions and those that could be used practically within the timeframe available. As the systems under development mainly represented large, infrastructure systems, the majority of measures used came from the internal and customer perspective Scorecards, as was indicated in Chapter 6.

Effectiveness and efficiency of IT Infrastructure Management

The measurement of IT Infrastructure Management, called Data Center Operations at ANWB, focused on three main aspects:

- level of service to users (the customer perspective),
- technology resources employed in relation to the workload (internal and financial perspectives),
- human resources employed in relation to the workload (internal and financial perspectives).

The *level of service to users* was measured using the indicators of response time for on-line services (overall and during peak times) and availability of IT services. Measures were compared with benchmarks, as usual.

The measurement of technology *resources employed* focused on available and used CPU MIPS, disk space, tape capacity, printing capacity, etc., in relation to the workload (measured in used capacity of the mainframe computers).

The measurement of *human resources* employed focused on the number of people performing data center-related tasks, in relation to the workload.

Finally, as with IT development effectiveness and efficiency, the existence and actual application of methods, procedures, techniques, rules, and other management controls were verified, during workshop discussions with Data Center Operations' management and employees, using a series of measures on interval scales. Specific measures of the innovation and learning perspective were not applied in this case.

Again, measurement at this level did not face severe problems, other than discussions with IT professionals on definitions of measures and the interpretations of results, which is common.

As a result, the fourth question, "Are we capable of managing and implementing our projects?" was answered through the use of measures of the IT supply effectiveness and supply level of the BTRIPLEE framework. In fact, we also looked at the efficiency and effectiveness of IT supply beyond the project and implementation phases, namely the operational stage of IT systems once they are managed by IT infrastructure management processes. Both the IT development and IT infrastructure measures, classified by the Balanced Scorecard concept, proved to be workable and demonstrated their value in the measurement of IT supply effectiveness and efficiency measurement at ANWB, leading to an action plan for improvement in both.

CONCLUSION

The concepts of the valuation of IT, extensively discussed in Chapters 3, 4, 5, and 6, were applied at the Royal Dutch Touring Club ANWB, a truly information-based organization. The objective of this case study was aimed at providing practical evidence for the application and business relevance of the BTRIPLEE framework and classes of associated measures, in terms of content, context, and process.

The value of IT proved to be measurable at all levels of the BTRIPLEE framework. The questions raised by ANWB's board members could be answered satisfactorily, while it was necessary to invoke all three levels of the BTRIPLEE framework and associated classes of measures to answer these questions, underpinning the business relevance of the BTRIPLEE framework and each of its levels.

Overall, ANWB management took far-going actions in relation to the management, application, and supply of IT, in order to obtain higher value from their IT expenditures. These actions included, but were not limited to, ANWB-wide control of IT costs, a re-distribution of IT supply efforts in favor of maintenance at the cost of new development of IT capabilities, the restriction of the scope of some projects under development, and the actual stop, re-definition, and re-start of a major infrastructure IT system under development at the time of measuring.

ANWB also decided to adopt the major components of the approach described to measure the value of IT more systematically and consistently.

REFERENCES

Brynjolfsson, E. (1993). The productivity paradox of information technology. *Communications of the ACM*, December, 36(12), 67-77.

Henderson, J.C. and Venkatraman, N. (1993). Strategic alignment: Leveraging information technology for transforming organizations. *IBM Systems Journal*, 32(1), 4-15.

Appendix C

IT Supply Scorecards of Measures

IT Supply Management
Customer Perspective
Internal Perspective
Innovation and Learning Perspective
Financial Perspective

IT Development Management
Customer Perspective
Internal Perspective
Innovation and Learning perspective
Financial Perspective

IT Infrastructure Management
Customer Perspective
Internal Perspective
Innovation and Learning Perspective
Financial Perspective

Account Management
Customer Perspective
Internal Perspective
Innovation and Learning Perspective
Financial Perspective

Client Support
Customer Perspective
Internal Perspective
Innovation and Learning Perspective
Financial Perspective

Supply Management Scorecard-Customer Perspective

Goals	Measures
Be an attractive supplier	Awareness score of the suppliers product and service portfolio
	% of proposals that are converted into a contract
	Overall client satisfaction score
Be a preferred supplier	Market share-IT supplier's revenue as a % of total IT expenditure of client organization, number of workstations served as a % of total workstations
	Number of formal/informal client visits per time period
Be a business partner	Agreed upon total annual budget vs. realization
	% of supplier revenue covered by formal contracts
	% of bills sent out on time

IT Supply Management Scorecard-Internal Perspective

Goals	Measures
Be a good employer	Employee satisfaction score
	Employee turnover rate
	% of employee absence, illness days
	Salary competitiveness
Be a lean organization	Ratio direct/support personnel
	Ratio direct/indirect hours
Be competent	Lost business because of lack of capability
	Usage of external consultants to compensate for lack of skills as a % of own staff

IT Supply Management Scorecard-Innovation and Learning Perspective

Goals	Measures
Be an innovative supplier	% of budget spent on IT staff training
	% of budget spent on IT research and development
	Average ages of hardware and IT applications
	Mix of new and old technology and extent of their usage
	Number of new products/services launched per year
Foster innovative thinking	Number of employee improvement ideas made, approved and implemented per year
Create new markets	% of revenues from new applications, products, and/or relationships

IT Supply Management Scorecard-Financial Perspective

Goals   **Measures**

Be a profitable business   ROS, ROA,
                               profit/revenue per employee
Be a reliable planner   Performance to budget
Be in financial control   Mix of budget by activity (development/
                                   maintenance/operations and communications)
                               Mix of budget by resource (personnel,
                                   technology, other)

IT Development Management Scorecard-Customer Perspective

Goals	Measures
Be a responsive supplier	Response time for enhancements: number of hours/days for small changes/to fix reported incidents
	Average initial time to respond to requests for new applications
	Elapsed time to deliver projects (large changes and new development): number of LOC/FP's per calendar month
Be cost effective	Total development costs per delivered Function Point
	Total maintenance costs per Function Point in operation
Be a reliable planner	Performance to budget (cost, time) within reasonable level of tolerance (e.g. 10%)-% projects delivered in time, within budget
Be a quality supplier	Customer satisfaction score
	Required training days per user to exploit new systems
	Number of versions (rework) of written documentation
	Number of software defects in acceptance test by size
	Number of software defects, e.g., in first three months of operation by size
	Number of functional changes, e.g., in first three months of operation by size
	Size of functional changes, e.g., in first three

	months of operation divided by the initial implementation size
Be a team player	Number of upper management arbitrages as a result of conflicts per year

IT Development Management Scorecard-Internal Perspective

Goals	Measures
Be an efficient developer	Number of staff days by project size and by project phase
	Number of staff days maintenance effort by system size Relative PI, MBI (Putnam)
	Extent of reuse by type of component: designs, modules, lines of code, documentation, etc.
	Degree of productivity tools penetration
Be a quality developer	Number of defects in unit test and system integration test by size
	Quality measures/ratings by development staff: design and maintainability,
	Quality measures/ratings by operations staff: operability,
	Quality measures/ratings by EDP auditors: auditability, security, and controllability
Be competent	Capability/experience level in number of years by job class
	Rubin's CASE-readiness rating
	SEI capability maturity model rating
	Business knowledge rating
Be in operational control	Performance to plan by project phase (cost, time) within reasonable level of tolerance (e.g., 10%)-% project phases completed in time, within budget
	Number of change requests per year per application/user group
	Average number of project requests in backlog

% of applications under release management

% of applications under configuration
management

IT Development Management Scorecard-Innovation and Learning Perspective

Goals	Measures
Be a quick adopter	Average elapsed time to (fully) master new development approaches/techniques / tools
	Average elapsed time to (fully) implement new development approaches/techniques/tools
Foster innovation	Number of state of the art projects per year/% of total number of projects
	Number of experiments with new packages/IT solutions per year
	Number of training days per year/% of total time devoted to training

IT Development Management Scorecard-Financial Perspective

Goals

Measures

Be a profitable developer

Profit/recovered costs per development project

Profit/recovered costs per maintained system

Profit per employee

Charged hours as a % of available hours per
   group or individual

Be in financial control

Costs of maintenance as a % of maintenance +
   development costs

Costs of maintenance as a % of total operations
   costs

IT Infrastructure Management Scorecard-Customer Perspective

Goals	Measures
Be a responsive supplier	Response time-at the terminal-for on-line transactions by type of transaction (classified by complexity)
	Elapsed time for regular-planned-batch jobs
	Elapsed time for ad hoc-not planned-batch jobs
Be cost effective	Processing cost per-on-line-business transaction
	Processing costs per -batch- report (e.g. per page)
	Data center and communications costs per business user/workstation
	Processing costs as a % of a business measure (e.g. order, shipment, customer, passengers flown, etc.)
Be a reliable planner	On-time delivery of-key-batch output (performance to plan)
	Performance to annual budget
Be a quality supplier	Customer satisfaction score
	% of technologies in use that don't adhere to standards
	Availability: mean-time-between-failures (MTBF) per application in hours or days, mean-time-to-repair (MTTR) in minutes or hours,
	Number of hassle-free days per period
	Number of business transaction failures as a % of total business transactions

Accuracy of key output: Processing errors in
   reports as a % of total number of reports
Number of incidents in conflict with agreed
   upon SLA's per year
Number of upper management arbitrages as a
result of conflicts per year

IT Infrastructure Management Scorecard-Internal Perspective

Goals	Measures
Be efficient	Total spending per used MIPS/1.000 network nodes
	Hardware spending per used MIPS/1.000 nodes
	Software spending per used MIPS/1.000 nodes
	Personnel spending per used MIPS/1.000 nodes
	Communications spending per 1.000 nodes
	Other spending per used MIPS/1.000 nodes
	Cost per generic unit of work (mount a tape, store a gigabyte of DASD for a month, print a page, manage 1.000 network nodes, etc.)
Optimize assets utilization	CPU usage (%) overall, prime shift, non-prime shift
	DASD usage (% allocated, % actually used)
	Tape usage (number of mounts/job, % multiple tape files, % small tape files, % optimally blocked files)
	Printer usage (% busy)
	Network usage (% occupied)
Optimize staff levels	Degree of productivity tools penetration
	Total staff per used MIPS/number of shifts/ 1.000 nodes
	Console operators per used MIPS
	I/O operators per 10.000 production jobs/ 100.000 printed pages/10.000 tape mounts
	Schedulers per 10.000 production jobs
	System programmers per Operating System/ used MIPS

	Data Base administrators per 10.000 files
	Capacity planners per used MIPS/1.000 network nodes
	Security specialists per used MIPS/1.000 nodes
	Network managers per 1.000 nodes
Be a quality operator	Number of outages/defects/incidents
	% reruns of batch jobs
	% of data backed up
	% of data files covered by access control mechanisms
Be competent	Capability/experience level in number of years by job class
Be in operational control	Performance to budget by application/user group
	Average size of outstanding network change requests
	Average size of outstanding ad hoc batch jobs
	% of network change requests per year accomplished in time
	% of hardware and software under configuration management
	% of procedures passed, e.g., ITIL tests

IT Infrastructure Management Scorecard-Innovation and Learning Perspective

Goals	Measures
Be a quick adopter	Average elapsed time to (fully) master new technology/tools
	Average elapsed time to (fully) implement new technology/tools
Foster innovation	Number of training days per year/% of total time devoted to training
	Number of experiments with new technology per year

IT Infrastructure Management Scorecard-Financial Perspective

Goals

Measures

Be profitable

Profit/recovered costs per unit of service

Profit/recovered costs per user group

Profit per employee

Be in financial control

Size of equity (for capital investments)

ROA, ROI, etc.

Account Management Scorecard-Customer Perspective

Goals	Measures
Be informative	Awareness score of the suppliers product and service portfolio
	% of user groups for which informative sessions are held on a regular basis
	% of information requests answered in one call/ visit
	Number of complaints about miscommunication per year
Be available	Time spent with clients as a % of available time
	% telephone calls returned the same day
Be a preferred supplier	Market share-IT supplier's revenue as a % of total IT expenditure of client organization, number of workstations served as a % of total workstations
	Number of formal/informal client visits per time period
	% of won contracts in competition with other suppliers
Be a business partner	Agreed-upon total annual budget vs. realization
	% of supplier revenue covered by formal contracts
	Number of improvement ideas generated by supplier
	% of bills sent out on time
	Average collection period of amounts receivable
	Overall client satisfaction score

Account Management Scorecard-Internal Perspective

Goals	Measures
Be marketing oriented	% of user groups for which a marketing plan is available
	% of user groups of which IT use and awareness is tracked consistently
	% of user groups of which profiles are maintained listing all their important characteristics
Be efficient	Costs of marketing programs, events, promotion material, etc., as a % of revenue
Be informed	Number of internal (other IT functions') meetings attended per year

Account Management Scorecard-Innovation and Learning Perspective

Goals	Measures
Be an innovative marketer	% of budget spent on market development
	New promotion material as a % of total promotion material
	Average age of promotion material
	Number of new products/services launched per year
Foster innovative thinking	Number of marketing improvement ideas made, approved and implemented per year
	% of budget spent on -marketing and IT-training
Create new markets	% of revenues from new applications, products and/or relationships

Account Management Scorecard-Financial Perspective

Goals   **Measures**

Be a profitable business   ROS

Revenue per user group

Marketing and sales expenditures as a % of

revenue

Client Support Scorecard-Customer Perspective

Goals	Measures
Be responsive	Number of hours per day/week that client support can be contacted
	Average number of rings/seconds before staff answers calls
	Average number of abandoned calls per week
	Average elapsed time before support staff appears on-site after support request
	Average elapsed time before education sessions are held after request
	Average waiting time for users who "walk in" support center
	Degree of statistical support information supplied per user group
Be cost effective	Charged cost per call
	Charged cost per on-site assistance
	Charged cost per training/training day
	Charged cost per full-service contract per user/ workstation
Be a reliable planner	On-time delivery of agreed upon training/ support services
Deliver quality support	Customer satisfaction score
	Number of incidents in conflict with agreed upon SLA's
	Number of upper management arbitrages as a result of conflicts
Be informative	Number of newsletters, help desk cards, telephone stickers, etc. distributed per year

Client Support Scorecard-Internal Perspective

Goals	Measures
Be efficient	Average number of users/workstations supported per staff member
	Number of calls handled per staff member per month
	Number of on-site assistance's handled per staff member per month
	Number of training days given per staff member per year
Be a quality support center	% of calls / visits administrated
	% of incidents logged/resolutions administrated /elapsed resolution time administrated
	Degree of automation to support client support personnel
Be competent	Capability/experience level in number of years by job class
Be in operational control	Performance to budget by application/user group

Client Support-Innovation and Learning Perspective

Goals	Measures
Be a quick adopter	Average elapsed time to fully support new client applications/client technology
	Average elapsed time to (fully) master new technology/support tools
	Average elapsed time to (fully) implement new technology/support tools
Foster innovation	Number of training days per year/% of total time devoted to training
	Number of experiments with new support technology per year

Client Support Scorecard-Financial Perspective

Goals   **Measures**

Be profitable   Profit / recovered costs per unit of service

Profit / recovered costs per user group

Profit per employee

REFERENCES

Humphrey, W.S. (1989). *Managing the Software Process*. Reading, MA: Addison-Wesley Publishing Company.

Rubin, H. (1991). Using readiness to guide CASE implementation. *CASE Trends*, January/February, 37-41.

Index

Han van der Zee

Prof. Dr. Ing. Han T.M. van der Zee is director of the Nolan Norton Institute, an international research arm of KPMG / Nolan, Norton & Co. Management Consultants in De Meern, The Netherlands. He is in charge of thought leadership and innovation of consulting approaches for business strategy, organizational development, and IT strategy and management.

He is also a professor at the Dutch Tilburg University, where he teaches and researches on the impact of information technology on businesses and business transformation.

Prior to re-joining Nolan, Norton & Co. in November 1996, he was managing consultant for Nolan, Norton & Co. from 1986-1991. He also worked for Arthur D. Little and the Index Group in senior consulting positions. Prior to that he worked in managerial IT positions for multinational companies.

He is the author of several articles and books, and speaks regularly at public conferences on this subject. He has university degrees in Computer Science and Business Administration, and obtained a doctorate degree on "Measuring the Value of IT" from the Economic Faculty of Tilburg University in The Netherlands.